Springer Series on Cultural Computing

Cultural Computing is an exciting, emerging field of Human Computer Interaction, which covers the cultural impact of computing and the technological influences and requirements for the support of cultural innovation. Using support technologies such as location-based systems, augmented reality, cloud computing and ambient interaction researchers can explore the differences across a variety of cultures and provide the knowledge and skills necessary to overcome cultural issues and expand human creativity. This series presents the current research and knowledge of a broad range of topics including creativity support systems, digital communities, the interactive arts, cultural heritage, digital museums and intercultural collaboration.

More information about this series at http://www.springer.com/series/10481

Jocelyn Spence

Performative Experience Design

 Springer

Jocelyn Spence
Digital World Research Centre
University of Surrey
Guildford, UK

Mixed Reality Lab,
University of Nottingham,
Nottingham, UK

ISSN 2195-9056   ISSN 2195-9064   (electronic)
Springer Series on Cultural Computing
ISBN 978-3-319-28393-7   ISBN 978-3-319-28395-1   (eBook)
DOI 10.1007/978-3-319-28395-1

Library of Congress Control Number: 2016933033

Printed on acid-free paper

This Springer imprint is published by SpringerNature
The registered company is Springer International Publishing AG Switzerland.

Preface

I used to make a living as a user experience architect. I was working to contribute in some way to the quality of life of individual human beings: never purely rational, prone to whim or passion, forever dancing through a process of being and becoming. This was my perspective after decades of study in the arts—theatre, music, filmmaking, and creative writing. But every digital artefact in my workday was a static, fixed unit—the very opposite of human experience—and people were not people, they were 'users'. Of course, there is a substantial tradition of digital art that is anything but static, but such art figures very little in most people's everyday lives. The digital technology that tends to matter to irrational, passionate, mutable human beings is the media with which they identify: digital photos, music, videos, animations, social networking interactions, games, sites, apps, and the like.

I want to shine more light on the meanings that digital media technologies have for people and performance—well, insert your own 'spotlight' or 'limelight' joke here. I know from experience that performance is more than a transmission of information and that being in an audience is more than processing information. Performance is a sometimes exhilarating, sometimes exhausting experience, made up of but experientially very different from a person's normal activities. I wanted to experiment with digital technologies as a trigger for emotional and 'artistic' engagement with self and other, reflecting and incorporating media technologies as an integral part of the person's lived experience.

Relatively recently, the fields of human-computer interaction (HCI) and performance studies have taken tentative steps towards each other. The need to address felt experience has occupied the minds of some HCI researchers. Similarly, performance researchers have tried to make sense of new media technologies in performance. Debates on the ontologies of liveness and mediation have given way to more nuanced examinations of the interplay among their various permutations. At the same time, online social networking is reconfiguring the basic ways that millions, even billions, of people conceive of interacting with and displaying themselves for others. Surely performance studies can contribute to HCI, and HCI to performance studies, if the right focus can be found.

This book attempts to bring together the convergent elements of two different disciplines to forge a new way of understanding the phenomena of performance and performativity in a world saturated with digital media technologies. The aim is performance, understood as an emergent event unique to each constellation of performers and audience members. *Performative Experience Design* stakes a claim to a new field, framework, and methodology for creating and making sense of the everyday performance of twenty-first-century selves.

Nottingham, UK   Jocelyn Spence
December 2015

Acknowledgements

To all my colleagues at the University of Surrey, everyone who helped with technical and/or moral support in building *Collect Yourselves!*, people who contributed such stellar comments on the manuscript, and for wise words along the way: Ernest Adams, Stuart Andrews, Jon Back, Tom Bartindale, Steve Benford, Alicia Blum-Ross, Janko Calic, Rachel Clarke, Angharad Dalton, Owen Daly-Jones, Kristen Ali Eglinton, Phil Ely, David England and the CHI Digital Arts committee, Mary Ellen Foley, David Frohlich, Hamish Fyfe, Connie Golsteijn, Dave Green, Toby Harris, Jon Hook, Kristina Langhein, Andy Lavender, Karen Lewis, Chris Lim, Roisin McNaney, Mog (aka Chris Morgan), Simon Pipe, John Shearer, Barrie Stephenson, Robyn Taylor, Stephen Taylor, Jane Vincent, Annika Waern, Julie Williamson, Mike Wilson, Peter Wright, and Miki Yamanouchi.

To all my anonymous participants and non-anonymous performers. Special thanks to Alex Kelly for being so gracious with his time and to Claire Murphy-Morgan, my collaborator in intermedial autobiographical performance. I'm also very grateful for the existence of the Live Art Development Agency, whose study room provided me with ideas and research material for days on end. My biggest thanks, of course, go to Ian Spence.

Contents

Chapter 1
Introducing Performative Experience Design

Abstract Chapter 1 begins with an introduction to the concept of Performative Experience Design (PED) as a methodology, a field, and a framework for understanding interactions with technology in which the device, system, or situation creates an opportunity for the user to engage in performance for and/or with others. It works from concrete examples in the HCI literature to paint a picture for readers who may have any number of conflicting or confusing ideas of what 'performance' or 'performative' means, particularly in the context of experience design. The chapter defines the aims and design space of PED, which indicates its scope in terms of the continuing developments of third-wave HCI. It then raises the questions: what is the point of pursuing performative experience design? What use is it to designers and researchers, and what larger purposes does it serve? Several initial responses are proposed: as a development of critical design, an exploration of speculative and transformative interactions, and a design-oriented methodology that addresses the ethical dimensions of design research into interactions with technologies that are deeply personal and yet often widely disseminated. The chapter concludes with an overview of the argument presented in the text.

The Scope of the Field

Performative Experience Design: three incredibly broad words that could mean almost anything you want them to mean. For decades now, every type of event from operas to basketball games to courtroom proceedings have been analysed using the tools of performance studies, a discipline with close but sometimes antagonistic connections to theatre and drama. Performativity can refer to the uttering of 'I do' in a wedding ceremony (Austin 1962), the power of discourse to create gender (Butler 2002), or the opposite of the artifice implied by the term 'theatricality'. Experience can describe anything to which we bring our consciousness, or it can be a key element of pragmatist philosophy: 'the result, the sign, and the reward of that interaction of organism and environment which, when it is carried to the full, is a transformation of interaction into participation and communication' (Dewey 2005, p. 22). Design is simultaneously the increasingly complex skill set of professionals, even visionaries, and a predisposition to action that separates all humans, and even *Homo habilis*, from most other animals (Friedman and Stolterman 2015, p. 9).

© Springer International Publishing Switzerland 2016

J. Spence, *Performative Experience Design*, Springer Series on Cultural Computing, DOI 10.1007/978-3-319-28395-1_1

Even within design as a profession and research method, co-design and participatory design have positioned us all as potential contributors to the design of actual products. 'Experience design' is itself a contested field, with some proponents yearning for the use of knowledge-based models to guide a theory-driven design process (Hassenzahl 2010) and others seeking 'a more interpretive and qualitative approach' (Wright and McCarthy 2010, p. xiii) to preserve the complexities of felt experience in the face of imperatives to 'reduce it to design implications, methods, or features' (McCarthy and Wright 2004, p. 11). Where did a term like Performative Experience Design come from, and how useful can it be?

This book sets out a clear remit for Performative Experience Design (PED) as a methodology, a field, and a framework for understanding interactions with technology in which the device, system, or situation creates an opportunity for the 'user' to perform for others. Performance is not limited to the professional acting of roles on a stage, but the conscious display of behaviour that others might observe. In other words, PED directs our attention away from a technological device or even the user's interaction with that device, towards the powerful internal and interpersonal shifts in perception that are brought about by *displaying* our interactions with technology and *appearing* to others as beings engaged with others through technology.

A hypothetical example: in the British television series *How to Look Good Naked*, which has inspired numerous spin-offs around the world, fashion guru Gok Wan leads people with a negative image of their bodies through a process of learning to dress in a way that emphasises their natural beauty. The culmination of each episode involves a nude or semi-nude photo session. One of those photos—with the person tastefully positioned so as to avoid breaking obscenity laws—is then projected onto the side of a building, and the object of the week's confidence-building exercises embraces that newly attractive self-image in front of hundreds of passers-by, as well as the future viewing audience of friends, family, and a few million complete strangers. What if this display mechanism were set up to surprise people with their own semi-salacious photos? How would they react? How would you?

A real-world example: Humanaquarium is an interactive artwork with a glass screen that spectators can touch. Different gestures control different elements of the artwork, but these gestures are not explained anywhere. The only way to find out what happens is to try, or to watch others trying. Some people experiment readily but others are too shy to touch the artwork while other spectators are watching. So far, this description could apply to any number of interactive artworks over many years. However, in this case, the artwork included live human beings—two musicians performing behind the glass, inches from the interacting participants, making eye contact and encouraging participation. Passers-by became participants, performers and collaborators. Clearly this is a radically different experience than simply touching the screen on an iPad in the privacy of your own home—but how can we articulate the difference, and how can we pursue it further? (Fig. 1.1)

A less 'artsy' example: Five friends gather around the dinner table. A small, four-sided centrepiece catches their attention with photographs drawn automatically from their Facebook albums. As the images float from one screen to the next around

Fig. 1.1 Performers behind the touchscreen glass of Humanaquarium (Image © Cassim Ladha, courtesy of Robyn Taylor, used with permission)

the centrepiece, they foster free-flowing conversation and reminiscence around personal stories (Fig. 1.2).

The display is called 4Photos (ten Bhömer et al. 2010).[1] In field studies, groups of friends and family interacted with 4Photos while sharing a meal. The photographs guided topics of conversation and created an opportunity for participants to learn more about each other's lives (2010, pp. 57–58). The talk was highly interactive and depended upon seating position and the ongoing flow of conversation. Hence much of the analysis focuses on spatio-temporal arrangements, dynamics of use, and the moment-by-moment access to displayed media. 4Photos calls attention to the need for careful design of both media content and media player in conversational settings, and a sensitivity to the experiential effects of mediated encounters that unfold over time. It facilitates reminiscing and storytelling encounters that allow people to express themselves as much as they wish and discover unexpected new levels of intimacy and participation.

---

[1] 4Photos would seem to have much in common with commercially available photo frames or research projects such as an affect-responsive frame (Dibeklioğlu et al. 2011) and the *Cherish* digital photo frame (Kim and Zimmerman 2006). Their primary function seems to be the choice of image to display, in the hope of provoking affective or behavioural changes. As the aim of PED is to explore performative interactions, display systems will not be discussed further.

Fig. 1.2 4Photos (Photograph © Martijn ten Bhömer, used with permission)

The perspective of this book lies within human-computer interaction (HCI), interaction design, and experience design. Performance studies can inform experience design in ways that usefully—and critically—extend the field. The argument is that performance provides a lens for understanding and designing for the emotionally and aesthetically powerful interactions that involve perceptions of engagement with digital technology. However, that is only half of the argument, as I believe that HCI and experience design have a lot to offer performance studies, as well. In fact, PED goes beyond the idea of one discipline informing another: it occupies its own space between experience design and performance studies. PED constitutes its own small but important and growing field that draws on the shared perspectives of both of its parent disciplines. To make this argument as straightforwardly as possible, I will approach PED primarily from the point of view of an HCI researcher and explain how a thorough understanding of performance can contribute to the work of that field—contribute so much, in fact, that the new field of PED is the result.

Defining Performative Experience Design

PED is the setting of technological and social parameters to create opportunities for performative experiences with interactive technologies. The term 'performative' will be explored further in Chap. 3, but for the time being, it can be taken to mean an action that one is aware may be witnessed by others—and that awareness may affect the nature of the action, the perception of that action, and/or an evaluation of the self who is undertaking that action. For example, the action of moving a finger along a touchscreen might be very different if the 'user' is alone in a studio, or surrounded on all sides by curious onlookers and standing and only inches away from a woman in Victorian dress singing directly at her (Taylor et al. 2011). One person might shrink from the singer's gaze, poke hesitantly at the touchscreen, and flee in embarrassment, while another might join in enthusiastically and walk away from the experience feeling a sense of pride and accomplishment.

In PED (as in other types of experience design, mixed reality performance (Benford and Giannachi 2011), or participatory performance), a user might take on the role of a performer or audience member, perhaps become an 'orchestrator' (Benford and Giannachi 2011) or 'bystander' (Benford et al. 2006), or shift between roles. These opportunities move people out of their everyday comfort zone and into the risky space of the aesthetic by making their actions, words, and even their presence conspicuous to themselves and others. Challenge, risk, and vulnerability are key to the case study in this book and to PED as a whole. This focus puts PED at odds with much of interaction design and experience design, which has historically tended to reinforce rather than subvert the usability goals of efficiency, effectiveness, and satisfaction. PED also pushes third-wave HCI (described in Chap. 2) towards a fully performance-based and transformative engagement with others based on unconventional interactions with digital technology.

The use of the term 'audience' in this text accommodates the active part played by those who watch and listen to a performance, without delving too deeply into the intrapersonal mechanisms of spectatorship or emphasising its visual aspect. My interest lies in the interactions among performers and audience members as they co-create the 'autopoietic feedback loop' (Fischer-Lichte 2008, p. 165), the self-generating and emergent performance event that will be described in more detail in Chap. 3.

Figure 1.3 lays out the most basic elements of PED. The 'performance' axis refers to the degree to which a given experience announces itself as a performance for public consumption and aesthetic and/or cultural evaluation. At the top end would be theatrical productions, public carnivals or festivals, and the like. The performer undertakes actions in the full knowledge that an audience is perceiving those actions, or perhaps the mediated effects of those actions. Any changes in the participant's performance can be immediately perceptible by her audience. The bottom end would include performances that are private and hidden, not (primarily) in the sense of creating an exclusive audience but in the tradition of artists such as Roberto Cuoghi and Pawel Althamer (discussed in Chap. 3). At this extreme end of the axis,

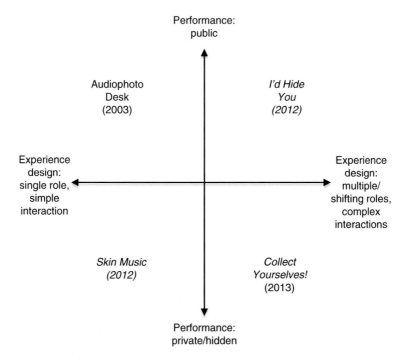

Fig. 1.3 The Performative Experience Design space

'performance' can be argued to elide with 'performativity'. It can include interactions performed in private while imagining how those interactions would appear from the perspective of an imaginary future onlooker (Dalsgaard and Hansen 2008). It is interesting to note that the idea of performing alone for a camera without any live, co-present audience would occupy a space near the bottom of this axis, where the participant shapes her performance for an as-yet imaginary audience.

The other main element represented in Fig. 1.3 is the 'experience design' element. On the left is an extremely simple interaction involving a single user functioning in only one role. Such an interaction might otherwise be studied using basic methods of usability evaluation. At the far right of the axis, the designed experience encompasses extremely complex interactions among many people in multiple, shifting roles, such as performer, audience member, and bystander. It might extend over long periods of time—in fact, it might take place across multiple time scales, either within and outside of the narrative structure incorporated in the experience (Benford and Giannachi 2011) or across the time frames represented by digital media (Spence et al. 2012). It might also extend over both virtual/technological and real/physical spaces. Although the 'experience design' element refers to complexities of interactions with technologies and interpersonal interactions in multiple roles, it should be clear that the more important of these two is the interpersonal. Anyone who has battled with a complex, user-un-friendly computer program has experienced the down side of complex interactions with a technological device, yet

I would not say that it created a complex experience in terms of PED. Some works that I would identify as performative experience designs, such as Blast Theory's *Day of the Figurines* (2006), involved fairly complex temporal and interpersonal interactions, yet it was conducted almost entirely through sending and receiving text messages (Benford and Giannachi 2011). The complexity of any interaction *may* follow the complexity of the interpersonal interactions, but complex interactions with technology on their own do not necessarily translate to complex experience design.

The top right quadrant of the PED space maximises both the performance nature of the interaction and the complexity of the experience in terms of interactions and user roles. Examples of this quadrant include many of the most frequently cited works of mixed reality performance by Blast Theory such as *I'd Hide You* (2012) or *Ulrike and Eamonn Compliant* (2009). The top left quadrant is occupied by designs such as the audiophoto desk (Frohlich et al. 2004), a physical desktop that plays back audio files associated with physical photographs. The user controls the volume and panning of the sound by selecting the photos to place on the desk and moving them forward, backward, left, or right. Multiple photos can be placed on the desk at the same time, giving the user real-time control over both the visuals and the sound mix, as well as the display of her own physical movement in doing so. This method of interaction encourages expressivity and engagement with the audiovisual media; if more than one person is present, there will also be some division among performer and audience roles (though these are not necessarily mutually exclusive). The bottom left quadrant of Fig. 1.3 holds works with simple interactions, little engagement with multiple roles, and a tendency for the user to engage in a relatively private, unselfconscious way. One example is *Skin Music* (2012) by Lauren Hayes, presented at the Creativity and Cognition conference in Glasgow, Scotland, in 2015. The user interacts with the technology by lying back on a chair that plays music haptically as well as aurally (Hayes 2015). Experiencing this work in a public setting does mark the user as taking an active part with one of the designs, but the activity consists simply of sitting comfortably in a normal-looking chair while wearing headphones. Thus the level of putting oneself on display as a performer remains low, as does the interaction between user, device, and anyone else present.

The bottom right quadrant may seem difficult to conceive of at first. It requires users to engage in a relatively unselfconscious way with a technology that is interpersonally and perhaps interactionally complex, involving at least some degree of multiple and/or shifting roles. This type of engagement is often framed in terms of game or play, as with many of the mixed reality performances described by Benford and Giannachi (2011) and created in partnership with Benford and colleagues through the University of Nottingham's Mixed Reality Lab and the artists of Blast Theory. Similar framings appear in Digital Live Art (e.g. Sheridan et al. 2007). In these cases, users tend to be acutely aware of their role as performers and invest themselves accordingly. There are at least two ways of reducing the strength of the performance frame and/or the game structure: one is to conduct the experience in private, and the other is to engage users in a private phase of preparing for a later performance. Both of these tactics are taken in the case study presented in Chaps. 5 and 6.

From the perspective of PED, digital technology is a contributor to rather than strictly a mediator of the connections among performers and audience members. The interaction among humans is primary. Some designs, such as the case study described in this book, are meant to be 'dwelled with' rather than simply 'used', as participants imagine the performance they will create using their own personal digital media as prompted and afforded by the design. Digital media are particularly potent for PED. Images, for example, can be not only displayed but also performed as the participant interacts with a personal photo to tell the story behind it. The story reflects not only the performer's present-moment reinterpretation of her memories but her ongoing interaction with her audience. She might have a striking insight about her previous interpretation of an event, but depending on the nature of the emerging relationship with her audience, she might or might not feel able to share that insight. All of these interactions can be shaped by an understanding of the processes and effects of performance. PED aims to create a time and space for participants to engage with the technology, the associations they hold with that technology, their own felt experiences and perceptions regarding the emerging event, their fellow participants and audience members, and their conceptualisation of themselves in the future as affected by their experience. It uses the specific context of performance to create intra- and interpersonal connections through the meanings and implications of interaction with digital technology that *cannot* be represented in digital form.

The relationship between performativity, performance, and experience design is explored by Jon McKenzie, a seminal theorist in performance studies who worked as an information architect in a web design company and directs the DesignLab, a digital media design consultancy at the University of Wisconsin, Madison. He defines experience design as 'the crafting and eliciting of affective and social experiences in such spaces as museums and retail stores, private homes and public spaces, video games and websites' (2008, p. 136). For him, experience design is a place where organisational performances, such as the production of goods and services, mix with cultural performances, such as works of theatre. His ability to see performance in experience design comes from his combination of training in the field of performance studies and practical work in the design industry. After studying performance, he 'went from seeing design in primarily—even exclusively—visual terms to feeling design in performative terms… an open, synesthetic, and processual approach to design, one that includes all the senses and, as important, the temporal *and* the spatial dimension' (2008, p. 127). Focusing on the 'open, synesthetic, and processual' elements of experience design—in other words, those that correspond directly to performance—McKenzie hopes to bridge divides between 'aesthetics and functionality', and between 'designers, engineers, and…those others called consumers, audiences, and users' (2008, p. 128).

McKenzie's ideas are presented in his contribution to a book on the emerging and interdisciplinary field of Performance Design, which has its roots in scenography but encompasses the process of designing 'places, things, gestures and imagery' to become 'more mobile, dynamic, and affective' (Hannah and Harsløf 2008, pp. 12–13). With case studies such as Hotel Pro Forma's 2002 performance of *jesus_c_odd_size* and the interactive installation *Plastic Forest* (2005) at the Universidad Técnica Federico Santa María in Valparaíso, Chile, Performance Design explores much of the same territory as PED. However, its focus lies in the design of the environment that makes performances and performative interactions possible, rather than specific technological interventions into performative interactions. There is no clear line separating these two, as evidenced by the many projects discussed under the heading of Performance Design that could just as easily be presented as interactive digital art (such as Plastic Forest), or the fact that two members of the seminal Performance Design programme at Roskilde University in Denmark also publish on experience design (Strandvad and Pedersen 2015). PED is not trying to fight for intellectual or artistic territory with Performance Design, but rather to welcome the upsurge in interest in how performative interactions can be constructed and understood, regardless of the area of focus. After all, there is no way to achieve clarity on the relationships among performativity, performance, and experience design without a full view of their many interconnections.

PED opens a way of conceptualising, designing for, and performing a type of interaction that has emerged as computing technology has become increasingly personal, ubiquitous, and media-rich. The issues addressed by this book have been recognised and addressed by a number of researchers, and the interest is increasing: see Popat and Palmer 2005; Sheridan and Bryan-Kinns 2008; Salter 2010; Benford and Giannachi 2011; Chatzichristodoulou 2011; Nitsche 2013; Nam and Nitsche 2014; Rust et al. 2014; Williamson et al. 2014. The case study in this book focuses on personal digital media, but PED is not limited to these types of interactions. It can encompass interactions with digital media that do not belong to or have personal significance for the user; interactions with personal devices such as smartphones, in which users have invested a measure of identity or personal connection; group interactions using digital technology in almost any way; pervasive computing scenarios in which the user's interactions with technology are masked or automated; public performances involving bystanders, audience members, and participants; or asynchronous, distributed performances in applications ranging from telematic performance to online social media. It is unwise to assume that all of the properties of live performance can be created in the context of asynchronous and/or distributed interactions, but that is all the more reason to investigate their potential.

One of PED's potential drawbacks—or benefits, depending on the point of view—is the tendency I am already demonstrating to conflate the first-person perspective of a designer with the first-person perspective of a performer, particularly one who also creates her own performances. This text is a reflection of my own experiences, and I would not want to implicate anyone else in any of my missteps or misstatements. However, as with any design or any performance, the development of PED was very much a collaborative effort. People to whom I owe a huge debt of gratitude are named in the acknowledgements. For now, I would like to make the simple disclaimer that my use of 'I' nearly always stands in for a shifting group, a 'we' whose collective background and insights have created the scope for PED.

What Is the Point?

Those of you who have followed this argument so far might be asking yourselves the same thing I asked myself when I embarked on this path several years ago. What is the point? Even if experience design and performance can speak to each other, why should we listen? For a long time, I struggled to articulate the significance that I felt certain PED could have in the context of experience design, interaction design, and HCI. Part of my certainty came from the 'humanist agenda' (Wright and McCarthy 2010, p. vi) in much of the work of John McCarthy and Peter Wright and their colleagues (e.g. McCarthy and Wright 2004, 2015; Wright et al. 2008). As they put it, the aim of experience design is 'to give people the chance to have a richer life' (Wright and McCarthy 2010, p. 2). This is about as lofty of a goal as I can think of, not to mention one that sounds suspiciously 'artistic'.

As I looked more closely at the strands of research within HCI and interaction design that aimed for 'humanist' or quasi-artistic goals, I realised that a substantial body of work within performance studies could contribute to each of them. I eventually concluded, though, that performance can do much more than provide the odd helpful method or bit of theory. Performance is best suited as a full partner to experience design. My attempts to discover how exactly performance and experience design could work together—and why anyone should pay attention—took me through critiques of experience design and participatory design, the shift from problem solving to problem setting, Anthony Dunne and Fiona Raby's seminal work on critical design (e.g. Dunne and Raby 2001), the renaissance of critical design as reconceived by Jeffrey Bardzell and colleagues, critiques of critical design, and the principle of 'uncomfortable interactions' (Benford et al. 2012). A brief explanation of how performance relates to these ideas, and how they relate to each other, will clarify the 'point' of PED.

Anyone interested in experience design as opposed to traditional ergonomics or usability research, for example, is likely to be captivated by the depth and breadth of what the term 'experience' connotes. It implies both the most deeply held values and searingly felt emotions that mark the extremes of an individual's experience, combined with attention to the myriad material, temporal, and socio-cultural contexts of that internally experienced feeling. However, there is still no consensus as to how design research might come to understand depth and breadth at the same time. McCarthy and Wright (2004) trace the development of 'experience' as a topic and practice of technology design with the aim of challenging the 'rationalist assumptions' that I would argue persist in much of HCI, interaction design, and even experience design research. They appreciate but ultimately reject previous attempts to move beyond rationalism such as phenomenology, ethnography, and ethnomethodology. They see phenomenology as focusing too much on the depth of internally felt experience, while McCarthy and Wright criticise ethnography and ethnomethodology for overemphasising an analytic approach to the breadth of external contexts that implies an impossibly objective researcher (2004, pp. 35–41).

Interestingly, McCarthy and Wright also criticise the 'Scandinavian approach to human/computer interaction' that emphasises reflexivity and engagement on the part of the researcher, leading to the development of participatory design—despite their eventual commitment to work that positions users as participants in the design process (2010, p. xiii). In the hands of design researchers more familiar with the field of performance studies, these same emphases on reflexivity and engagement might easily have led towards something closer to practices of contemporary performance. For example, Baz Kershaw and Helen Nicholson identify reflexivity as a 'methodological key' connecting disparate performance methodologies that create space for reflection on the paradoxes and contradictions that almost inevitably emerge in the process of creating and researching new works (2011, p. 5). This leads to a continual questioning of the researcher's own choices and an iterative process of refining, reshaping, and rethinking. However, within the context of performance studies, the iterative process is likely to address the performance creator's developing sense of what her performance might achieve, rather than what the 'user' or audience expects out of the experience.

What McCarthy and Wright name as 'engagement' might find a performance studies parallel in the recent attention paid to audience research, which has gained sudden and sustained popularity in the past several years. Audience research ranges from theory-based (e.g. Fearon 2010) to empirical (e.g. Reason 2010), but virtually all of it positions audience members as active co-creators of each performance event (see also Oddey and White 2009; Rancière 2011; Boenisch 2012; Fensham 2012; Reason 2015). However, this does not necessarily mean that this research aims to include audiences in the process of co-creating the next performance. Where participatory design shares responsibility for the design output with its potential users, audience research tends to support performance makers—whether or not those makers then choose to create a substantially participatory performance. 'Reflexivity' and 'engagement' may have guided Scandinavian design researchers towards participatory design, but in the context of performance, those same traits seem to have opened up an entirely more authorial process, driven less by what users say they need and more by what designers speculate they might benefit from. The strong similarities in focus between Scandinavian experience designers and Anglophone performance makers lead me to suspect that performance studies might provide options for relieving some of the tension between the pursuit of (interior) depth and the pursuit of (contextual) breadth.

The shift towards designing for a richer life is also reflected in the move that experience design takes from problem solving to problem setting. Tara Mullaney (2015) identifies the call for this move in the work of several researchers and presents her own call for designing 'transformative' experiences. Again, the terminology used—in this case, 'transformative'—overlaps with performance studies and points towards similar aims, as I will describe in Chap. 3. Mullaney advocates an imaginative stance in which researchers 'suspend reality' in order to create new perspectives on existing situations using 'a critical lens' (2015, p. 152). She gives the example of a process of designing new experiences for a bank. She added two 'disruptive' design exercises into the process, both of which were inspired by criti-

cal design. The second disruption, 'critical objects', aimed to get designers to imagine how a bank might interact with elements of their personal lives, regardless of
whether banks have traditionally held that role or performed that service. From the
perspective of user-centred design, Mullaney's designers were creating solutions to
problems that might not exist—and thereby creating new 'problems' for design
teams to solve (and for clients to pay for). Yet some of these designs were far more
'humane' in how they could serve a potential user's wants and needs than any incre-
mental improvement to an existing bank service. One of these designs, *Mino*, pre-
dicts what the user's future health, social life, and global environment will look like
based on the choices they make today (2015, p. 156). The users of these designs
may or may not undergo any personal transformation, but any bank that implemented them would certainly initiate a process of transforming what it means to be
a bank.

Like Mullaney, I was impressed by critical design as described in foundational
work by Dunne and Raby (e.g. Dunne 1999; Dunne and Raby 2001). It does more
to challenge the assumptions of user-centred design than any of the examples given
so far. In fact, it often results in designs that raise questions or explore contradictions, resulting in objects that may be beautiful, unwieldy, or physically impossible
to use. This was work at the extreme opposite end of the spectrum from concerns of
efficiency, effectiveness, and satisfaction, with a thoroughly aesthetic bent and anti-
consumerist feel. Surely this was the apotheosis of humane design, and therefore the
best possible match for a performance studies approach?

I soon ran into many of the same problems with critical design as put forward by
Jeffrey Bardzell and colleagues (Bardzell and Bardzell 2013a, b; Bardzell et al.
2012). They challenge Dunne and Raby's lack of attention to methods of conducting or even identifying critical design practice (Bardzell and Bardzell 2013b,
pp. 3299–3300). Where Dunne and Raby sound the rallying cry for a socially and
politically active design perspective, Bardzell and colleagues propose a specific set
of mechanisms for putting that perspective into practice. Jeffrey and Shaowen
Bardzell explain what they see as the value of critical design as put forward by
Dunne and Raby:

> critical design is a design research practice that foregrounds the ethical positioning of
> designers; this practice is suspicious of the potential for hidden ideologies that can harm the
> public; it optimistically seeks out, tries out, and disseminates new design values; it seeks to
> cultivate critical awareness in designers and consumers alike in, by means of, and through
> designs; it views this activity as democratically participatory. (2013b, p. 3300)

This description of the point of adopting a critical design perspective aligns very
closely with my own sense of why performance and performativity are so important
to experience design. Performativity foregrounds the ethical positioning of designers by revealing the intra- and interpersonal costs of interacting with technology and
exposing potential harms to the public. Performance as an artistic practice could be
beautifully described as an optimistic exploration and dissemination of values: not
only social values embedded in the content of an acted text, but the 'design values'
embedded in every dramaturgical choice. And by bringing performative designs to

the public, consumer/citizens become viscerally aware of the results of those designs—designs which cannot fully exist without their participation as audience members of one kind or another.

The Bardzells go on to offer a five-point definition of critical design as they have formulated it, after an exhaustive exploration of critical theory and metacriticism in philosophy and aesthetics. In their definition, a design is critical

> to the extents that it proposes a perspective-changing holistic account of a given phenomenon, and that this account is grounded in speculative theory, reflects a dialogical methodology, improves the public's cultural competence, and is reflexively aware of itself as an actor—with both power and constraints—within the social world it is seeking to change. (2013b, p. 3304)

The clarity and specificity of this definition revealed to me why critical design seemed to hold such promise for the development of a humane and enriching field of experience design. More importantly, it revealed how performance studies could contribute to its aims. One could argue that the aims of at least some performance practice and research coincide with this definition. It is certainly easy to interpret some performance practice and research as aiming to change perspectives with a holistic account of the performance event; to offer speculative points of view rather than claims to objective truth; to aim for liminal and transformational experiences (analogous to Gadamer's 'luminous moment', Bardzell and Bardzell 2013b, p. 3303); to contribute to the viewer's (or reader's) ability to understand her sociocultural environment; and to understand itself as ethically and reflexively embedded in the world. This rethinking of performance aims according to the five points of the Bardzells' definition of critical design offers a springboard for understanding the reasons that PED is a constructive next step for some strands of experience design (and performance studies) to take.

Any discussion of performance and critical design needs to address the issue of art and aesthetic practices. This will be treated more fully in the discussion of 'making special' (Dissanayake 2003) in Chap. 3. In relation to critical design, though, Bardzell and Bardzell again offer an extremely useful critique of Dunne and Raby's original framing of the relationship between design and art. Dunne and Raby assert that critical design cannot be art because art is too far from everyday experience to be taken seriously by most people, either because it is easy to go through daily life without encountering art, or because it is too shocking for people to integrate into their everyday lives. Bardzell and Bardzell reply with the fundamentally pragmatist stance that art and daily life are irrevocably intertwined, and that examples of the first impressionists or Damien Hirst notwithstanding, relatively little art shocks its audience. They include examples from the visual arts such as 'fine art photography on magazine covers' or 'graffiti' (2013b, p. 3299). I argue that performance only strengthens and extends their critique. Performance is deeply rooted in the tropes and rhythms of everyday life, particularly those genres of performance that eschew stages and greasepaint in favour of a more immediate connection with audience members. From Allan Kaprow's Happenings and Activities from the 1950s onwards, through Bobby Baker's autobiographical performances in her own kitchen, the boundaries between performance and everyday life are very easily blurred. From this perspective, it might be difficult to tell where the experience of interaction with a design ends and the experience of performance begins. It might be important, as the Bardzells argue, to prevent a critical design from being 'absorbed into the social practices of the artworld' (2013b, p. 3304). Any design that is created only for artists to use within a strongly demarcated art framework runs the risk of being dismissed in the way that Dunne and Raby originally foresaw. However, it is possible that this stricture against embedding a critical design firmly within the art world might be less of a rule and more of a challenge to be eventually and ingeniously overcome.

In the short time since the Bardzells and their colleagues began publishing on critical design, the topic has generated a number of responses and a fair amount of debate. Some researchers have used critical design in ways that are very much in line with PED. It has been a framework for clarifying emerging social norms that designers could work to understand, strengthen, or subvert (Lundmark and Normark 2014; Boer et al. 2015). It has been used to explore phenomena as diverse as databases (Feinberg et al. 2014) and hypnosis (Liang and Chang 2013). It forms a point of reference for speculative design (DiSalvo 2012) and critical making (Grimme et al. 2014), two of many practices that overlap to some degree with critical design. Criticisms include the lack of cultural sensitivity and postcolonial theory in this and related design fields (Sun 2013), where postcolonial theory has a fair track record within performance studies. Still others argue that critical design as described by the Bardzells should be de-emphasised in part because the epistemologies of critical theory and metacriticism are incompatible with the already existing critical practices available to design (Pierce et al. 2015). Many of the protests levelled at critical design seem well founded: for example, the challenge of 'design authorship' to user-centred design (2015, p. 2088) and the substitution of 'provisional exemplars' for the idea of a canon of critical design (2015, p. 2089) resonate strongly with PED. However, I believe that the definitions and methods put forward so far, whether in 'critical design' in the mould of the Bardzells or in the various forms of design identified by Pierce et al. (2015, p. 2088) are far from exhausted, and PED may make significant contributions to the aims of this type of design before the arguments over ontology and terminology are resolved. In terms of how performance and critical design can productively work together, I am convinced of the potential for performance theory and practice to inform a design practice that exists within the context of academic research. I am not alone in this, either, as critical design research into interactive performance can attest (Cerratto-Pargman et al. 2014). Performance theories, like critical theories, may be textual works that emphasise clarity, argument, and (arguably) ontology, but this does not prevent them from informing the generative, inspiration-driven, and tactical practice of design (Pierce et al. 2015, p. 2087).

The use of design to alternative ends is not limited to proponents of critical design. It is also shared by researchers who subscribe to Steve Benford et al.'s notion of 'uncomfortable interactions', which 'cause a degree of suffering to the user' (2012, p. 2005). Any request for people to engage in performance is very likely to provoke at least a mild sense of discomfort or anxiety, as so many experience nervousness or shyness when speaking in public or otherwise drawing attention to themselves—a situation noted by the designer/performers of Humanaquarium and in *Collect Yourselves!*, the case study for this book. In turn, though, these discomforts can lead to strongly pleasurable feelings as participants transcend their discomfort and release their tensions. Some uncomfortable interactions even aim for an aesthetic experience that users might experience as enlightening: 'demanding a deep personal commitment, reducing the risk of trivialisation, and in turn, promoting empathy and respect' (2012, p. 2006). It is also notable that uncomfortable interactions are theorised within a performance framework: Freytag's pyramid of exposition, rising action, climax, falling action, and dénouement (2012, p. 2011). While neither critical design nor uncomfortable interactions draw explicitly on each other's work, they share an interest in an ethical means of challenging users, rather than spoon-feeding them the product they say they want.

PED actively seeks to challenge emerging norms, not necessarily because they must be bad, but because there is value in questioning assumptions behind rapidly evolving technological practices. Explorations of experience design, participatory design, critical design, and uncomfortable interactions reveal places where performance theories and practices can contribute to the discussion within HCI and design. More importantly, though, they indicate an area of design research that performance is uniquely suited to explore: the ethical relationships among people, and between people and technology, where the constraints and affordances of the technology form a constitutive part of how the 'user' creates, understands, and performs her own identity. PED challenges emerging digital practices, not necessarily because the designer has decided that they are bad, but because there is value in questioning assumptions that are helping to shape our sense of self in the world. In light of the principles of critical design, the technologies that are created through PED need not be intended for immediate consumption by the general public. Instead, they may function primarily as a mechanism for exploring relationships between people and the digital media technologies that occupy a significant part of their performance of self and relationships. But in all cases, their aim is to gently push users away from the comfort zones that they have adopted, perhaps unthinkingly, around their digital technologies, towards a novel, possibly uncomfortable, and potentially transformative experience.

The Need for New Methodologies

As mentioned above, HCI has deep roots in positivist or postpositivist methodologies. In first- and even some second-wave HCI, usability was at the heart of the methodologies for approaching 'a confined problem space with a clear focus that adopted a small set of methods to tackle it' (Rogers 2009, p. 2). Usability is an ISO standard judged by measuring the efficiency, effectiveness, and satisfaction of an interaction through such classic methods as user testing (ISO 1998). For example, although Balabanović et al. provide a rich set of findings about digital media sharing behaviour, their methodology was the straightforward design of a prototype whose 'efficacy' was 'evaluated' (2000, p. 568) with straightforward HCI user tests. Incidentally, these tests excluded the process of selecting the photos used in the evaluation process, indicating the emphasis these researchers placed on the usability of their design's interface rather than the overall experience of engaging with personal photos when using the device. In the early years of this century, Yvonne Rogers identified common usability or user experience 'design methods, including scenarios, storyboards, sketching, lo-tech and software prototyping, focus groups, interviews, field studies and questionnaires and use cases' (2004, p. 24). These methods can provide rich, qualitative data, but do not push the bounds of understanding user experience within second- or third-wave HCI.

With the expansion of usability to user experience and now beyond user experience to 'emotional, eco-friendly, embodied experiences … context, constructivism and culture' (Rogers 2009, p. 2), HCI and design researchers require new methodologies to guide both the success of their suggested products and the decision of which research questions are most worthwhile to pursue in the first place. Rogers (2009) makes an eloquent argument for exploring as fully as possible the ethical dimensions of technologies that can become integrated into people's daily lives and by consequence into their sense of self and relationship to others—an argument that resonates with the aims of critical design. She calls for a rich, transdisciplinary mixture of methods to develop deeply contextualised user experiences (2009, p. 17) designed 'not in terms of time and errors, but in terms of the weighing up of the various moral, personal and social impacts on the various parties who will be affected by the proposed technology' (2009, p. 15). Similar concerns about the limitations of traditional HCI methodologies are seen in Erik Stolterman's compelling argument for rigorous yet 'designerly' methods such as sketching and working iteratively on multiple design alternatives at once (2008, p. 61). His term 'designerly' leaves space for the creation of novel goals as well as the design of solutions that effectively meet those goals. Tracee Vetting Wolf et al. seem intent on broadening the remit of HCI methodologies as well, describing a 'praxis' of 'creative design' that begins with 'a **non-linear process** of intent and discovery' (2006, p. 524, emphasis in the original). In line with these inclusive, responsible points of view is Johan Redström's caution to design for contexts rather than for users *per se*, lest designers over-constrain the actions and attitudes of the people who come to use their products (2006).

A key approach that enables boundary-pushing within HCI methodology is design-oriented research, which Daniel Fällman (2003) argues 'should have truth or knowledge of some sort as its main contribution, specifically such knowledge that would not have been attainable if design—the bringing forth of the research prototype—were not a vital part of the research process' (2003, p. 231).[2] The methodol-

---

[2] It can be argued, as Fällman does, that design is the foundational field and HCI merely one of the disciplines that it can address (2003, p. 225). I take instead his position that HCI is inherently oriented towards design, though that orientation requires investigation (2007). I do not intend for my

ogy in design-oriented research is neither art nor science but 'an unfolding activity which demands deep involvement from the designer' (2003, pp. 231–232). However, this critically important activity is often obscured by activities that are perhaps easier to specify and certainly more acceptable to the majority of HCI gatekeepers in research and publication, such as evaluative user testing—an observation made in print by Fällman and echoed by myself and most of the other experience design researchers I know. This obscuring of design happens in the struggle for researchers to establish the validity and relevance of their work, whether in reference to the natural sciences, as in first-wave HCI, or to the social sciences, as in second-wave HCI and design-oriented research itself (2007, p. 3). Fällman argues that design-oriented research should be valued for the quality of knowledge that is produced through the design process, particularly 'exploring possibilities outside of current paradigms' (2007, p. 4). He does not exclude the potential for other traditions, theories, and methodologies to contribute to the research process, which is especially important when exploring complex experiences such as those involving the performance of identity or social relationships.

Design-oriented research is a valuable HCI methodology for the purposes of PED, but it is insufficient. It allows for, but does not provide all the tools for, research into performative experiences with technology. It does not hold the answers to the third-wave goal of exploring the furthest reaches of personally and socio-culturally meaningful experience. Several years ago, Ron Wakkary et al. pointed out that 'performance, theatre, dance, architecture, conceptual design, industrial design, and visual art each contain rich knowledge and rigorous methodologies for constructing experience' (2004, p. 1709). While many inroads have been made since then, none has yet done justice to the full range of possibilities offered by performance. In fact, even PED as it is laid out in this text takes only a few steps down what is certainly a long road towards a full understanding of how performance and HCI can inform each other.

Steve Benford and Gabriella Giannachi (2011) offer a methodology of mixed reality performance that incorporates the basic ideas of design-oriented research but is tailored for the very public, artist-led technological experiments that they specialise in. Although they do not frame mixed reality performance within the field of experience design, their work is devoted to 'articulat[ing] design strategies for creating future experiences' (2011, p. 13), particularly 'the experience of real audiences' (2011, p. 11). They never intended to limit themselves to strict evaluations of a product, or even a qualitatively rich evaluation of an experience of a product. Instead, they and their colleagues gradually developed a methodology for developing 'compelling and tourable new experiences' with technology (2011, p. 8) that they could study in situ, with actual audiences participating in these publicly available mixed-reality performances.

---

arguments about methodologies to weigh in on the question of whether design or HCI is the dominant field. For the purposes of understanding HCI methodologies, I am framing design-oriented research as a methodological approach for researching human-computer interaction.

Their methodology has three major components. First, it is 'led by artistic practice' and prioritises taking 'risks' (Benford and Giannachi 2011, p. 10). Although research is an important part of the motivation and development of these mixed reality performances, they are conceived and driven as aesthetic events that aim to 'compel' audiences. Second, their methodology uses 'quick and dirty ethnographies' that are 'informed by sensitising concepts, which provide lenses through which to attack the challenge of analyzing a novel application' (2011, p. 11). In other words, new experiences can call for new ways of conceptualising what it means to understand those experiences. The 'quick and dirty' approach allows researchers to stay alert to the experiences of audiences coming to these mixed reality performances with fresh eyes and few expectations. Finally, their methodology derives generalisable theories, frameworks, platforms, and tools from these ethnographic studies. They work in the most 'designerly' ways to create utterly novel performance/game/technology hybrid experiences, yet they aim to derive from their research a body of information that can be of use to other researchers, to at least some degree bringing together the 'design-based UX research camp' and the 'model-based UX research camp' (Law 2011, p. 4). Their highly inclusive and adaptable methodology emphasises unpredictable individual agency in a performative interaction and provides a compelling model for the design of experiences based on performance.

The methodology developed for PED provides a very different type of guidance than the mixed reality performance methodology, but it aims for many of the same things: a pushing of boundaries, the generation and exploration of novel types of experience, and a set of tools that can be adapted by other researchers working with performative interactions in HCI (Williamson et al. 2014). This methodology lies at the heart of the overall framework of the emerging field described in this book.

Structuring the Argument

This book is divided into eight chapters. Chapter 1, this introduction, sets out the scope, aims, and definition of PED. It lays out the question that the book as a whole aims to answer: how can HCI and performance studies be brought together to enrich a design-led understanding of the personally significant interactions between people and digital technology?

Chapter 2 explores the slippery concept of performativity in greater detail. This term can mean radically different things depending on the context, which often goes unspoken, and yet much of the relevant work in experience design and performance studies hinges on it. After exploring the various meanings and their relevance to the topic of this book, the chapter traces the twin lineages of PED. It first takes a viewpoint that would be familiar to many people working in performance studies, then presents the parallel viewpoint of experience design, also drawing on interaction design and HCI.

Chapter 3 delves into more detail on the elements of performance studies that share the goals and perspectives of third-wave HCI and arts-based approaches to experience design. This chapter does not anticipate any background knowledge, or even a particular interest, in performance studies. It begins with a brief sketch of the main ways that performance has been treated in the HCI literature. It goes on to describe two seminal but not necessarily famous examples that ground discussion of the key theoretical perspectives, topics, and methodologies. Having explained the most salient traditions of live performance, the chapter then offers an overview of intermediality, a strand of performance research that emphasises how digital technologies and mediated elements can co-exist productively with live performance. The chapter concludes with a discussion of how performance seen from these points of view can inform PED.

The elaboration of the PED methodology, Chap. 4, begins with a discussion of how the concept of 'experience' has been treated in both performance studies and HCI. These perspectives are beginning to resonate in useful ways. The chapter then presents the six-part PED methodology in detail: (1) developing a line of enquiry, (2) selecting performances to watch that would inform the line of enquiry, (3) performance analyses on some of those performances, (4) design exploration based on the first three steps, (5) the 'performed experience' of the designed prototype in use, and (6) multiple analyses of the prototype being 'performed' in use. This methodology incorporates standard and accepted methods from the fields of design-oriented research and experience design, including investigation, design exploration, prototyping, and analysis. It also adopts the method of performance analysis alongside the argument within performance studies that methodologies must be reflexive and take into account the unpredictability of research processes (Kershaw and Nicholson 2011). This hybrid methodology involves the creation of a hybrid method: 'coded performance analysis', which combines HCI's thematic analysis techniques with performance analysis. The chapter concludes with a discussion of how the PED methodology can adapt to a range of possible projects.

Chapters 5 and 6 are devoted to the main case study, a digital media sharing project called *Collect Yourselves!* Chap. 5 charts the process by which the PED methodology resulted in a functioning prototype. The first step identifies lines of research and gaps in the literature around co-located digital media sharing. Step 2 explains the reasoning process by which I decided on a long list of autobiographical performances to watch, culminating in performance analyses on four of those (Step 3). Only one of these four is presented here, in full, as an example of the type of performance analysis that can be useful for PED. The performance analyses indicated key generative properties of autobiographical performance: self-making; a 'heightened attention' (Bauman 1975; Fischer-Lichte 2008) to the objects, bodies, and structures that make up the performance; situatedness, meaning attention to the spatiotemporal and social context of the performance; and the 'aesthetics of the event' (Fischer-Lichte 2008) that distinguish performance from ordinary conversation. The chapter concludes with a discussion of the design exploration that resulted in the *Collect Yourselves!* prototype.

Chapter 6 covers the last two steps of the PED methodology. It is concerned with the description, analysis, and findings derived from seeing *Collect Yourselves!* being performed. Four performances were created and analysed, of which again only one is presented in this text. Each performance was analysed from four perspectives, according to the methodology: two thematic analyses, an interaction analysis, and a coded performance analysis. The result was a technological design that created the conditions in which non-professional participants created performances that contained all of the identified properties of professional autobiographical performance. They experienced moments of connection, intimacy, risk, vulnerability, and liminality, in which emotions were heightened and attitudes might shift. The chapter concludes with new knowledge and theories generated by this process that extend both the HCI and the performance studies literature.

Chapters 7 and 8 explain what you, the reader, might take away from this book. Chapter 7 sets out guidelines for design, while Chap. 8 takes a broader view of the impact of PED on emerging trends in research—both in HCI and in performance studies. Both of these chapters consider PED as a field of study that may focus on any type of performance or performativity, using any technological intervention, including any type of digital media (or none at all). There is a virtually endless scope for pursuing a better understanding of interactions with technology in which people invest something of the self that they reveal, display, or perform for others. While the case study in Chaps. 5 and 6 concerns digital photo sharing, and therefore many of the examples in other chapters reflect that concern, Chaps. 7 and 8 attempt to open the field to other possibilities. They discuss the contributions PED might make in terms of HCI and performance studies research, not to be re-absorbed by these two fields but to open a dialogue among all three. From this perspective, performance is not some rarefied or optional realm that exists only for its own sake, but rather a personally meaningful, possibly risky, and potentially transformative experience that PED is uniquely well suited to explore.

References

Austin JL (1962) How to do things with words: the William James Lectures delivered at Harvard University in 1955. Oxford University Press, Oxford

Balabanović M, Chu L, Wolff G (2000) Storytelling with digital photographs. In: Proceedings of the SIGCHI conference on human factors in computing systems. ACM Press, New York, pp 564–571

Bardzell J, Bardzell S (2013a) Practical quagmires. Interactions 20(6):10–11

Bardzell J, Bardzell S (2013b) What is critical about critical design? In: Proceedings of the SIGCHI conference on human factors in computing systems. ACM Press, New York, pp 3297–3306

Bardzell S, Bardzell J, Forlizzi J, Zimmerman J, Antanitis J (2012) Critical design and critical theory: the challenge of designing for provocation. In: Proceedings of the designing interactive systems conference. ACM Press, New York, pp 288–297

Bauman R (1975) Verbal art as performance. Am Anthropol 77(2):290–311

Benford S, Giannachi G (2011) Performing mixed reality. MIT Press, Cambridge, MA/London

Benford S, Crabtree A, Reeves S, Sheridan J, Dix A, Flintham M, Drozd A (2006) The frame of the game: blurring the boundary between fiction and reality in mobile experiences. In: Proceedings of the SIGCHI conference on human factors in computing systems. ACM Press, New York, pp 427–436

Benford S, Greenhalgh C, Giannachi G, Walker B, Marshall J, Rodden T (2012) Uncomfortable interactions. In: Proceedings of the SIGCHI conference on human factors in computing systems. ACM Press, New York, pp 2005–2014

Boenisch PM (2012) Acts of spectating: the dramaturgy of the audience's experience in contemporary theatre. Crit Stages (7), np

Boer L, Mitchell R, Caglio A, Lucero A (2015) Embodied technology: unraveling bodily action with normative types. In: Proceedings of the 33rd annual ACM conference extended abstracts on human factors in computing systems. ACM Press, New York, pp 1711–1716

Butler J (2002) Gender trouble: feminism and the subversion of identity. Routledge, New York

Cerratto-Pargman T, Rossitto C, Barkhuus L (2014) Understanding audience participation in an interactive theater performance. In: Proceedings of the 8th Nordic conference on human-computer interaction: fun, fast, foundational. ACM Press, New York, pp 608–617

Chatzichristodoulou M (2011) Mapping intermediality in performance. Contemp Theatr Rev 21(2):230–231

Dalsgaard P, Hansen LK (2008) Performing perception: staging aesthetics of interaction. ACM Trans Comput-Hum Interact (TOCHI) 15(3):1–33

Dewey J (2005) Art as experience. Perigee Books, New York

Dibeklioğlu H, Ortega HM, Kosunen I, Zuzánek P, Salah AA, Gevers T (2011) Design and implementation of an affect-responsive interactive photo frame. J Multimodal User Interface 4(2):81–95

DiSalvo C (2012) Spectacles and tropes: speculative design and contemporary food cultures. Fibrecult J 20:109–122

Dissanayake E (2003) The core of art: making special. J Can Assoc Curric Stud 1(2):13–38

Dunne A (1999) Hertzian tales: electronic products, aesthetic experience, and critical design. MIT Press, London

Dunne A, Raby F (2001) Design noir: the secret life of electronic objects. Birkhäuser, Basel, Boston, Berlin

Fällman D (2003) Design-oriented human-computer interaction. In: Proceedings of the SIGCHI conference on human factors in computing systems. ACM Press, New York, pp 225–232

Fallman D (2007) Why research-oriented design isn't design-oriented research: on the tensions between design and research in an implicit design discipline. Knowl Technol Policy 20(3):193–200

Fearon F (2010) Decoding the audience: a theoretical paradigm for the analysis of the 'real' audience and their creation of meaning. About Perform 10:119–135

Feinberg M, Carter D, Bullard J (2014) Always somewhere, never there: using critical design to understand database interactions. In: Proceedings of the SIGCHI conference on human factors in computing systems. ACM Press, New York, pp 1941–1950

Fensham R (2012) Postdramatic spectatorship: participate or else. Crit Stage (7):1–8

Fischer-Lichte E (2008) The transformative power of performance: a new aesthetics. Routledge, London

Friedman K, Stolterman E (2015) Series forward. In: Taking [a]part: the politics and aesthetics of participation in experience-centered design. MIT Press, Cambridge, MA/London, pp ix–xiii

Frohlich DM, Clancy T, Robinson J, Costanza E (2004) The audiophoto desk. In: Proceedings of 2AD, second international conference on appliance design, HP, Bristol, np

Grimme S, Bardzell J, Bardzell S (2014) "We've conquered dark": shedding light on empowerment in critical making. In: Proceedings of the 8th Nordic conference on human-computer interaction: fun, fast, foundational. ACM Press, New York, pp 431–440

Hannah D, Harsløf O (2008) Introduction. In: Hannah D, Harsløf O (eds) Performance design. Museum Tusculanum Press, Copenhagen, pp 11–19

Hassenzahl M (2010) Experience design: technology for all the right reasons. Morgan & Claypool, San Rafael

Hayes L (2015) Skin music (2012): an audio-haptic composition for ears and body. In: Proceedings of the 2015 ACM SIGCHI conference on creativity and cognition. ACM Press, New York, pp 359–360

ISO (1998) Ergonomic requirements for office work with visual display terminals (VDTs) – Part 11: Guidance on usability. ISO 9241–11:1998. ISO, Geneva

Kershaw B, Nicholson H (2011) Introduction: doing methods creatively. In: Kershaw B, Nicholson H (eds) Research methods in theatre and performance. Edinburgh University Press, Edinburgh, pp 1–15

Kim J, Zimmerman J (2006) Cherish: smart digital photo frames for sharing social narratives at home. In: CHI '06 extended abstracts on human factors in computing systems. ACM Press, New York, pp 953–958

Law Effie Lai-Chong (2011) The measurability and predictability of user experience. In: Proceedings of the 3rd ACM SIGCHI symposium on engineering interactive computing systems, ACM Press, New York, pp 1–10

Liang R-H, Chang H-M (2013) Hypnotist framing: hypnotic practice as a resource for poetic interaction design. In: Proceedings of the 6th international conference on designing pleasurable products and interfaces. ACM Press, New York, pp 241–250

Lundmark S, Normark M (2014) Designing gender in social media: unpacking interaction design as a carrier of social norms. Int J Gend Sci Technol 6(2):223–241

McCarthy J, Wright P (2004) Technology as experience. MIT Press, Cambridge, MA

McCarthy J, Wright P (2015) Taking [a]part: the politics and aesthetics of participation in experience-centered design. MIT Press, Cambridge, MA/London

McKenzie J (2008) (Almost) all you need is love. In: Hannah D, Harsløf O (eds) Performance design. Museum Tusculanum Press, Copenhagen, pp 127–142

Mullaney T (2015) Suspending reality: a disruptive approach to designing transformative experiences. In: Benz P (ed) Experience design: concepts and case studies. Bloomsbury Publishing, London/New York, pp 151–158

Nam HY, Nitsche M (2014) Interactive installations as performance: inspiration for HCI. In: Proceedings of the 8th international conference on tangible, embedded and embodied interaction. ACM Press, New York, pp 189–196

Nitsche M (2013) Performance art and digital media. Digital Creat 24(2):93–95

Oddey A, White C (2009) Modes of spectating. Intellect, Bristol

Pierce J, Sengers P, Hirsch T, Jenkins T, Gaver W, DiSalvo C (2015) Expanding and refining design and criticality in HCI. In: Proceedings of the 33rd annual ACM conference on human factors in computing systems. ACM Press, New York, pp 2083–2092

Popat S, Palmer S (2005) Creating common ground: dialogues between performance and digital technologies. Int J Perform Arts Digit Media 1(1):47–65

Rancière J (2011) The emancipated spectator. Verso, London

Reason M (2010) Asking the audience: audience research and the experience of theatre. About Perform 10:15–34

Reason M (2015) Participations on participation: researching the active theatre audience. Particip J Audience Recept Stud 12(1):271–280

Redström J (2006) Towards user design? On the shift from object to user as the subject of design. Des Stud 27(2):123–139

Rogers Y (2004) New theoretical approaches for human-computer interaction. Annu Rev Inf Sci Technol 38(1):87–143

Rogers Y (2009) The changing face of human-computer interaction in the age of ubiquitous computing. In: Miesenberger K, Holzinger A (eds) HCI and usability for e-inclusion. Springer, Berlin/Heidelberg, pp 1–19

Rust K, Foss E, Bonsignore E, McNally B, Hordatt C, Malu M, Mei B, Gumbs HK (2014) Interactive and live performance design with children. In: Proceedings of the 2014 conference on interaction design and children. ACM Press, New York, pp 305–308

Salter C (2010) Entangled: Technology and the transformation of performance. MIT Press, Cambridge, MA

Sheridan JG, Bryan-Kinns N (2008) Designing for performative tangible interaction. Int J Arts Technol 1(3):288–308

Sheridan JG, Bryan-Kinns N, Bayliss A (2007) Encouraging witting participation and performance in digital live art. In: Proceedings of the 21st British HCI group annual conference on people and computers: HCI…but not as we know it. British Computer Society, Swinton, pp 13–23

Spence J, Andrews S, Frohlich DM (2012) Now, where was I? Negotiating time in digitally augmented autobiographical performance. J Media Pract 13(3):269–284

Stolterman E (2008) The nature of design practice and implications for interaction design research. Int J Des 2(1):55–65

Strandvad SM, Pedersen KM (2015) Co-producing a festival experience: a socio-material understanding of experience design. In: Benz P (ed) Experience design: concepts and case studies. Bloomsbury Publishing, London/New York, pp 105–112

Sun H (2013) Critical design sensibility in postcolonial conditions. Sel Pap Internet Res 14.0(3):1–4

Taylor R, Schofield G, Shearer J, Wallace J, Wright P, Boulanger P, Olivier P (2011) Designing from within: humanaquarium. In: Proceedings of the 2011 annual conference on human factors in computing systems. ACM Press, New York, pp 1855–1864

ten Bhömer M, Helmes J, O'Hara K, van den Hoven E (2010) 4Photos: a collaborative photo sharing experience. In: Proceedings of the 6th Nordic conference on human-computer interaction: extending boundaries. ACM Press, New York, pp 52–61

Wakkary R, Schiphorst T, Budd J (2004) Cross-dressing and border crossing: exploring experience methods across disciplines. In: CHI '04 extended abstracts on human factors in computing systems. ACM Press, New York, pp 1709–1710

Williamson JR, Hansen LK, Jacucci G, Light A, Reeves S (2014) Understanding performative interactions in public settings. Pers Ubiquit Comput 18(7):1545–1549

Wolf TV, Rode JA, Sussman J, Kellogg WA (2006) Dispelling design as the black art of CHI. In: Proceedings of the SIGCHI conference on human factors in computing systems. ACM Press, New York, pp 521–530

Wright P, McCarthy J (2010) Experience-centered design: designers, users, and communities in dialogue. Synth Lect Hum-Centered Inf 3:1–123

Wright P, Wallace J, McCarthy J (2008) Aesthetics and experience-centered design. ACM Transact Comput-Hum Interact (TOCHI) 15(4):1–21

Chapter 2
Performativity

Abstract This chapter helps clarify the concept of PED by examining the concept of performativity, a term with any number of distinct meanings and implications in HCI, performance studies, and beyond. The introductory section sketches four definitions of performativity: as a capacity for action (though not always individual agency), as a process of performance, as active engagement (embodied, mental, energetic, and the like), and as an indication of markers of theatricality or a performance frame. These definitions inflect the primary sense of the performative in PED, which is the concept of putting one's actions on display. Performativity is therefore implicit in every interaction with technology that may result in another person perceiving and potentially passing some judgement on the user. As a result, the *how* of any interaction becomes a key consideration. With this perspective established, the chapter provides a brief overview of the field of performance studies and its point of view on performative interactions with technologies, followed by an overview of the move in HCI, interaction design, and experience design towards third-wave concerns. The chapter concludes with an explanation of how these two points of view come together in PED.

Performativity

Probably the trickiest part of PED is the word that starts it all: 'performative'. Everyone who reads that word will have some sense of what it means, or what they assume it must mean. The term has any number of meanings, though, and it is fairly easy to find examples of research where it is used with no clear referent at all. What it *can* mean is enormously exciting for researchers and practitioners in HCI, and it is occupying an increasingly important role in current research. Researchers and practitioners in experience design, digital or intermedial performance, or technology studies can all benefit from a solid understanding of what performativity might mean for their work. In general, 'performativity' is used to refer to one of four basic concepts: first, the capacity for something other than a living creature or force of nature to act on the world; second, a focus on the processual nature of an event; third, a focus on a person's active engagement with the world as distinguished from a more passive perception or experience of it; and fourth, as an adjective for 'performance' in the sense of theatrical performance. The first three of these readings

© Springer International Publishing Switzerland 2016

J. Spence, *Performative Experience Design*, Springer Series on Cultural
Computing, DOI 10.1007/978-3-319-28395-1_2

underscore the contextualised, durational, and meaningful aspects of interaction, while the fourth often implies artifice. However, all four point towards a meaning of performativity that is particularly useful in the context of interaction design: a contextualised, durational, heightened, and meaningful interaction with others that reflects something of the person in that interaction.

The first concept, referring to the capacity to act on the world, is usually traced back to the work of J.L. Austin (1962), a philosopher of language who was active in the mid-twentieth century. He was the first to identify uses of language that act on the world. Saying that the sky is green does not change the colour of the sky, while saying 'I do' at the right point in a wedding ceremony gives you all the privileges and obligations of marriage. Other things need to happen as well, such as signing the right documents. And if you happen to say 'I do' while sitting next to a stranger on the bus, you will not suddenly marry the person you are sitting next to. However, the speaking of the words 'I do' are necessary to the act of getting married (at least in the traditional situation imagined by Austin)—saying 'I have changed my mind' would invalidate the entire procedure. Austin's term for these words that actually accomplish the action they describe is 'performative utterances'. Incidentally, while Austin argued that any of the trappings of theatrical performance would weaken the power of a performative utterance, later interpretations have indicated that those utterances are actually strengthened by being perceived as part of a socio-cultural performance (Bauman and Briggs 1990, p. 65).

This idea that in some cases '*by* saying or *in* saying something we are doing something' (Austin 1962, p. 12) is vital for the development of another extremely influential philosophical concept, this time in the area of gender theory. Judith Butler's work on gender performativity (2002) is extremely dense and detailed, and she has elaborated on it several times in the more than two decades since its initial publication. For Butler, gender is neither simply a biological fact nor an act of choice on the part of the individual. For her, 'gender proves to be performative— that is, constituting the identity it is purported to be' (2002, p. 33). Being a girl, for example, isn't the simple fact of having the anatomy of a female, but a composite of every action that girl makes that would mark her out as different from a boy. One easy mistake to make in trying to use this theory is to assume that the person in question has the power to act like a girl, a boy, or anything else. According to Butler, each individual has very limited scope for acting outside the norms around her. This limitation has two main causes. First, performativity means that there is no such thing as an essence of girlness, or boyness, or any other attribute, that an individual could choose to act out or modify. Butler explains this by saying that 'gender is always a doing, though not a doing by a subject who might be said to preexist the deed' (2002, p. 33). The second cause is that performativity does not come solely from the individual. After all, we do not invent the actions that indicate gender; we learn them, repeat them, and even if we make some change, we still cite them in context. It is an act of discourse, deeply embedded in social norms, that acts on an individual. A girl is made a girl by other people's reactions to her just as much as she is made one by her own actions. Butler's complex and subtle theoretical points support the idea that an individual does not have full and immediate control of every element of her own identity, but that identity is shaped in relation to others.

Although Butler is writing about gender, her theories have been applied to any number of aspects of personal identity. Many performance theorists rely on her work, particularly those who deal with autobiographical performance. This is particularly relevant to performativity, because autobiography involves performers using their own life experiences as their material. They perform themselves, or at least a version of themselves, not unlike how people in everyday life will 'perform' differently at Sunday dinner with their parents than they will on a weekend night out with their friends. People are not entirely fake in one context or entirely authentic in another, because there is no essence of who they are that they can decide to fully conceal or fully reveal. This extension of Butler's theory underpins most of contemporary thinking of what it means to perform the self, whether in staged and scripted works of autobiographical theatre or more visceral and immediate forms of body art where the performer uses his or her (often naked) physical presence as the primary medium. And, if there is no essential self to reveal, there is no point in aiming for a perfectly truthful or unmediated connection between two people, even when they are sharing deeply personal life experiences as accurately as they can (Heddon 2008, p. 6).

Even the most fundamental elements of identity exist only as they are lived in encounters between people (Watson and Smith 2005, p. 20; Sandbye 2005; Heddon 2008; Fischer-Lichte 2008b). The sharing or performance of the self in terms of self-disclosure will mean different things to different audiences, and each act of self-disclosure (or refusal to disclose) will alter the identity it is in the process of constructing. The idea that there is no essential self to know has found support in the basic tenets of postmodern theory as well as cognitive science research into how autobiographical memories—those memories that tell us who we are—are formed and retrieved (which will be explained further in Chap. 3).

Austin's performative utterances, Butler's gender theory, and the consequent understanding of the self as unstable and multilayered, all point to a way of understanding the world in which power is held in surprising ways. Spoken words have the power to change the world. Repeated, culturally determined actions have more power to create gender identity than a person's own body does (as for example with the many babies born with bodies that do not fit the norms of 'girl' or 'boy', where the family and/or medical establishment decide how to raise the child). A person's entire identity is made up of what she does, over time, rather than any one thing that she perfectly and permanently 'is'. In all these cases, performance is a very powerful action, but it is not fully controlled by an individual person exerting her will alone. Words act, discourse acts, cultural norms act, action itself acts.[1] This is the

---

[1] Performativity is also invoked by theorists and practitioners such as Chris Salter, who works in performance, media, and technology, to explain one way in which technological devices can have agency of their own to perform (Salter 2010, p. xxix). Within performance studies, there are strong arguments that inanimate objects such as photographs (Auslander 2006) or written documents (Phelan 2004) of a past performance can be said to do their own performing. For the purposes of

first set of ideas that performativity can refer to, and it is extremely helpful for keeping experience designers from assuming that their users or experiencers have a unified, static identity that they are fully in conscious control of when responding to a designed intervention.

The second meaning is that performativity points to a *process* of performance rather than a single object or result. This is entirely in line with the first meaning of performativity in the sense that all of those actions take place over time—particularly Butler's theory, in which the entire lifetime of an individual is just one segment of a much longer process of cultural activity. However, this second idea focuses on the duration and process of each individual 'performance'. This might seem to be a trivial differentiation to make, but it was at the heart of a fundamental upheaval in performance studies in the 1990s. As performance theorist Erika Fischer-Lichte (2008a) explains, the study of performance had been dominated by semiotics, which reads the signs of a performance as if they were a text. For example, a semiotic reading of a performance might dissect the props, gestures, and lighting of a performance for what they contribute to the performance's meaning. In the 1990s, many performance researchers felt the need to acknowledge what makes performance different from other cultural 'texts', namely how people feel and experience the 'performative process' of a performance as it unfolds over time (2008a, p. 71). This led to a turn to phenomenology, which was combined with semiotics to produce the dominant form of performance analysis over the past two decades and more.

'Performativity' is often used in this second sense within HCI because 'it stresses the event character of action and interaction, as it is about bringing something to completion that has an initiation and a consummation' (Ehn et al. 2007, p. 64). Others in HCI acknowledge this temporal structure and then extend performativity to perception, as well: 'Following this, particular expressions and experiences can be understood as choreographing a user's active or passive participation in a "performance"' (Williamson and Hansen 2012). Paying attention to the ongoing and shifting nature of an event helps to direct our attention to ways that we might choreograph not just the course of the event or the user's participation, but also her range of experiences over the course of the interaction. Performance as an event that begins, evolves, and then ceases to exist in an age where people expect the (semi-)permanence of digital media also provides a way of 'knowing that takes us beyond the quotidian…why its stubborn makers still seek to create artificial events that remind us that the everyday is extraordinary only when we can observe and experience it as such' (Salter 2010, p. 352). The processual nature of performance is a significant means of choreographing perception in this way.

Performativity's third meaning is of an active engagement with the interaction or event in question. Recent work within performance theory that studies audiences promotes some version of the idea that spectators are always active in some way,

---

the work discussed in this book, it is helpful to know that these perspectives exist, but it is not critical to go into precisely how a non-human element would act. It is also arguable that HCI and design communities have the advantage over some performance theorists in their familiarity with concepts such as actor network theory.

even if they are sitting still in a traditional theatre. These theories (e.g. Oddey and White 2009; Rancière 2011; Boenisch 2012; Fensham 2012; Reason 2015) also have some empirical, neuroscientific weight to them, as individuals pay attention to different parts of a performance in different ways, attach significance to different elements, associate based on personal memories and attitudes, etc. However, 'performativity' is sometimes used to draw attention to the actions of spectators or audience members beyond perception and meaning-making, particularly within HCI research. For example, Benford and Giannachi describe 'designing for spectating', in which 'it can be argued that it is the very presence of these spectators that transforms an interaction with a computer into a performance' (2011, p. 156). Other HCI and performance researchers are less specific in their definition, but also intend to convey a sense of the 'power' or 'energy' that comes from an active and shared experience (as in many of the contributions in Hannah and Harsløf 2008). Within HCI, a similar intention is seen in the many projects that use 'performativity' to refer to how interactions are physically embodied and what that sense of embodiment can mean for designers (e.g. Jacucci et al. 2009; Loke and Robertson 2010; Wallis et al. 2010; Nam and Nitsche 2014). Any discussion of performativity involving humans must deal to some degree with their physical, mental, and/or energetic engagement with an interaction, particularly when that engagement is shared amongst people holding the same or different roles in the engagement.

The fourth and last of the main definitions that I have identified is the sense of artifice or staging that underlies some uses of the word 'performativity'. As Lone Koefoed Hansen et al. (2011) point out, sociologist Erving Goffman created one of the seminal works for understanding how human interactions can be understood—metaphorically—as a performance. Therefore his use of 'performativity', which has influenced scholars in HCI and performance studies (recently Benz 2015, who uses the term to mean anything related to cultural performance), makes many references to the strategies of creating theatrical productions such as taking on roles; creating a harmony amongst the setting, appearance, and manner of performance; and the 'awe and distance' that audiences can feel towards performers (Goffman 1959, p. 76). It would be pointless to try to argue that these have absolutely no place in the experimental performance pieces that underpin the examples and theories of PED, but they are certainly not the focus.[2] In the types of performance described in Chap. 3, performers play aspects of themselves, are often relatively unconcerned with settings, and strive to overcome the physical and emotional distance between performers and audiences. However, Goffman has more traction outside of performance studies than most of the scholars dealing with performativity from within the field, so the conflation of performativity and theatricality continues.

It is unfair to make Goffman shoulder all the blame for this situation, when the English language itself does not have a separate word referring to those aspects of a performance that frame it as such,[3] distinct from the normal interactions of everyday

---

[2] For a brief overview of the complex relationship between performativity and theatricality in the context of mediatised performance see Barton 2013.

[3] See Goffman 1974; Schechner 2006; Benford et al. 2006.

life. If the word 'performancey' existed, we could reserve 'performative' for self-constituting actions that are committed and repeated over time, and use 'performancey' to refer to all those other characteristics of performance that are not bound by traditional constraints such as a stage, costumes, roles, tickets, seats, etc. It is probably just as well that such an ungainly word does not exist, because the self-constituting nature of performance is critical to its aesthetics (Fischer-Lichte 2008b) and therefore to any design that would attempt to create something like a performance. Instead, I propose thinking about performativity from the point of view of an experience designer. To design an experience, we need to focus on how an individual participant would perceive and feel her interaction with the technology we are designing, with other participants, with any bystanders, with anyone who might later hear about this interaction or view its documentation, with her memories and self-image as they emerge and shift during the experience, with any moments of dissonance or risk, and with changes to these perceptions and feelings over time, including far beyond the end of the interaction per se. We need to focus on a wide range of potential responses to all of these elements, as different participants in different combinations create new and unexpected interpretations of their experience. Perhaps most importantly of all, we need to focus on how we, the designers, come to interact with the participants through the technologies we have developed. We are generally far more knowledgeable and comfortable with the technology we have designed than the participants will be—but they are the ones who have, shape, and reflect on the experiences we are so anxious to design. This calls for a radically simplified, but inclusive, definition of the performative, which places a participant's experience at the heart of the inquiry.

This can be accomplished by adopting seminal performance researcher Richard Schechner's definition of performance as a 'showing doing': 'pointing to, underlining, and displaying doing' (2000, p. 28). The term 'performative' then refers to this self-conscious and audience-conscious act of not only taking some action, but taking it in just the way an individual *would* take it, on that day, in that context, in front of those people. The *how* becomes important, tied just as much to an individual's layered and shifting sense of self as it is to the culturally coded mannerisms through which she makes the act her own. Siân E. Lindley and colleagues (2009) express performativity in a non-theatrical context as 'how memories are enacted in conversation, stories, photos, and so on' (2009, p. 2). The *how* of that interaction cannot be fully planned: it generates the experience that it describes, and both the designer and the participant (not to mention the full spatiotemporal and sociocultural context of the situation) must share the credit for the result of the design. The sometimes uneasy mixture of the 'performative' and the 'theatrical' also gives us enormous insight into exactly *how* design can shape a performance, thanks to empirically based theories of performance aesthetics that hinge on 'heightened attention' (Fischer-Lichte 2008b; Bauman 1975) like the 'heightened vitality' described by United States pragmatist philosopher John Dewey (2005, p. 18) that underpins so much current work in experience design (McCarthy and Wright 2004 and their many adherents). Performativity in this sense is not limited to cultural performances: a similar interplay of performativity and performance takes place in ordinary conversational storytelling, where performativity not only describes but creates a performer, audience, and experience each time a particular storytelling 'performance' occurs (Langellier 1999). In all cases, from the most everyday to the most sublime, performativity refers to a contextualised, durational, heightened, and meaningful interaction among people—sometimes mediated or influenced by digital technologies (Bardzell et al. 2010, p. 35)—through which performer, audience, and experience are created. The aesthetics of performance will be explained in Chap. 3, and the methodology for applying these aesthetics to design will follow in Chap. 4.

A Performance Studies Point of View

PED draws equally from both experience design and performance studies, but these are two wide-ranging fields harbouring a range of sometimes clashing points of view. Both of them, arguably, rely on the concept of performativity to distinguish them from closely related fields such as interaction design on the one hand, or theatre studies on the other. This section sets out in more specific terms the traditions that PED inherits from performance studies and the challenges it seeks to take on.

To someone not steeped in the performance studies literature, the first question might be: is there any difference between performance, theatre, and drama? After all, books and papers on conventional theatre are published under each of these headings, and the terms are often used interchangeably. The answer is that it depends on whom you ask. The simplest answer I can offer is that unlike much of what falls under the heading of 'theatre' and 'drama', 'performance' tends to focus on those situations that closely parallel the interactions or experiences that an HCI practitioner or designer might recognise. For example, performance does not need to take place on a stage, or be conducted by a professional actor taking on a fictional role. My favourite example is of a street performer I encountered on a busy pavement in the middle of London. He was upside down, with his head in a bucket, casually maintaining his balance and occasionally giving a 'thumbs up' sign with one hand. No one passing by called the emergency services to report a man with his head stuck in a bucket. We all understood that he was standing there for the purpose of being seen, and probably to earn some spare change from his performance, despite the fact that there was no stage, no costume, no ticketing, no fictional role, no situation being enacted. This performer was working solely with his ability to influence people's perceptions and interactions as they walked by. As with the difference between performativity and theatricality, there are no hard and fast rules, but Upside Down Bucket Man is as good an example as any of why you are reading about PED rather than Theatrical Experience Design or Dramatic Experience Design. Chances are you use technology rather than buckets to accomplish your goals, but the principle of experience and interaction is the same.

The field of performance studies is a broad church. Arguably its most influential denomination, at least in the Anglophone world, was born from the fusion in the

1970s and 1980s of theatre studies, under Schechner, and anthropology, under Victor Turner (Phelan 1998, p. 3). Performance as identified by Schechner and colleagues is well equipped to study interactions with technology that have cultural, discursive, representational, and identity-forming elements. They combined their fields of expertise to imagine a new field of performance studies in the United States. Their goal in the early stages was 'to approach the genres of theatre, dance, music, sports, and ritual as a single, coherent group, as performance' (Schechner and Appel 1990, p. 3). Their colleague Barbara Kirshenblatt-Gimblett observes that the field 'sets no limit on what can be studied in terms of medium and culture. Nor does it limit the range of approaches that can be taken' (2007, p. 43). This perspective has led to a situation in which performance is at least as broad and ill-defined a term as performativity, as different fields adopt a performance metaphor for their own uses. It has even led performance theorist Jill Dolan (1993) to plead for performance and performativity to be returned to performance and theatre studies, where they would ideally be applied to actual cultural performances. While I appreciate Dolan's concern, I argue that PED generates actual performances that can be analysed and understood as such, using the tools of performance studies alongside the methods of experience design.

Schechner's and Kirshenblatt-Gimblett's version of performance studies at New York University was not the only one: at Northwestern University, Dwight Conquergood saw performance studies as an extension of the oral interpretation of literary texts rather than as a direct challenge to theatre studies (Kirshenblatt-Gimblett 2007, p. 45). In their different ways, though, both the East Coast (New York University) and the Midwestern (Northwestern) approaches aimed attention at what Conquergood described as the 'finely nuanced meaning that is embodied, tacit, intoned, gestured, improvised, coexperienced, covert—and all the more deeply meaningful because of its refusal to be spelled out' (2002, p. 146). Despite the fact that the Midwestern approach is rooted in written texts, it seeks to understand exactly those elements of live performance that are separate from, and unattainable by, the written text on its own. This provides a different angle on the study of the meanings and significances in human interaction that 'refuse to be spelled out' in positivist, scientific terms. This tradition comfortably includes practises of storytelling, oral history, and performing narrative that help to connect cultural performances with everyday performances of the self, and thereby connect the more arcane elements of performance theory and practice with designs that will be experienced by people outside of an artistic context.

The development of performance studies in relation to theatre and oral interpretation, while influential in the Anglophone world, was a latecomer compared to the German field of Theaterwissenschaft. Since the 1920s, this field has studied 'theatre as a social event and a process of embodied action rather than the communication of a literary text' (Carlson 2008, p. 4). This approach maintains a direct relationship to theatre without the unfortunate side effect of setting up performance and theatre studies as antagonists. There is no surprise, then, that the foundational performance theory behind PED comes from the German theorist Erika Fischer-Lichte. Her work is widely influential in continental Europe, but has only recently begun to have a significant impact in the Anglophone performance community.

I am by no means attempting to establish (or resurrect) a division between performance studies and theatre studies on the spurious claim that all theatre is text-based fiction, or that performance studies excludes text-based fiction. However, the focus of performance studies on 'behavior [as] the "object of study"' (Schechner 2006, p. 1) rather than on the staging of a given fictional text makes performance studies particularly useful for PED. In contrast to much of the theatre or drama studies literature, performance studies tends not to assume a literary script brought to life by actors playing fictional roles. Instead, it makes room for interactions between people that break every rule or assumption about theatrical performance. Performance studies even embraces those performers who hide or obscure their work: some, like Tehching Hsieh, perform in solitude, leaving almost no trace of their performances for anyone to see. Others, like Pawel Althamer, stage works in public that for the most part go totally unnoticed, such as setting performers to undertake utterly unremarkable actions for half an hour in a square in Ljubljana amongst regular, unsuspecting inhabitants and passers-by. It is not my intention to contribute to the disparaging of theatre or theatricality that some in the field identify (States 1996, p. 9); much of the work that is so useful to PED (and fascinating in its own right) draws directly from traditional theatre and is discussed in those terms. On the whole, though, 'performance' is usually the more useful term for PED.

Given the technological orientation of PED, it might seem practical begin with a survey of digital performance. Steve Dixon's encyclopaedic work (2007) still stands as a landmark in the field, laying out a dazzling array of approaches to the use of digital technology in performance. Until recently, the study of digital performance has been dominated by analyses of the functions of particular technologies on stage, on screen, in virtual reality, or via cyborgs. Dixon's definition of digital performance is one of any kind 'where computer technologies play a key role rather than a subsidiary one in content, techniques, aesthetics, or delivery forms'. This definition leaves little room for exploring how digital media might shape performance beyond the way in which its display technology impacts the events on stage. Even Dixon's single chapter on interactivity (2007, Chapter 23) focuses more on how certain digital performances replicate or problematise the performer-audience relationship established in pre-digital performances than on the role that digital media might play in forming a new set of relationships through performance. This 'theatrical' understanding of performance can say a great deal about how those technologies are perceived in an artistic context, but it does not tend to prioritise the nuances of felt experience, particularly among individuals engaging with the technology in various or shifting roles outside the confines of an easily identifiable theatrical context.

Since 2007, the use of digital elements in performance has hardly abated, and the number of performance-oriented interactive projects or artworks studied within HCI continues to grow. However, Dixon's approach would be extremely limiting for a field of enquiry that is devoted to exploring performative interactions—contextualised, durational, heightened, and meaningful interactions among people—which are mediated or influenced by technology. Analyses based on digital performance tend to valorise the technology, sometimes at the expense of a full understanding of the performative interactions among people. A crude but possibly useful metaphor would be to imagine studying why social media is so popular starting from the premise that people are seeking a digital interaction. In the real world, people have developed expectations around their personal technologies, and social media services met those expectations with new ways of connecting online *with other people*. Of course the technology is key to any study of social media, because the types of interaction it affords are in many ways different to anything we have had before. But the fact that technology is key to the phenomenon being studied does not mean that it should be the main focus of that study. The main motivation for engagement with social media is the engagement itself. As with performativity, the question of focus is enormously important. HCI, interaction design, and experience design already have a rich tradition of developing and understanding technological advances. What is needed now is a better understanding of how to develop interactions in subtle and complex interpersonal situations (Williamson et al. 2014).

A strong focus on the technology involved in a performance also feeds the debate that raged through much of the 1990s and still bubbles up from time to time in the twenty-first century, between live and mediatised performance. It began in earnest with Peggy Phelan (1993) with her assertion that live performance is by its nature an act of disappearance that cannot be reproduced. Live performance is therefore incapable of being claimed or captured by another medium, and not even the most sophisticated documentation can recreate it. Phelan therefore argues that live performance is a radically different thing from any mediatised form, and it is politically and ethically empowered to oppose the dominant Western 'commodity culture' (2003, p. 294) that privileges the mediated, static, and commodifiable. It is extremely difficult to argue against Phelan's premise that there is a qualitative difference between a performance given by a living, co-present human being and a performance viewed on a screen, or that the precise conditions of live performance can never be recreated, if for no other reason than live performance always carries within it the potential to deviate from its plans (Fischer-Lichte 2008b). However, the cultural and political thrust of her argument helped to set live performance in fierce opposition to mediated forms including film, television, and computer-based representations.

Phelan's position is vigorously contradicted by Philip Auslander in the book *Liveness: Performance in a Mediatized Culture* (1999), which continues to underpin the bulk of the responses to the debate. Auslander sees live and mediatised performance as 'rivals' (1999, p. 1), but not because of any ontological opposition between the two. He points out that in its early days, television was promoted as a live experience in contrast to film (1997). It is only as norms changed and expectations moved on—and as replay became possible—that people began to think of television in terms of its mediatising power and separation from the live performance being broadcast. Moreover, he points out that media degrade over time, contradicting the immutability of media implied by Phelan. For Auslander, mediatisation is not a technologically determined quality but a function of 'media epistemology', the ways in which we expect to perceive the world (1999, p. 32). By treating media-tised performance as historical events shaping and shaped by political and economic forces, Auslander rejects Phelan's ontology of performance and allows a space for various combinations of live and mediatised performance to emerge. A number of other performance theorists have likewise turned away from ideas of a zero-sum battle between the live and mediatised. These see live performance as incorporating the digital through tangible interfaces (Sheridan and Bryan-Kinns 2008) or being enhanced by mediatisation (Dixon 2007, p. 29); they identify mediation as a site of performance (Boenisch 2006, p. 195), or conversely argue that the co-present human body is always mediated through the audience's expectations of what it means to perform in a media-saturated world (Kappenberg 2011). Media technol-ogy and performance researcher Chris Salter neatly encapsulates the current frame of the debate between live human performance and technical or mediated elements, as a 'tension' that is 'artificial but continually propagated' (2010, p. xiv).

Performativity provides a helpful way of making this tension productive. When someone begins to perform in front of an audience, that activity creates the perfor-mance—it distinguishes a performer, an audience, and the performance taking place between them. This will happen when a live performer starts her act and the people near her choose whether to pay attention (forming an audience) or go about their business (which impedes the performance in some way but does not make it cease to exist). However, it will also happen when someone starts playing a recorded per-formance. A room full of people having conversations now need to choose whether to pay attention, forming an audience for the recorded performer, or go about their business. To this degree, both situations are 'performative' in the first sense described above. In the mediatised situation, audience members can also be studied as they go through a process of spectating and possibly become more engaged in their experi-ence of spectating. It can be extremely helpful to study how different audience members shape each other's experience of spectating, as well. What the asynchro-nous mediatised situation cannot do is to create a performance in which both per-formers and audience members have the power to shape each other's experience.[4] The felt experience of live performance is one in which both performers and audi-ence members interact with each other, creating a dynamic and fluctuating exchange. This interaction gets to the heart of what interaction and experience designers do: to create and try to understand how people interact with technologies. PED seeks to create and try to understand how this works in situations where technologies are not just the object being spectated, but a factor in how people interact with each other. This points to performance studies and performativity as fruitful ways of exploring interactions among people where technology is a condition but not exclusive focus of study. However, there is a way to approach digital technology in performance that operates from a premise of interconnection rather than opposition: intermedial performance.

---

[4] Telematic, virtual reality, and other synchronous performances would be 'live' in these terms, though more research is needed to fully understand how the mediatisation at work in these situa-tions may influence the many levels of performativity at work.

Intermedial research covers any combination of media or mode, from movie adaptations of novels to mixed-media performance.[5] Rather than exalting the technology or positing a conflict between live and mediatised performance, intermedial research attempts 'to mark the concrete effects of being definitively multiple and interrelational' (Nelson 2010, p. 17). This work sees digital culture in terms of the 'relationships' and 'interdependencies' it creates—like the social media example described above—where the technologically shaped interactions of performers and audience members are the primary objects of study. An emerging concept in this field, *sensibilité* (sensibility), indicates the move towards embodied and immersive experiences demanded by intermedial performances that engage users more deeply than simply seeing and hearing an activity happening on a stage (Lavender 2013). Moreover, the aim of intermedial studies is to understand 'how—singularly and collectively—intermedial performances may have elicited a new cultural way of seeing, feeling and being in the contemporary world' (Nelson 2010, p. 18). The inverse of this broad question is at the centre of Salter's investigation of technology in performance, which uncovers how technologies and what Salter refers to as 'socio-political-cultural-economic contexts' have changed how performances are created and perceived (Salter 2010, p. xiii). Intermediality looks at performances that are marked by digital technology in any way and interrogates their reciprocal relationship with their performers and audiences. This perspective allows for a rich investigation of the processes of interactivity and performativity of interest in experience design and PED.

An Experience Design Point of View

In broad terms, HCI examines the ways in which people interact with digital technology. However, HCI is anything but homogeneous. According to Susanne Bødker (2006), three 'waves', or epistemological assumptions, have driven the field over the past 30 years or more. First-wave HCI, which emerged during the early 1980s, focused on making it possible for an individual to use a computer to complete a task without knowing how that computer had been built or programmed (Bannon 1991). The 'hegemonic discursive practices of rationalism' (McCarthy and Wright 2004, p. 24), underpinned by the 'dominant paradigm' of cognitivist psychology (Kaptelinin et al. 2003, p. 692), attended to one generic user performing one task on one machine.

This focus on the single, decontextualised and almost disembodied user gave way to second-wave HCI, which took a broader perspective. Researchers in this wave viewed users in a larger context and paid more attention to the situations in which they found themselves performing tasks on computers. New theories were brought into play, such as activity theory and distributed cognition (Kaptelinin et al. 2003). McCarthy and Wright describe this shift as a change from perceiving the

---

[5] See the work of the International Society for Intermedial Research.

user as a 'cog' (2004, p. 6) in the 1970s and 1980s to perceiving the user as contextualised, situated, relational 'social actor' (2004, p. 7) in the 1980s and 1990s.

In recent years this second wave has been overtaken by a third wave, which moves even further from the original focus on one user applying only cognitive processes to a single task. Third-wave HCI looks to understand a multiplicity of users, bringing their minds, emotions, bodies, and full personalities to bear on each situated interaction. Thus third-wave HCI is inherently a performative area of inquiry. Bødker, the first to describe this third wave, sees these interactions as 'non-work, non-purposeful, non-rational', concerned with culture, aesthetics, emotions, and a pragmatic approach to experience (2006, pp. 1–2). These areas of focus open a Pandora's box of potential motivations, requirements, modes of interaction, and social implications, any of which might interconnect.

First-wave HCI involved many things that were physical and relatively easy to measure. Second-wave HCI began to require a way of accounting for context and social interactions. Third-wave HCI is now pushing the boundaries of what can be effectively conceptualised, much less studied or measured. Emotions and aesthetics can be complex things: the extremely public display of one's own nude photo is doubtless a positive experience for most of Gok Wan's participants in the UK television show *How to Look Good Naked*, but it is also a mixed bag. Many speak of dreading the moment and physically cringe in terror at being exposed. I doubt that any Likert scale would do justice to the powerful process of self-acceptance triggered by the simple act of standing near an enlarged photo of oneself in public.

Along with HCI, interaction design stands as an inclusive and well recognised discipline directly concerned with people's relationship to technology. Interaction design is defined pithily as 'the specification of digital behaviors in response to human or machine stimuli' (Goodman et al. 2011, p. 1061). Although the work of interaction design involves the creation and refinement of technological devices and systems, the unit of analysis is the way in which the device or system creates or constrains opportunities for use. This requires attention to the way the interaction is experienced by uniquely situated individuals and implies the possibility for a shift in focus from first-wave to second-wave concerns. Interaction design has undergone a 'recent dramatic rise in popularity' in both research and practice, indicating the importance of this shift in focus:

> Increasingly often, "interaction design," rather than "HCI," is being used as an umbrella term to refer to a collection of research areas having a common interest in understanding and supporting the interaction between people—individuals or small groups—and digital technology. (Kaptelinin and Nardi 2012, p. 279)

Interaction design moves away from HCI's first-wave roots by focusing attention on the process by which a particular design is achieved, which leaves room for a good deal of exploration based on theoretical inputs and reflective insights. After all, it is easier to pursue inspirations for third-wave designs and analyse user responses through ethnographic methods than it is to devise accurate ergonomic measurements for 'fun'. However, interaction design still tends to retain a focus on the individual digital product as experienced by these 'individuals or small groups', which can pose a problem for interactions that extend over time, or across multiple users in different roles, or ones that alter relationships among people not directly engaged with the product in question. In these cases, it can be more useful to think in terms of a holistic 'experience' than a series of singular 'interactions'.

The exact relationship between experience design and interaction design is, like everything else in this area, murky and contested. What is commonly agreed is that experience design and other related terms emerged within HCI and interaction design since the turn of the millennium or so, and their popularity continues to increase (Wright and McCarthy 2010; Wakkary et al. 2004, p. 1710). Thus experience design can be seen as an upstart within the parent fields of HCI and interaction design, and discussions of experience design can both reflect on and be at least partially informed by discussions of HCI and interaction design. In all cases, though, experience design can be understood as performative in one or more uses of the term, especially considering the potential for a lone user to be the spectator of her own experience (Dalsgaard and Hansen 2008).

Jodi Forlizzi, a prominent researcher in experience design and user experience, frames experience design as a field of inquiry very much in line with third-wave HCI interests in culture and, of course, experience: it is 'the practice of designing products, services, events, and environments with a focus on the quality of the user experience and culturally relevant solutions, rather than a focus on increasing and improving functionality of the design' (2010, p. 60). For her, experience design goes beyond the interaction of a single user (or small group) with a single device, to take in not only broad cultural issues that would affect those interactions but also wider time spans—'even a lifetime' (2010, p. 61)—during which the experience created with the device might change significantly. This wide perspective is thrilling in its promise to encompass cultural, temporal, holistic, and ever-shifting perspectives on human relationships with specific technologies.

Given the fact that such experiences are less immediately accessible to a researcher than, say, the amount of time it takes to click a button, much of experience design research celebrates unusual techno-social and/or artistic interventions such as Humanaquarium, a combination of interactive device and live audiovisual performance that results in exploratory participative events (Taylor et al. 2011). These researchers' studies of the experience may be rigorous, but they are to some extent tied to the unique situation of each design implementation. Therefore, they are best positioned to offer suggestions or reflective questions (McCarthy and Wright 2004). The language used by Erik Stolterman in his discussions of design practice suit these projects well: Humanaquarium, for example, might be seen as an 'ultimate particular' that should 'prepare' but not 'guide' designers 'to address the people and situations *at hand*' (2008, p. 59, emphasis in the original). The many examples of experience design articulated by Benford and Giannachi as mixed reality performance also align with this perspective: for example, there is little discussion of any 'product' in research projects with Blast Theory, but a significant theorising of the 'trajectories' through a performance that can be shaped by design and by performers' interactions with the design (Benford and Giannachi 2011).

Mark Blythe et al. specify the key way in which experience design differs from product design: 'Experience must be narrated, described and interpreted. By that, experience design becomes intimately concerned with the construction of meaning. But experience is not limited to sense making' (2009, p. 123). It extends beyond the cognitive into potentially any other aspect of human life. Experience design is also not simply product design with the added 'spice' of emotion, but a complex task of creating meaning that might be at odds with the desire to give users (consumers) a pleasant experience with a new technology (2009, p. 124). This task is all the more challenging because designers cannot plan precisely what experience their design will trigger in an individual, and therefore experiences are subject to less control than a product is.

However, Marc Hassenzahl retains a strong focus on the product itself: he refers to it as the creation of 'experiences through products' (2010, p. 8). He and others push back against some of the more exploratory, open-ended research and are deeply suspicious of any reluctance to generalise or deduce guidelines for design based on the many commonalities of experience. This attitude is connected to a tension in the area of user experience (UX) between the predominantly qualitative 'design-based UX research camp' and the predominantly quantitative 'model-based UX research camp' as described by Law (2011, p. 4). The former values qualitative methods to unearth emotional responses to designed interactions, while the latter values more positivist attempts to derive models on which to base interaction designs (2011, pp. 4–5). While neither Law nor I argue that these camps are diametrically opposed, with one camp's methods off limits to the other, the tensions between the two reveal the structural effects of the development of third-wave HCI as it attempts to address topics such as 'affect' (Picard 2003), 'fun' (Blythe et al. 2002), 'enchantment' (McCarthy et al. 2005; Sengers et al. 2008), and 'aesthetics' (Petersen et al. 2004; Dalsgaard and Hansen 2008).

One thing that should, and usually does, unite researchers and practitioners in experience design is the deceptively simple observation made by Marc Davis: '*experiences are not data*' (2003, p. 46, emphasis in the original). The entire premise of PED rests on this observation and the conclusions that can be drawn from it, namely that experiences cannot be transmitted as objects or data can, but must rather be 'occasion[ed]' in others, a process through which new experiences are generated (2003, p. 46). This perspective implies a deep sense of interpenetration with the world around us and an unfolding of experience over time as found in Dewey, whose work forms a cornerstone of the seminal text *Technology as Experience* (McCarthy and Wright 2004). Dewey defines experience as 'the result, the sign, and the reward of that interaction of organism and environment which, when it is carried to the full, is a transformation of interaction into participation and communication' (2005, p. 23). PED uses digital technology to 'occasion' new experiences that cause 'organisms' to view their 'environments'—including the digital aspects of those environments—in a different light.

One of the common ways of thinking that PED challenges is the notion of how an experience can be 'occasioned' in someone else. Experiences are no more transmittable than information is, at least when human interpretation is involved.

Davis's observation about experience is a radical departure from the 'conduit metaphor' described by Michael Reddy in 1993, which describes the familiar idea of getting a message across to someone. In the conduit metaphor, ideas (or 'repertoire members') are packaged into words and conveyed from one person to another. Any design approach or theoretical stance that assumes such a transmission of felt experience from one person to another would lead to gross errors, because no matter how convenient this metaphor is for describing the simple transmission of facts between two entities (devices) with identical points of view on the world, it fails to stand up to rigorous scrutiny (see Davis 2003, p. 48). Reddy replaces the overly simplistic conduit metaphor with his 'toolmakers paradigm', in which meaning is made (and experiences can be occasioned) through an iterative process of sense-making using only the individual's own point of view and frame of reference. According to McCarthy and Wright, Dewey, Reddy, and philosopher G.H. Mead (to name some of the thinkers in this area discussed by experience design researchers), the individual does not exist outside its relationship to others. Rather, the individual maintains a 'source of spontaneity that can surprise the person themselves as much as other selves' (McCarthy and Wright 2004, p. 110). Through a dynamic interplay between the self—which is not fully known or accessible to the conscious mind at any given point—and the environment—including the digital world of social media, multimedia, information and connection—experiences can be occasioned, though never 'transmitted'.

The idea of occasioning an experience is a far richer prospect than the idea of transmitting information. In a similar way, a performative experience can be more challenging, meaningful, and personal than many other types of experiences. Performativity involves the most deeply intimate and unique elements of the self, and puts those on display to an audience. This sense of performing for an audience in turn involves concepts of aesthetics. Far from being frivolous, aesthetics are 'the paradigm' for all experience according to Mead and Dewey. 'Art… intensifies and clarifies its energy… in the very operation of creating, by means of new objects, new modes of experience' (Dewey 2005, p. 253). Aesthetic experiences have the potential to tap precisely the types of non-task-oriented, emotional, affective, and interpersonal realms that third-wave HCI tries to investigate. I argue that any framework of experience design or user experience that fails to account for the aesthetic in this sense is incomplete.

PED is an extension of experience design. It pushes experience design in the direction set out by McCarthy and Wright, among others, to explore the most nebulous elements of experience with as much rigour as the pioneers of HCI studied the speed of pointing at an on-screen target. But rather than attempting this exploration with the incredibly wide-ranging concept of 'aesthetics', it uses the aesthetic or artistic mode that directly addresses engagements between people over time: performance. Thankfully, the field of performance studies has been working to make sense of the nebulous for decades.

A Shared Perspective

So far, I have sketched out the basics of the two points of view that most strongly inform PED: performance studies, with its close cousins performativity and intermedial research, and experience design within the broader field of HCI. For all their differences, performance studies and experience design each have areas of interest whose aims and even some methodologies tend to converge. The case study that forms the backbone of this text explores one of these areas of convergence, which has been termed *intermedial autobiographical performance*. However, any number of other convergences exist in works that I believe share the design space of PED. Digital Live Art, as formulated by Jennifer G. Sheridan et al. (2007), emphasises emergent behaviours around physical challenges that do not involve personal digital media in any way. Mixed reality performance (Benford and Giannachi 2011) explores a complex mix of games, performance, digital technologies, and role-playing. Projects by Robyn Taylor and colleagues explore concepts in performance and performativity from a number of perspectives, including a visceral engagement with the human voice in dream.Medusa (Taylor et al. 2008) and Humanaquarium (Taylor et al. 2011). The content of a performance does not need to be spoken, factual, or deeply revelatory: what is important is that the technology involved is carefully designed to explore the felt experience of displaying one's interaction with that technology for others. Whether telling a personal story about a treasured photo, creating intricate light shows at a festival, scanning a crowd for real-life runners represented as avatars in an online game, or self-consciously waving a hand across a screen just inches from the face of a classically trained singer in mid-flow, people engaging with PED put something of themselves on the line—in front of others—when they interact with the technologies we have created. It is that sense of display, or performance, that is the ultimate object of design: the technology is the fulcrum for exploration.

References

Auslander P (1997) Ontology vs history: making distinctions between the live and the mediatized [online]. Available at: http://webcast.gatech.edu/papers/arch/Auslander.html

Auslander P (1999) Liveness: performance in a mediatized culture. Routledge, London/New York

Auslander P (2006) The performativity of performance documentation. PAJ: J Perform Art 28(3):1–10

Austin JL (1962) How to do things with words: the William James lectures delivered at Harvard University in 1955. Oxford University Press, Oxford

Bannon L (1991) From human factors to human actors: the role of psychology and human-computer interaction studies in system design. In: Design at work: cooperative design of computer systems. Erlbaum Associates, Hillsdale, pp 25–44

Bardzell J, Bolter J, Löwgren J (2010) Interaction criticism: three readings of an interaction design, and what they get us. Interactions 17(2):32–37

Barton B (2013) New betrayals: intimacy in mediatised performance. E&I, 3, np

Bauman R (1975) Verbal art as performance. Am Anthropol 77(2):290–311

Bauman R, Briggs CL (1990) Poetics and performance as critical perspectives on language and social life. Annu Rev Anthropol 19:59–88

Benford S, Giannachi G (2011) Performing mixed reality. MIT Press, Cambridge, MA/London

Benford S, Crabtree A, Reeves S, Sheridan J, Dix A, Flintham M, Drozd A (2006) The frame of the game: blurring the boundary between fiction and reality in mobile experiences. In: Proceedings of the SIGCHI conference on human factors in computing systems. ACM Press, New York, pp 427–436

Benz P (2015) Experience design: concepts and case studies. Bloomsbury Publishing, London/New York

Blythe MA, Overbeeke K, Monk AF, Wright PC (2002) Funology: from usability to enjoyment. Kluwer Academic Publishers, New York/Boston/Dordrecht/London/Moscow

Blythe M, Hassenzahl M, Law E (2009) Now with added experience? New Rev Hypermedia Multimed 15(2):119–128

Bødker S (2006) When second wave HCI meets third wave challenges. In: Proceedings of the 4th Nordic conference on human-computer interaction: changing roles. ACM Press, New York, pp 1–8

Boenisch PM (2006) Aesthetic art to aisthetic act: theatre, media, intermedial performance. In: Chapple F, Kattenbelt C (eds) Intermediality in theatre and performance. Editions Rodopi B.V., Amsterdam/New York, pp 103–116

Boenisch PM (2012) Acts of spectating: the dramaturgy of the audience's experience in contemporary theatre. Crit Stage (7):np

Butler J (2002) Gender trouble: feminism and the subversion of identity. Routledge, New York

Carlson M (2008) Introduction: perspectives on performance: Germany and America. In: The transformative power of performance: a new aesthetics. Routledge, London, pp 1–10

Conquergood D (2002) Performance studies: interventions and radical research 1. TDR/Drama Rev 46(2):145–156

Dalsgaard P, Hansen LK (2008) Performing perception: staging aesthetics of interaction. ACM Transact Comput-Hum Interact (TOCHI) 15(3):1–33

Davis M (2003) Theoretical foundations for experiential systems design. In: Proceedings of the 2003 ACM SIGMM workshop on experiential telepresence. ACM Press, New York, pp 45–52

Dewey J (2005) Art as experience. Perigee Books, New York

Dixon S (2007) Digital performance: a history of new media in theater, dance, performance art, and installation. MIT Press, Cambridge, MA/London

Dolan J (1993) Geographies of learning: theatre studies, performance, and the "performative". Theatr J 45(4):417–441

Ehn P, Binder T, Eriksen MA, Jacucci G, Kuutti K, Linde P, De Michelis G et al (2007) Opening the digital box for design work: supporting performative interactions, using inspirational materials and configuring of place. In: Streitz N et al (eds) The disappearing computer: interaction design, system infrastructures and applications for smart environments. Springer, Berlin/Heidelberg, pp 50–76

Fensham R (2012) Postdramatic spectatorship: participate or else. Crit Stage (7):1–8

Fischer-Lichte E (2008a) Sense and sensation: exploring the interplay between the semiotic and performative dimensions of theatre. J Dramat Theory Crit 22(2):69–81

Fischer-Lichte E (2008b) The transformative power of performance: a new aesthetics. Routledge, London

Forlizzi J (2010) All look same?: a comparison of experience design and service design. Interactions 17(5):60–62

Goffman E (1959) The presentation of self in everyday life. Doubleday, Garden City

Goffman E (1974) Frame analysis: an essay on the organization of experience. Harvard University Press, Cambridge, MA

Goodman E, Stolterman E, Wakkary R (2011) Understanding interaction design practices. In: Proceedings of the 2011 annual conference on human factors in computing systems. ACM Press, New York, pp 1061–1070

Hannah D, Harsløf O (2008) Performance design. Museum Tusculanum Press, Copenhagen

Hansen LK, Rico J, Jacucci G, Brewster S, Ashbrook D (2011) Performative interaction in public space. In: CHI '11 extended abstracts on human factors in computing systems. ACM Press, New York, pp 49–52

Hassenzahl M (2010) Experience design: technology for all the right reasons. Morgan & Claypool Publishers, San Rafael

Heddon D (2008) Autobiography and performance. Palgrave Macmillan, Basingstoke

Jacucci G, Spagnolli A, Chalambalakis A, Morrison A, Liikkanen L, Roveda S, Bertoncini M (2009) Bodily explorations in space: social experience of a multimodal art installation. In: Proceedings of the 12th IFIP TC 13 international conference on human-computer interaction: Part II. Springer, Berlin/Heidelberg, pp 62–75

Kappenberg C (2011) Screendance. Seminar at University of Surrey, Department of Dance

Kaptelinin V, Nardi B (2012) Affordances in HCI: toward a mediated action perspective. In: Proceedings of the SIGCHI conference on human factors in computing systems. ACM, New York, pp 967–976

Kaptelinin V, Nardi B, Bødker S, Carroll J, Hollan J, Hutchins E, Winograd T (2003) Post-cognitivist HCI: second-wave theories. In: CHI '03 extended abstracts on human factors in computing systems. ACM, New York, pp 692–693

Kirshenblatt-Gimblett B (2007) Performance studies. In: Bial H (ed) The performance studies reader, 2nd edn. Routledge, London/New York, pp 43–55

Langellier KM (1999) Personal narrative, performance, performativity: two or three things I know for sure. Text Perform Q 19(2):125–144

Lavender A (2013) Feeling engaged: intermedial *mise en sensibilité*. In: FIRT/IFTR conference. Barcelona, Spain, 22–26 July 2013

Law Effie Lai-Chong (2011) The measurability and predictability of user experience. In: Proceedings of the 3rd ACM SIGCHI symposium on engineering interactive computing systems. ACM Press, New York, pp 1–10

Lindley SE, Randall D, Sharrock W, Glancy M, Smyth N, Harper R (2009) Narrative, memory and practice: tensions and choices in the use of a digital artefact. In: Proceedings of the 23rd British HCI group annual conference on people and computers: celebrating people and technology. British Computer Society, Swinton, UK, pp 1–9

Loke L, Robertson T (2010) Studies of dancers: moving from experience to interaction design. Int J Des 4(2):39–54

McCarthy J, Wright P (2004) Technology as experience. MIT Press, Cambridge, MA

McCarthy J, Wright P, Wallace J, Dearden A (2005) The experience of enchantment in human–computer interaction. Pers Ubiquit Comput 10:369–378

Nam HY, Nitsche M (2014) Interactive installations as performance: inspiration for HCI. In: Proceedings of the 8th international conference on tangible, embedded and embodied interaction. ACM Press, New York, pp 189–196

Nelson R (2010) Introduction: prospective mapping. In: Bay-Cheng S et al (eds) Mapping intermediality in performance. Amsterdam University Press, Amsterdam, pp 13–23

Oddey A, White C (2009) Modes of spectating. Intellect, Bristol

Petersen MG, Iversen OS, Krogh PG, Ludvigsen M (2004) Aesthetic interaction: a pragmatist's aesthetics of interactive systems. In: Proceedings of the 5th conference on designing interactive systems: processes, practices, methods, and techniques. ACM Press, New York, pp 269–276

Phelan P (1993) Unmarked: the politics of performance. Routledge, London

Phelan P (1998) Introduction: the ends of performance. In: The ends of performance. New York University Press, New York, pp 1–19

Phelan P (2003) Performance, live culture and things of the heart. J Vis Cult 2(3):291–302

Phelan P (2004) On seeing the invisible: Marina Abramovic's the house with the ocean view. In: Heathfield A (ed) Live: art and performance. Routledge, New York, pp 16–27

Picard RW (2003) Affective computing: challenges. Int J Hum-Comput Stud 59(1):55–64

Rancière J (2011) The emancipated spectator. Verso, London

Reason M (2015) Participations on participation: researching the active theatre audience. Participat J Audience Recept Stud 12(1):271–280

Reddy MJ (1993) The conduit metaphor: a case of frame conflict in our language about language. In: Ortony A (ed) Metaphor and thought, 2nd edn. Cambridge University Press, Cambridge, pp 164–201

Salter C (2010) Entangled: technology and the transformation of performance. MIT Press, Cambridge, MA

Sandbye M (2005) Performing the everyday: two Danish photo books from the 1970s. In: Gade R, Jerslev A (eds) Performative realism: interdisciplinary studies in art and media. Museum Tusculanum Press, Copenhagen, pp 117–144

Schechner R (2000) Post post-structuralism? TDR/Drama Rev 44(3):4–7

Schechner R (2006) Performance studies: an introduction, 2nd edn. Routledge, New York

Schechner R, Appel W (1990) By means of performance: intercultural studies of theatre and ritual. Cambridge University Press, Melbourne/New York/Cambridge

Sengers P, Boehner K, Mateas M, Gay G (2008) The disenchantment of affect. Pers Ubiquit Comput 12(5):347–358

Sheridan JG, Bryan-Kinns N (2008) Designing for performative tangible interaction. Int J Arts Technol 1(3):288–308

Sheridan JG, Bryan-Kinns N, Bayliss A (2007) Encouraging witting participation and performance in digital live art. In: Proceedings of the 21st British HCI group annual conference on people and computers: HCI...but not as we know it. British Computer Society, Swinton, pp 13–23

States BO (1996) Performance as metaphor. Theatr J 48(1):1–26

Stolterman E (2008) The nature of design practice and implications for interaction design research. Int J Des 2(1):55–65

Taylor R, Boulanger P, Olivier P (2008) dream.Medusa: a participatory performance. In: Proceedings of the 9th international symposium on smart graphics. Springer, Berlin/Heidelberg, pp 200–206

Taylor R, Schofield G, Shearer J, Wallace J, Wright P, Boulanger P, Olivier P (2011) Designing from within: humanaquarium. In: Proceedings of the 2011 annual conference on human factors in computing systems. ACM Press, New York, pp 1855–1864

Wakkary R, Schiphorst T, Budd J (2004) Cross-dressing and border crossing: exploring experience methods across disciplines. In: CHI '04 extended abstracts on human factors in computing systems. ACM Press, New York, pp 1709–1710

Wallis M, Popat S, McKinney J, Bryden J, Hogg DC (2010) Embodied conversations: performance and the design of a robotic dancing partner. Des Stud 31(2):99–117

Watson J, Smith S (2005) Introduction: mapping women's self-representation at visual/textual interfaces. In: Smith S, Watson J (eds) Interfaces: women, autobiography, image, performance. University of Michigan Press, Ann Arbor, pp 1–46

Williamson JR, Hansen LK (2012) Designing performative interactions in public spaces. In: Proceedings of the designing interactive systems conference. ACM Press, New York, pp 791–792

Williamson JR, Hansen LK, Jacucci G, Light A, Reeves S (2014) Understanding performative interactions in public settings. Pers Ubiquit Comput 18(7):1545–1549

Wright P, McCarthy J (2010) Experience-centered design: designers, users, and communities in dialogue. Synth Lect Hum-Center Inf 3:1–123

Chapter 3
What Exactly Is Performance?

Abstract This chapter begins with a brief overview of the major ways in which performance theories and practices have been used in the HCI literature. It then describes two performances drawn from the Live Art canon: *Kitchen Show* (1991) by Bobby Baker and *Bubbling Tom* (2000) by Mike Pearson. These intimate, low-tech performances might seem odd choices for a book for HCI researchers and designers, but they serve to indicate exactly the kinds of experiences that are so difficult to articulate within HCI paradigms. They anchor the subsequent discussions of the key theoretical perspectives, topics, and methodologies in performance studies as they relate to PED: postdramatic and presentational theatre, performance art and Live Art, aesthetics and liminality, autobiographical performance, storytelling, devising, participatory performance, reflexivity, unpredictability, applied theatre, and making strange. Having established important insights into how performance can shape and illuminate interactions among human beings, the chapter presents 'intermediality' as an appropriate and generative way of understanding digital technologies within performance. The chapter concludes with a discussion of how these performance concepts integrate with concerns in HCI and design, all under the umbrella of PED.

Performance

This chapter aims to present a sufficiently substantial overview of some aspects of performance studies that will shed light on the purpose and promise of PED. Read in conjunction with the 'performance studies point of view' in Chap. 2, this chapter gives a basic grounding in performance as a discipline and a topic of study relevant to PED, from which an HCI researcher can begin to explore according to her own specific interests. The chapter begins with a taxonomy of major ways that performance has been treated in the HCI literature to date. From this basis, it offers a description of two performances in which the shaping of performer-audience interactions can be clearly seen: Bobby Baker's *Kitchen Show* (1991) and Mike Pearson's *Bubbling Tom* (2000). With these two performances as a touchpoint, the chapter moves on to explain a few of the key theoretical perspectives, performance types, and methodologies that overlap most strongly with interaction and experience design and therefore are most immediately applicable to PED. The chapter

© Springer International Publishing Switzerland 2016   45
J. Spence, *Performative Experience Design*, Springer Series on Cultural
Computing, DOI 10.1007/978-3-319-28395-1_3

concludes with an argument for 'intermediality' as a forward-looking and generative framework for understanding digital technology in performance, and a brief discussion of how all of these elements of performance theory and practice come together.

The topics covered here are not at all exhaustive; I have no doubt that PED research will greatly expand the range of relevant work within performance studies. It is also important to remember that although this chapter presents the discipline of performance studies to an HCI audience, I am in no way suggesting that HCI researchers should extract nuggets of performance theory or practice out of context and import them into a static HCI or design process. These 'useful' strands of performance research are intended to be brought into productive relationships with HCI and design processes, resulting in new ways of working that reflect the contributions of both disciplines.

Performance in HCI

PED is by no means the first time that the HCI community has incorporated elements of theatre and performance studies. For many years, performance has been understood as a potentially fruitful means of conceptualising HCI. Brenda Laurel's *Computers as Theatre* (1993) sets out drama as a theoretical framework, choosing Aristotle's *Poetics* as 'appropriate to the state of the technology to which we are trying to apply it' (1993, p. 36). This was a forward-thinking statement when first published in 1991 and has influenced the thinking of many HCI researchers over the past two decades. Over a similar period, the Creativity and Cognition conferences have included performance in their investigation of the creative process. Recently, though, the HCI community has begun to search for stronger and more varied contributions from the very broad field of performance studies, primarily through conference workshops (Wakkary et al. 2004; Rico et al. 2010; Hansen et al. 2011; Leong et al. 2011; Hook et al. 2012; Williamson and Hansen 2012; Bowers et al. 2014; Spence 2015) and the 2013 Inputs-Outputs Conference: An Interdisciplinary Conference on Engagement in HCI and Performance. At the same time, the Digital Arts Community of the Association for Computing Machinery's Special Interest Group on Computer-Human Interaction (ACM SIGCHI) has pursued both digital and the arts to 'push the boundaries of HCI research and practice' (England et al. 2011, p. 609; England et al. 2014), including performing arts.

The range of works responding to these calls varies widely in terms of how sustained its engagement is with performance. Some are complex and thorough studies, such as Giulio Jacucci's investigation of physical interfaces (2004) and his subsequent work in media, performance, and interaction. However, some invoke performance as an approach while providing only fleeting mentions of a single source within the field of theatre or performance studies. Some even limit themselves to citing Goffman (e.g. 1959), a sociologist who uses performance as a metaphor for everyday interactions. It is not my intention to pass judgement on researchers or their projects based solely on individual papers, because even lengthy publications will make use of only a small fraction of an author's range of knowledge and expertise, and it may be the case that these authors make fuller use of performance studies than they reveal in their publications. Unfortunately, though, it can be difficult for an HCI researcher interested in performance to decide how to navigate the vast array of performance research based on just one or two references. One might use performance to understand aesthetic experience (e.g. Dalsgaard and Hansen 2008; Laurel 1993), investigate story and narrative (e.g. Geigel and Schweppe 2004; van Doorn and de Vries 2006), develop theories of presence (e.g. Wagner et al. 2009), explore audience perception of digitally mediated performance (Corness et al. 2011), or penetrate deeply felt audience reactions to performance (Leong and Wright 2013). Using a term like 'performance' to refer to only one of these approaches can bring up unintended implications for readers more accustomed to another use of the term, and causes the HCI community to miss all but a small fraction of performance's potential to contribute to HCI. The following overview sketches out the key purposes to which performance research has been put in HCI over the years, using only a handful of examples from the HCI literature, and indicates how these uses may develop in the near future.

The most basic way of using performance in terms of the number of interactants is what I have termed 'portrayal'.[1] In these cases, performance is used as an example of narrative communication. For example, Katri Mehto et al. (2006) look to drama for 'representing and communicating a scenario' (2006, p. 979) and allowing 'the design/research group [to] experience the information' that is 'represented' in this way (2006, p. 984). This is very different from Peter Dalsgaard and Lone Koefoed Hansen's intention 'to understand performance as a very physical thing; it is the actual actions taking place and not a dramaturgical or narrative term' (2008, p. 9). They and many other researchers use performance, particularly dance, to explore the embodied nature of human interactions with technologies (Corness and Schiphorst 2013) or to leverage that understanding to enhance a performer's experience (Fdili Alaoui et al. 2013). In the 'embodiment' category, researchers emphasise the physicality and/or emotional nature of a person's interaction with technology. The third category, 'enactment', turns its attention to the social aspects of performance. It examines the interactions of several audience members or performers with a device or system. As Mark van Doorn et al. put it, they aim for '[v]iewing life as social theatre' (2008, p. 1) along the lines of Goffman's *The Presentation of Self in Everyday Life* (1959).

The final category, 'engagement', refers to multiple users adopting different roles in their interactions with a technological device or system. 'Engagement' opens up an opportunity for performance to function as more than a metaphor (for a similar critique from within performance studies see States 1996), or as a pointer towards embodiment or multi-user interaction. 'Engagement' is a narrower but potentially richer application of performance, as it makes use of specific practices and theories that can be applied, tested, and extended through HCI and design

---

[1] An extended version of this section has been published in Spence et al. 2013.

research. In fact, the Inputs/Outputs conference on 'the intersection of HCI and performance' had 'engagement' as its theme, and several of its speakers advocated a similarly rich overlap between the two fields.[2] Perhaps the most substantial and sustained body of work in the 'engagement' category is the collaboration between Blast Theory and the Mixed Reality Lab at the University of Nottingham to 'create projects that merge different technologies and dramaturgical structures, converging disciplines such as live performance, media arts and games' (Chatzichristodoulou 2009, p. 107). These mixed reality performances (Benford and Giannachi 2011, p. 1) often take place in dense, urban environments, drawing audiences from the general public and engaging them with game mechanics. Other work along similar lines uses performance art as a basis for reimagining what engagement with instrumental technologies such as 3D printing might mean (Devendorf and Rosner 2015).

One particularly interesting contribution of four key papers in the 'engagement' category is their appreciation of the various roles that people adopt in relationship to a performance or performative interactions. The first of these is 'A Manifesto for the Performative Development of Ubiquitous Media' (Jacucci et al. 2005), which separates the role of performer and spectator in 'activities with interactive technology' (2005, p. 24). The second and third papers offer taxonomies that address spectatorship, one centred on 'manipulations' and 'effects' (Reeves et al. 2005), and the other differentiating 'audience' members from 'bystanders' who are unaware of the performance going on around them (Benford et al. 2006, p. 434). Sheridan et al. usefully expand on this awareness in terms of 'wittingness', technical skills, and interpretive skills on the parts of performers, participants, and spectators in a public space (2007, pp. 15–16). Dalsgaard and Hansen (2008), the authors of the fourth work, distinguish between the 'participant roles' played by a single user of an interactive system: the operator of the interactive system, the performer, and the spectator perceiving her surroundings as well as herself performing for others (2008, p. 20). Their insight into how performers project the spectator's view of their ongoing performance in their own minds requires an understanding of performance as three simultaneous acts of 'interacting' with the technology, 'perceiving' the context of that interaction, and 'performing' while conscious of how the performance may be viewed by others (2008, pp. 9–10).

These terms complicate the notion of the 'user' in different, sometimes contradictory ways. Where Joe Geigel and Marla Schweppe distinguish between 'audiences' that are 'active' or 'passive' (2004); Dix et al. identify 'performers', 'participants', and 'bystanders' (2006); Reeves et al. identify 'performers' and 'spectators' (2005); and Benford and his colleagues identify 'performers', 'audience', 'bystanders' (Benford et al. 2006), and 'orchestrators' (Benford and Giannachi 2011). As Dalsgaard and Hansen point out, the term 'performer' is not used in the same way by Reeves et al. and Benford et al., due most likely to their different contexts: interactive art in the former, and mixed reality performance in the latter (2008, p. 8). Not even the term 'user' is stable: Johan Redström (2006) observes that '[a] "user" is something that designers create' (2006, p. 129). Research

---

[2] Held 26 June 2013 at the University of Sussex, Brighton, UK.

in the 'engagement' category might be fragmented at the moment, at least in its terminology, but it makes the fullest use so far of performance within HCI. PED extends 'engagement' by examining more closely how performers and audiences create potentially transformative experiences.

Certain discussions of interactive art can also support or extend PED's interest in audience engagement of all types, particularly in public. Ernest Edmonds uses interactive art to drive what he identifies as the most important concerns of experience design: 'kind of experience', 'mode of engagement', 'phase of involvement', and 'viewpoint of evaluation' (2010, p. 263), while Hye Yeon Nam and Michael Nitsche point out the function of some interactive art in 'positioning the audience in a critical stance in a new sociopolitical context' (2014), much like many of the seminal mixed reality performances (Benford and Giannachi 2011). The better we can understand subtleties of user roles, particularly of participants or audiences for works of PED, the more we will be able to offer experiences that can transcend the expectations of traditional HCI research.

The rest of this chapter presents some of the aspects of performance theory and practice that have for the most part gone unrepresented in HCI research. The work described here is by no means an exhaustive list or an assertion of a 'correct' way to interpret performance studies, and it in no way implies that existing HCI research using performance (such as the projects described above) is unworthy of attention. The intention of this chapter is to add breadth, depth, and consequently a new perspective on a line of enquiry whose promise has not yet been exhausted. The areas covered below have been chosen because they correlate strongly with the interests of interaction and experience design, such as traditions that draw on the actual life experiences of the performers. Beyond these theoretical and practical examples, it sketches out some of the surprising methodological overlaps between HCI and performance studies. In total, this chapter aims to give an insight into those elements of performance studies that have an immediate and clear connection to interaction and experience design. My hope is that before too long, this list will be eclipsed by the number of insights in the performance literature that this text has not even hinted at.

Performance Practice: *Kitchen Show* (1991) and *Bubbling Tom* (2000)

Kitchen Show (1991)

You walk into the kitchen of an unexceptional terraced house in north London. The owner offers you a tea or coffee. While she fixes your drink, she confides that she never feels comfortable until her guests have a hot drink in their hands. Then, to mark this self-disclosure on her body, she wraps a plastic bandage around her thumb and forefinger, binding them in the perfect position for stirring milk and sugar into tea.

The kitchen was the performer's own, arranged to seat up to 25 people for performances of the 'very structured' (Baker quoted in Iball 2007, p. 186) 70-min work called *Kitchen Show*, produced as part of the London International Festival of Theatre (LIFT) 1991. *Kitchen Show* is frequently discussed in performance studies and Live Art literatures (Baldwyn 1996; Heathfield 1999; Aston 2000; Ferris 2005; Barrett 2007; Harris and Aston 2007; Iball 2007; Heddon 2008; Lawson 2009). *Kitchen Show* was made up of 13 actions rooted in the practices of everyday life including making tea, resting a wooden spoon on a pan, opening a new tub of margarine, and dancing to opera while cooking. Each action had an associated story, often intimate and always implicitly autobiographical. Through performance, Baker turned the commonplace into the extraordinary:

> What Kitchen Show is trying to convey is the whole range of associations and experiences of being in a kitchen doing routine tasks. It makes you think about why you do things—out of habit, upbringing, indoctrination. It's not a simple thing. ... Some cry—which pleases me. I feel deeply harrowed by a lot of it myself. (Baker quoted in Brown 1993, np)

Baker 'marked' each action on her body, as in the bandage example, or by applying lipstick, so that by the end of the show she was ready for her thirteenth action: '[s]howing all the marks whilst standing on a cake stand placed on a coffee table and showing this image to the public' (Barrett 2007, p. 54). Baker did not offer a photograph, digital or otherwise, but held her pose long enough to achieve the effect of 'showing this image'.

The final image is a startling one, funny and poignant because of the ties to Baker's autobiographical stories of habit, frustration, and desire. According to Geraldine Harris and Elaine Aston (2007), the 'autobiographical stories ... tend to provoke a personal identification with Bobby' (2007, p. 112). Baker notes the same of her audiences: 'People relate to these shows by constantly and to an extraordinary degree relating them to their own experiences' (quoted in Iball 2007, p. 188).[3] This sense of personal connection comes from the 'heightened potential of blurring the borders between performance, theatricality and autobiography' (Iball 2007, p. 186) that Helen Iball sees as central to Baker's work. It is important to point out that there is no way to isolate any of these components as if they were elements in a scientific experiment. An autobiographical performance does not necessarily suffer if some of its details are inaccurate – which is a good thing for the genre, as memory has been shown to be a perpetually shifting phenomenon, often making it impossible to say how accurate a given recollection actually is. As explored in the discussion on performativity in Chap. 2, 'performance' is at work in everyday life as well as on stage, and 'theatricality' can serve to amplify the sense of connection between performer and spectator just as much as it can signal a lack of authenticity. *Kitchen Show* engaged with its audiences intellectually, emotionally, and aesthetically because of the combination of the everyday and the theatrical, rooted in Baker's lived experience, and performed with Baker's own subtleties of tone and manner – in her own home.

---

[3] Baker is referring to re-stagings of *Kitchen Show* that she has done throughout the world.

The subtleties of *how* a show is performed are particularly interesting in terms of interaction and experience design, because regardless of the physical environment (like Baker's kitchen) or the theatricality of the content (like Baker's bandages and wooden spoons), any interaction or experience design will revolve around at least one person engaging with that design. The *how* is even more interesting in PED, where the person engaging with the design has an audience watching all of the subtleties of their engagement, and that self-conscious and self-reflecting engagement can shape the ongoing experience for everyone involved. Each person brings her expectations, mannerisms, and peculiarities to bear, potentially turning an everyday interaction into 'an experience' in Dewey's terms (2005) – notable, memorable, and possibly even aesthetic. For example, Baker's performance is marked by 'a slight physical and vocal "awkwardness" [that] guarantees the "ordinariness" of her persona in ways that invite trust and identification' (Harris and Aston 2007, p. 111). A more impressionistic view is that one 'characteristic of her language … is the sense that she is speaking aloud an inner, private monologue. We are privy to her personal thoughts' (Ferris 2005, p. 194). These impressions of being awkward and ordinary, of being caught speaking to herself out loud, form a large part of *how* Baker performs, and this *how* can at times be more powerful than the actual content of her words or gestures. In other words, Baker's autobiographical content works with her manner of performing to build the intimacy with her audiences that so many critics and researchers focus on. This intimacy is enriched by the audience's exposure to the traces of Baker's lived experience: the 'anecdotes, photographs, mugs and spatulas' (Iball 2007, p. 185) that surround them during the performance.

This interplay of autobiography and manner, or content and presence, does not have to be a comfortable experience. *Kitchen Show* was made up of charming eccentricities like the wooden spoon in Baker's hair, but it also included disturbing and violent actions such as hurling a piece of ripe fruit against the door in anger, sending bits of fruit flying across the room and making the audience wonder what other damage Baker would inflict on her own home (and possibly the spectator/guests within it). These are not idle suppositions: Baker explains how she tried throwing wine bottles and typewriters onto the floor. Some of her words imply threat or transgression directed outwards, while others direct that energy against herself. For example, when describing her urge to say the Lord's Prayer, Baker also explains the embarrassment and self-criticism that she feels in her attempts. This is a strikingly personal confession to make and one that opens Baker up to judgement or criticism. Some of her audience members can experience 'a discomforting sense of complicity in witnessing the public exposure of profoundly personal and painful experiences' (Harris and Aston 2007, p. 110). After all, it may be difficult to look someone in the eye after they have struggled to pray, right in front of you, in their own kitchen, while you drink the cup of tea they made for you. The physical violence (against a pear), the deeply personal confessions, and the everyday gestures of making each spectator her preferred drink all contribute to visceral senses of intimacy and transgression. As Baker says, 'The kind of transgression I am after is very slight, but nonetheless present. The danger is there in small gestures rather than large ones; the risk in intimacy' (quoted in Heathfield 1999, p. 102). On the most basic level, *Kitchen Show* is a grouping of a couple of dozen people listening to someone describe and sometimes re-enact her own thoughts and actions in her own home. Through performance, Baker is able to transform these descriptions and re-enactments into an experience for her audience that goes beyond the norms of everyday communication: an experience full of surprise, confusion, entertainment, trepidation, discomfort, intimacy, and transgression.

Bubbling Tom (2000)

Mike Pearson's *Bubbling Tom* (2000) was a site-specific performance in Hibaldstow, the remote village in Lincolnshire, England, where he had lived as a small boy nearly fifty years previously. Pearson identified ten locations about which he had personal stories to tell, nine of which had a corresponding personal photograph. The performance involved Pearson walking through the village with small audiences, stopping at these ten locations to talk about his memories. Pearson was less interested in straightforward explanations than in 'making strange' (2003, p. 175) the experience of coming back when both he and his former hometown had changed so much in the intervening decades.

Pearson is an internationally respected theorist and theatre maker who trained as an archaeologist. He and his colleagues have argued that there is no way of faithfully representing the past (Pearson and Shanks 2001), even with access to original artefacts such as the ten locations or the personal photographs. Any attempts to do so would be 'inevitably fictional and illusionary' (Pearson 2003, p. 175) because the process of representing the past happens in the context of a different moment, understood by people with different knowledge and expectations (Pearson and Shanks 2001). Along these lines, *Bubbling Tom* is Pearson's creation of 'a meaning, a narrative, a story, that stands for the past in the present' (Pearson 2007, p. 25). Pearson's desire to delve into the Hibaldstow he knew the 1950s led him to ask friends and family members about their recollections of the town at that time; to search for the physical traces of his presence in the town, such as his handprint in some paint; to physically re-embody past actions such as a mock gunfight with a childhood friend; and to find the traces of his own physicality in those years, from the way he stands to the scar above his eye that he received in Hibaldstow (2007, pp. 24–25). Above all, Pearson worked with his memories of gossip and storytelling in this place, where the sound of the voice and the richness of detail would give 'life' to his performance (2007, p. 26). His search for the past did not lead to a strict adherence to established facts, either: his performance text includes 'anecdotes, traveller's tales, poetry, forensic data, quotations, lies, jokes, improvised asides, physical re/enactments, impersonations and intimate reflections' (2003, p. 176). Through these many approaches, Pearson aimed 'to devise a "way of writing" springing directly from a "way of telling" that is intimate and self-reflective, that can mix useful information—about vernacular detail, people, events—with the pleasure of performing' (2007, p. 25).

Pearson's 'way of telling' created an intense and dynamic engagement with his audience. He wanted his performance to 'catalyse[] personal reflection and the desire on the part of the listener to reveal her own experiences, the minutiae of genealogy' (2003, p. 176). He achieved this to an extreme degree, as 'at times [he] could barely get a word in edgeways' (Pearson 2007, p. 22). Pearson's audiences were not merely taking in his story: they were generating their own memories, whether of Hibaldstow or of their own pasts, and often interjecting their stories into Pearson's performance. Two spectators elaborated on their own sense of engagement: theorist Adrian Heathfield was in the audience and reports a 'very acute recognition from people … . You don't have access to those things, but what you have access to is your sense in which they might be like some of your own things' (quoted in Heddon 2002, pp. 72–73). Theatre researcher Deirdre Heddon confirms this 'sense' by responding to Pearson's recollections of watching *The Lone Ranger* with her own *Dr Who* memories (2002, p. 82).[4] This triggering of personal reflection is not unique to *Bubbling Tom*, but Pearson's 'way of telling' created a work that clearly 'engages and re-engages the audience with material which is intimately familiar and infinitely other; as familiar as their own history, or as exotic as the strange sights and smells of the explorer's account' (Pearson 2003, p. 175).

The question of who made up Pearson's audience is also interesting. It consisted mostly of friends and family members, including his mother, some old enough to remember the facts of his stories better than he did himself (Wilkie 2004, p. 111). However, members of the public also attended, so Pearson needed to make his experiences understandable to people with no knowledge at all of the area. Pearson's audiences also had to make the effort to move from location to location, and to continually re-orient themselves to Pearson and to each other in each new location. As a result, the borders between everyday interaction and performance blurred. Audiences talked back to the performer and sometimes chatted amongst themselves. They commented on, questioned (Wilkie 2004, p. 130), corrected, and challenged (Heddon 2008, p. 101) Pearson's memories. Their active engagement helped to create an experience that Pearson describes as 'intimate, informal, at the edge of performance itself' (Pearson 2003, p. 175)—what I would call a performative experience for both Pearson and his audiences.

While Pearson's use of location in *Bubbling Tom* figures prominently in the literature on autobiographical performance (including Heddon 2002, 2008; Wilkie 2004; Gorman 2008), his use of personal photographs has received less attention. Pearson provided each audience member with a photocopied 'guidebook' containing, among other things, his personal photographs (Pearson 2003, p. 176). As observed by Fiona Wilkie, these guidebooks 'serve to remind us of the gaps conjured up by the performance: gaps in the act of recalling; gaps between (childhood)

---

[4] *Bubbling Tom* has also inspired at least two re-performances that operated through imagination at least as much as through memory, one by Heddon (2002) and one by Kris Darby (2010)—neither of whom grew up in Hibaldstow, or in the 1950s.

sites and the stories we tell ourselves about them (as an adult); gaps between performer's and spectator's experience of space' (2004, p. 132). The photos helped the audience to imagine their way into the gaps between the adult Pearson and the early memories he described.

Both *Kitchen Show* and *Bubbling Tom* reveal ways in which performers work with the material of everyday life to create vivid experiences for their audiences – charming, bizarre, threatening, inviting, co-creative, even nostalgic. Both of these works were rooted in the performer's own personal experience, though neither claimed to present a transparent view of their inner life or history. Both were sensitive to their spatiotemporal and interpersonal contexts and developed relationships between performer and spectators that sometimes included a sense of intimacy. Both involved a subtle but very real sense of risk where 'the danger is there in small gestures' (Baker quoted in Heathfield 1999, p. 102) and 'changes in status are possible' (Pearson 1998, p. 40). Throughout their lives, Baker and Pearson had been 'doing' the actions that made up their performances, like stirring milk into cups of tea for guests, or watching *The Lone Ranger* as a child. Now they were 'showing' that 'doing' for an audience (Schechner 2000, p. 28). Far from simply displaying or representing something static, these 'showing doings' shaped the relationships between performers and spectators. Baker and Pearson guided where the spectators moved, how they perceived their environment, the types of emotions they felt, and even the private memories and associations that might spring to mind.

These subtle but powerful forces are critical for any interaction or experience designer to understand when approaching projects that involve a user 'showing' her own 'doing' in front of others. The rest of this chapter lays out theories, practices, and methodologies in performance studies that help to unpick the forces at work in performances like these.

Key Perspectives

Performances such as *Kitchen Show* and *Bubbling Tom* may be grounded in personal experience and practices of everyday life, but they are unquestionably performances. Part of the certainty behind that statement comes from their context: both were supported by recognised national organisations and required the purchase of a ticket. However, on the level of interpersonal interaction, there is more at work than simply the official stamp of cultural norms. Performance can be 'poetic' (Langellier and Peterson 2004, p. 54) and 'intense' (Wilson 2006, p. 9), 'an experience' as opposed to the undifferentiated 'general stream of experiences' that make up so much of an ordinary day (Dewey 2005, p. 37). Salter refers to something similar when he notes how remarkable it is that people who rely on the relative permanence and fixity of media still seek to create the ephemeral experiences of live performance. For him, the reason is that performance 'yield[s] new knowing about the world through its sudden presence and equally sudden disappearance. It is in this sense that performance as knowing takes us beyond the quotidian' (2010, p. 352). Salter seems to capture the basic sentiments of many performance researchers when he says that 'the everyday is extraordinary only when we can observe and experience it as such' (2010, p. 352), and performance itself is one of those means of experiencing. This section introduces some of the important theoretical perspectives on how performance can transform the experience of everyday life: postdramatic theatre, presentational performance, performance art and Live Art, the aesthetics of performance, liminality, intensity of the performance frame, and making special.

Postdramatic and Presentational Theatre

The term 'theatre' in many places around the globe is likely to conjure images of a raised stage with dozens or hundreds of seats facing it. The auditorium goes dark, while lights come up on the stage, revealing actors who take on the roles of fictional characters in series of scenes that are intended to mimic possible events. For example, one might think of Benedict Cumberbatch (actor) playing Hamlet (character) in Lyndsey Turner's (director's) version of Shakespeare's (playwright's) *Hamlet* (title of play). The aim of a work such as this is often to present a fictional scenario. This type of work is referred to as the 'theatre of dramas' by Hans-Thies Lehmann, in contrast to the object of his interest—performances he calls 'postdramatic theatre' (2006, p. 21). These seek to avoid or downplay mimesis, or the acting out of an imitation of an event. Instead, postdramatic theatre involves 'the execution of acts that are real in the here and now and find their fulfilment in the very moment they happen' (2006, p. 104). Examples include performed narrations of fairy tales (2006, p. 109) that emphasise the personal relationship between performer and audience member, the spectacularly visceral productions of La Fura dels Baus, or the stark visuals of Robert Wilson. Marco De Marinis (1993) refers to a similar distinction with his terms 'representational theatre' and 'presentational theatre'. My imaginary, stereotypical version of *Hamlet* is an example of representational theatre, but in presentational theatre, 'the so-called *presentational* aspect variously prevails over the representational aspect' (1993, pp. 48–49, emphasis in the original). If Cumberbatch were to perform as himself rather than taking on a role like Hamlet, this might be a work of presentational theatre. Presentational and representational performance may seem like opposites in the abstract, but in practice they are descriptions of extreme ends of a spectrum. Neither Lehmann nor De Marinis claims that any performance would be wholly one or the other, and each type contains elements of the other. While it may be impossible to have a purely dramatic/representational or a purely postdramatic/presentational performance, any performance will emphasise one approach over the other. The emphases in presentational performance are on self-reflexivity and the production of reality.

Performance Art and Live Art

Self-reflexivity and the production of reality also drive much of the work within 'performance art' (the preferred term in the United States) or Live Art (the preferred term in the United Kingdom).[5] Performance art encompasses viscerally shocking works such as the renowned performance artist Marina Abramović's encounters with asphyxiation (*Rhythm 5*, 1974), Carolee Schneemann's reading of a text pulled from her vagina in *Interior Scroll* (1975), and Franko B's slow-motion bleeding up and down a white catwalk in *I Miss You* (1999–2005). On a less shocking note, performance art also includes some famous works such as *The Artist Is Present* at the New York Museum of Modern Art in 2010, in which Abramović sat in motionless silence for hours every day as members of the public sat opposite her. As theorist RoseLee Goldberg observes, 'performance defies precise or easy definition beyond the simple declaration that it is live art by artists' (2011, p. 9).

Performance art and Live Art often explore the space between performance and everyday life and can therefore contribute to an understanding of how performance practices might affect experience design. However, just as De Marinis (1993, pp. 48–49) sets out presentational and representational theatre as two extremes on a spectrum, or as Dewey finds the 'aesthetic' in the 'integration' of everyday experience (2005, p. 57), I argue that there is no single criterion distinguishing purely ordinary interactions from those that are 'like "Art art"' (Cull 2011, pp. 90–91). Rather, it is necessary to investigate the dynamics of the performer-audience interaction in the co-creation of any performance event. Putting a wooden spoon in your hair, or showing people around your hometown, or simply sitting silently in front of a stranger—actions like these can affect the relationship between performer and spectator every bit as powerfully as a more shocking or spectacular piece of performance can.

Performance art is also the heading under which many of the private and hidden works mentioned in Chap. 1 would tend to fall. Roberto Cuoghi spent years living as his father, copying every detail of how a man thirty years his senior speaks and moves. He conducted this work at all times, not only when being observed by an audience, yet it is framed as a performance outside the constraints of the art world (Hoffmann and Jonas 2005, p. 106). Similarly, Pawel Althamer creates performances set in public places, yet his performers undertake such common activities that only someone aware of his intentions—or someone with a keen eye who noticed these performers reappearing day after day—would detect any performance taking place. His work *Film* (2000) follows these performers (Hoffmann and Jonas 2005,

---

[5] Some will argue that these terms are not synonymous (see e.g. Johnson 2012, p. 7), or that they are closer than some in the UK would care to admit (Roms and Edwards 2012). However, the phenomena to which they refer are close enough for the purposes of this work that they may be used interchangeably except where noted. I use the term preferred by the writer I am referencing; in my own text, I use 'Live Art' to refer to British artists, including Pearson and Baker, both of whom have worked in association with the Live Art Development Agency in the UK – and 'performance art' as a more inclusive term that incorporates practices from other countries.

p. 112). These and many other works expand the notion of performance into subtleties of perception on the part of any spectators, as well as the subjective experience of the performer.

Aesthetics and Liminality

One substantial framework for understanding the types of performance described in this section is found in the work of Fischer-Lichte (2008b). She draws on performances since the 1960s, including many works of performance art, to establish an aesthetics of performance as an energetic, ephemeral event from which 'an extraordinary state of permanently heightened attention' (2008b, p. 168) can emerge. By 'heightened attention' she refers to the audience's awareness of the objects ('conspicuousness'), people ('intensity of appearance'), and structure ('deviation and surprise') of the performance event (2008b, pp. 165–166). This heightened attention 'transform[s] what has been ordinary into components of aesthetic experience' (2008b, p. 168). With these three categories, it is possible to understand and manipulate the components that can compel a spectator's attention, and therefore shape her experience of the performance event.

Fischer-Lichte's concept of aesthetic experience also comprises three components: the collapse of dichotomies, such as between the ethical and the aesthetic (see also Heddon 2008); autopoiesis and emergence, or the self-generating nature of the event; and 'liminality and transformation'. The first component refers to the fact that performances cannot be perfectly bracketed out from real life; performers and audience members feel the results of each other's actions, just as Marina Abramović would not have lived through *Rhythm 5* had her audience not pulled her unconscious body from the nearby flames that were unexpectedly asphyxiating her. The second refers to the unique and emergent nature of each performance, where audiences and performers contribute to the content and/or the 'feel' of each performance, and accidents or interruptions could disrupt events at any moment. Both of these first two components may alter 'the physiological, energetic, affective, and motoric state' (Fischer-Lichte 2008b, p. 177) of the audience, meaning that they can create physically perceptible emotional changes and 'enable experiences that always carry a liminal dimension' (2008b, p. 176).

The term 'liminal' within performance studies is often understood in terms of the writings of Victor Turner, an anthropologist whose work on ritual was vital to the development of performance studies in the United States. Fischer-Lichte uses 'liminality' as defined by Turner to imply a sense of ritual transformation whereby the audience member transitions from one state to another. In a social ritual, this transformation may be permanent, such as the transition from youth to adulthood through a religious or cultural ritual. When applied to performance, it is generally accepted that these transformations tend to lack the social recognition and permanence of religious or cultural rituals. Along those lines, Fischer-Lichte acknowledges that performance is likely to cause only temporary shifts in emotions, attitudes, and behaviours (2008b, p. 179). However, an individual audience member might experience a powerful internal transformation during a moment of liminality created through performance. Taken together, heightened attention converts the quotidian into an emergent performance event, and all of these components create the possibility for audience members to enter a liminal state in which their emotions, attitudes, and behaviours might be temporarily transformed.

Bearing in mind that the purpose of PED is not necessarily to explore artistic or cultural performance to the exclusion of other types of experience, it can be helpful to put Fischer-Lichte's very specific theories of the aesthetics of performance in a broader context. Like Fischer-Lichte, folklorist Richard Bauman (1975) is interested in studying performances in their own right rather than starting from a written text or script, but his topic is any type of spoken communication, whether framed as performance or conversation. For Bauman, the act of physically performing through speech is 'a unifying thread tying together the marked, segregated esthetic genres and other spheres of verbal behavior into a general unified conception of verbal art as a way of speaking' (1975, p. 291). By tying together 'personal narrative' (1975, p. 298) in regular conversation with cultural storytelling performances, Bauman links the everyday with the rarefied, and focuses his attention on how performance operates as an interaction between speaker/performer and audience. He draws conclusions that resonate with Fischer-Lichte's:

> Performance … is marked as available for the enhancement of experience, through the present enjoyment of the intrinsic qualities of the act of expression itself. Performance thus calls forth special attention to and heightened awareness of the act of expression, and gives license to the audience to regard the act of expression and the performer with special intensity. (Bauman 1975, p. 293)

Bauman views the variations in 'the degree of intensity with which the performance frame operates' as distinct from any notions of 'the relative quality of a performance' (1975, p. 297). This distinction helps to separate discussions of *how* the aesthetics of performance operate with a value judgement of *how well* the performance succeeds according to unspecified criteria. More specifically, his idea of varying intensities helps to further distance the concept of 'heightened awareness' or 'heightened attention' from any implications of defining an event as either aesthetic or non-aesthetic. Rather, 'heightened awareness' and 'heightened attention' point to specific actions and attitudes that can be consciously approached, analysed, and—I argue—designed for. The notion of 'aesthetics' can then be viewed as the emerging, self-generating condition in which the ordinary can 'appear as extraordinary' (Fischer-Lichte 2008b, p. 179), relatively free from notions of what a 'good' performance 'should' look like.

Using Bauman's language alongside Fischer-Lichte's runs the risk of simply replacing the terms 'aesthetic' and 'non-aesthetic' with 'extraordinary' and 'ordinary'. This can be resolved by a simple yet powerful analysis of what distinguishes the 'extraordinary'. Anthropologist Ellen Dissanayake defines the 'extraordinary' or 'aesthetic' in any field as the result of a 'making special' (2003), by which she means an 'intention to appeal to … another's faculty for apprehending and appreciating a specialness that is more than what is necessary to fulfill a practical end' (2003, p. 28). For Dissanayake, 'making special' applies to all art, as well as play and ritual (cf. Schechner 2006, p. 17), providing further grounding to the idea that there is no sharp line to be drawn between the ordinary and the extraordinary. Again resonating with Fischer-Lichte's discussion of the aesthetics of performance, Dissanayake's 'making special' happens as the result of behaviours through which 'everyday reality is transformed' (2003, p. 28). This phrase also echoes the over-arching purposes or hopes for performance as identified by a number of theorists: a heightened attention to others (Bauman 1975; Fischer-Lichte 2008b), a practice of empathy (Dolan 2005, p. 14), and the possibility of 'transformation' (Phelan 2004, p. 574; Fischer-Lichte 2008b). One way of understanding PED is as a way for people to make our everyday lives 'special' (Dissanayake 2003), including those elements of digital technology that have become embedded in our routines, by heightening attention to the elements of interaction and therefore creating opportunities for liminality and transformation.

Key Performance Topics

If we take as a starting point for PED the idea that everyday life can be understood and transformed through performance, it stands to reason that those types of performance that draw from the practices of everyday life can be fruitful places to examine. There are far more of these than can possibly be covered in a single chapter, including canonical examples such as the works of Bertolt Brecht, Augusto Boal, or Jerzy Grotowski. The work in this section offers points of departure for thinking about the design of performative experiences: autobiographical performance, storytelling, devised performance, and (briefly) participatory performance. Again, these four are useful starting points, and by no means an exhaustive list.

Autobiographical Performance

Autobiographical performance is a relatively underexplored area. Performance theorist Bonnie Marranca, writing in 1979, states that 'autobiography, in the sense of the "self as text," is one of the characteristic features of current experimental theatre and performance art' (1979, p. 86). Since 1979, autobiography has remained a vibrant genre, especially in 'the wider context of the contemporary glut of mass-mediated confessional opportunities—'reality tv' shows, chat shows, internet chat rooms, blogs, etc' (Heddon 2008, p. 17). A thorough examination of the history of autobiographical performance, particularly by women, can be found in Áine Phillips's doctoral thesis *Live Autobiography: An Investigation of Autobiographical Performance Practice* (2009). Further examinations of autobiographical performance can be seen in texts on individual performers or performances (e.g. Schechner 2002;

Ferris 2005; Bean 2006; Mock 2009; O'Bryan 2011; Blažević and Jablanovec 2012), or in full-length works focusing on particular categories of identity (e.g. Stephenson 2013).

The most substantial work on a range of autobiographical performance practices is Heddon's *Autobiography and Performance* (2008). Her key focus is the means by which performers negotiate their 'identity' and 'experience' (2008, pp. 96–97)—terms that make her work accessible to interaction and experience design researchers, especially those familiar with the theoretical frameworks put forward by McCarthy and Wright in their text *Technology as Experience* (2004) and subsequent works (Wright and McCarthy 2010; McCarthy and Wright 2015).

Of course, memory is a key factor in any performance or experience that deals with a person's life experiences. Heddon's approach to memory is nuanced, in line with the most widely accepted concepts among cultural theorists and psychologists working in memory research. This includes the rejection of the 'storage-space model', in which memories are stored away and then retrieved intact. Rather, memory should be conceived of using a 'work space model' (Andres et al. 2010, p. 8) in which memory becomes 'a site of identity formation, empowerment, and resistance for individuals and communities' (2010, p. 16). This model reflects the fact that memories change over time and are less reliable than many people believe. For example, autobiographical memories are affected by emotions experienced at the time of remembering (Holland and Kensinger 2010, p. 108). Similarly, cultural theorist Annette Kuhn (2007) examines performances of memory including 'performative viewings' of family photos (2007, p. 285). Her findings indicate that memory work is not a direct and unchanging insight into the soul: 'the task is not to psychoanalyse people but to be helpfully at hand at the birth of new insight and fresh understanding' (2007, p. 284). Autobiographical memory is best understood as a dynamic process that can change each time a memory is recalled. This makes each moment of recall a slippery but productive encounter with the self, the trigger for the memory, and anyone who might interact with the person experiencing that memory. In other words, autobiographical memory is itself a performative act that can amplify and be amplified by the process of creating a performance from those memories. Heddon reflects this view by describing memory as a tricky 'action' (2008, p. 63) marked by gaps and errors, placing autobiographical performance 'precisely and precariously on the intersection between imagination and memory' (2008, p. 64)—an apt description of at least some audience members' experience in *Bubbling Tom*.

Heddon identifies four constitutive themes in autobiographical performance: politics, history, place, and ethics. Her notion of ethics deals directly with the relationships among performers, audience members, and the people referred to or implied in the stories being told, both living and dead (2008, p. 124).[6] It is impossible to tell a life story without at least implying something of the lives of the people

---

[6] Ethics are of course not foreign to HCI. As Ann Light points out, design 'must recognise how the activity of interpreting technologies for use is charged with political possibilities' (2011, p. 431), especially when those technologies are directly mediating the construction of identity.

who interacted with the teller (or failed to interact with her). It is also impossible to tell a life story without implying something about the audience for that telling. For example, if the performer takes great pains to explain the background of the events she describes, she might imply that her audience would be unlikely to have shared her experience, while a performance that assumes background knowledge on the part of the audience might draw them into a sense of sharing her experiences. Stories about childhood tell or imply something about the teller's family, as in *Bubbling Tom*, and stories about daily life imply something about those whom the performer comes into contact with, as in *Kitchen Show*. For these reasons, ethics are an important concern in any autobiographical work (Heddon 2008, p. 127) and Heddon asserts that autobiographical performance's most powerful potential is in the structural relations between performer and audience in 'the shared time and space' of the live encounter (2008, p. 167).

Furthermore, Heddon believes that the emotional or political power of autobiographical performance can be increased by a move away from stages towards small or even one-to-one performances (2008, p. 168). In that genre, a single performer spends time in close proximity with a single audience member. The performer might be playing a role, but often that role is a version of the performer's self, as for example Adrian Howells sometimes performed as Adrienne (Heddon and Howells 2011). One-to-one performances can also be overtly participatory, as when Howells engaged his audience members in conversation or 'spooned' them on a bed in the 2006 performance *Held* (2011, pp. 4–5), though it can be argued that any one-to-one performance is participatory because the solitary audience member cannot hide from the performer's gaze. Such performances involve a great deal of 'risk' (2011, p. 2) of the type discussed in the context of *Kitchen Show* and can prove 'challenging' as well as surprisingly 'intimate' for audience members (2011, p. 7). They can also confront audience members with odd paradoxes in their own behaviour, as when Rachel Zerihan found herself unable to resist eating a detested strawberry in her self-imposed 'role of dutiful spectator' in Howells's *The Garden of Adrian* (Heddon et al. 2012, p. 123), or when Helen Iball felt threatened by memories triggered by getting into Sam Rose's bed in *Bed of Roses* (Heddon et al. 2012, p. 128). Creating a performance for one audience member at a time can result in any number of fascinating and unexpected responses rooted in each individual's life experiences and expectations in the particular time and place of that unique performance.

Perhaps the most important insight arising from autobiographical performance relates to its performativity in the first sense discussed in Chap. 2. Performativity implies that a person's (gender) identity is always being created: 'always a doing, though not a doing by a subject who might be said to preexist the deed' (2002, p. 33). This philosophical position is supported by research in other fields. Psychologist Craig R. Barclay writes that 'a unique remembered self does not exist, nor does a remembered self exist only as the current "text" of a life story or personal narrative' (1994, p. 57). Instead, 'self, and the remembered self especially, is initially a consequence rather than a cause of activity' (1994, p. 62). Barclay's term 'protoselves' reflects the multiplicity of experiences of the self that a person will have when engaging with autobiographical memory, and it does so without claiming a destructive fragmentation of the self that could so easily be assumed by invoking the idea of 'multiplicity' (1994, pp. 71–72). In a similar vein, psychologist Jerome Bruner extends cognition and emotion with the possibilities of narrative and imagination. He argues 'that Self is not an entity that one can simply remember … . Self is a perpetually rewritten story' (Bruner 1994, pp. 41–53). Bruner's self is not strictly tied to the 'facts' surrounding a remembered event. His theory allows for intentional or unintentional fictionalising on the part of the 'thinking' (1994, p. 43) subject. Bruner's 'self' is unstable and multiple, but like Barclay's 'protoselves', it is not necessarily fragmented in a postmodern understanding of the term. It is instead dialogical, outside the full control of the subject but still malleable to a certain degree—much like Butler's take on the performed self, or Fischer-Lichte's concept of performance as an 'autopoietic feedback loop' in which neither performers nor spectators are 'fully autonomous' or 'fully determined by others' (2008b, pp. 164–165). Most importantly, according to Barclay and Bruner, identity is imbricated with narrative, imagination, performance, and performativity, all of which are involved in autobiographical performance.

Just as memory research implies that individuals do not possess a static set of personal memories waiting to be revealed, unchanged, in any context, research on the self implies that the self that an individual experiences is not fixed. Instead, 'identity is performatively constituted by the very "expressions" that are said to be its results' (Butler 2002, p. 39). This includes everything from archival documentation like Pearson's photos in *Bubbling Tom* to Baker's precarious pose on the cake stand to conclude *Kitchen Show*. Every choice is performatively autobiographical, part of a contingent, shifting, moment-by-moment creation of the performer's sense of self.

Storytelling

Autobiographical performance is not the only performance practice that can address interactions between people who are 'showing' their own 'doing' to other people, especially when using digital technologies in the process. Writing about the generative properties of autobiographical storytelling, Tom Maguire chooses an apt term of reference:

> It allows the teller to establish social relations with others within which the identities, both of the teller and of the listener, are constituted in relation to each other through the act of telling. Autobiography thereby forms an *interface* between individuals… . (2015, p. 59, my emphasis)

The sharing of life experiences often takes the form of spoken stories, as does the co-located sharing of personal digital media (Balabanović et al. 2000). Storytelling is an important performance practice to understand, as the spoken word is a staple of interaction, whether human-to-human or, increasingly, human-computer. This is particularly relevant for social computing, social media, and perhaps even for the kind of internal narrative process that shapes people's perception of personal value (McCarthy and Wright 2004, p. 66).

Storytelling as a professional performance practice can vary widely. In the United States, the tendency is for performers to tell personal stories (Wilson 2006, p. xi), making the line between autobiographical performance and storytelling—and some types of standup comedy—almost impossible to draw. In the United Kingdom, as in many other countries within and beyond the Anglophone world, a storytelling performance will often imply the telling of an existing story, often based on the folklore of a particular place (2006, p. xi). Thus outside the US, one might assume that storytelling is generally a traditional practice unconcerned with emerging concerns in performance studies. However, Wilson traces the lineage of all kinds of storytelling to the 1960s (2006, p. 9), calling it 'a branch of vibrant alternative theatre' (2006, p. 16) that can embrace fragmented or non-linear narratives (2006, p. 121) along with more straightforward narrative styles. Recent work on storytelling in a theatrical context includes Live Art, specifically the work of Bobby Baker, and applied theatre (discussed below) in the remit of storytelling performance (Maguire 2015).

As practitioner Taffy Thomas puts it, storytelling is 'a reported art form in the way that you report the story, a couple of paces away from it' (quoted in Wilson 2006, p. 189). In part because of this emphasis on the reporting of a story (diegesis) over re-enacting the story (mimesis), storytelling breaks down the fourth wall of conventional theatre—the imaginary wall at the edge of the stage that separates the scene being represented from the world inhabited by the audience. The storyteller spends little time pretending behind that fourth wall, and instead reaches out to his audience as a co-conspirator, permitting the audience to see the teller as well as the story (Wilson 2006, p. 5). (While Wilson rightly includes this distinction in his *'false* acting/storytelling model' (2006, p. 46, my emphasis), it remains the case that many people associate theatre and acting with the fourth wall—see e.g. Benford and Giannachi 2011, p. 143.) Wilson's description of the performer reaching out to her audience is reminiscent of Walter Benjamin's (2006) definition of storytelling, the creation of a connection in a shared time and space between the storyteller and the audience, to whom she is attempting to offer a meaningful model or strategy for empowerment. In both cases, what emerges is an interaction between performer and audience member rather than a simple case of a spectator listening to whatever is placed before her. This type of interaction is not relegated to old-fashioned storytelling, either: these views are also reflected in what Bauman sees as the contribution of storytelling to 'emergent culture' (1975, p. 306) in whatever form it may take.

One style in particular, known as 'non-platform' storytelling, is relevant to performative experiences involving narrative. It involves minimal sets, props, or costumes (Wilson 2006, p. 71), and for the most part the storyteller does not attempt to inhabit the roles of her characters. Non-platform storytelling in particular raises interesting questions about the difference between an aesthetic or professional performance and the conversational kind of storytelling that everyone engages in from an early age. As Wilson is less concerned with the content of individual stories than with the ways in which they are performed, his 'performance continuum' (2006, p. 9) allows individual storytelling performances to be evaluated on the degree to which they diverge from the purely conversational (the left side of the spectra) and approach the highly professional (the right side of the spectra):

conversation .... cultural performance
low intensity .... high intensity
informal .... formal
subconscious .... conscious
low risk .... high risk
low rewards .... high rewards (Wilson 2006, p. 9)

The performance continuum is useful in analysing performances that break the traditions of mimetic theatre but which do not fit the mould of a stereotypical storytelling performance. For example, *Kitchen Show* would be highly 'conscious' in that it was meticulously devised and officially commissioned, with fairly 'high risk' for its experimentation with place. The 'formality' of Baker's performance was heightened by the unusual actions and marks on her body, which contrasted with the 'informality' of her making cups of tea for each audience member. Conversation such as the audience interjections into *Bubbling Tom* would tend to nudge a performance to the left side of that spectrum, though Pearson's performance was predominantly 'cultural' in that it was commissioned, planned, ticketed, and the like. Both *Kitchen Show* and *Bubbling Tom* had at least moments of intensity that are often lacking in everyday conversational storytelling, and they offered their performers and audiences rewards—financial, aesthetic, emotional—beyond the conversational norm as well.

Conversational storytelling has also been studied in some detail, though not within the performance studies literature. However, many draw from sources within performance. Key among these are the work of Kristen Langellier and Eric Peterson on 'performing narrative', a term which 'incorporates both performance and performativity' (2004, p. 3). In other words, they focus on stories as they are performed and negotiated in the moment of live performance, paying particular attention to the ways that audiences help shape the stories being told. They argue that stories people tell about themselves are integral to their sense of self; they are designed (if subconsciously) to meet the expectations of their recipients; and they are not to be understood as fixed or essential elements of a fixed and fully agentive self. For these reasons, the most important element for analysis is not a story's content but its singular, situated performance. Similarly, Neal R. Norrick (2000) extends the seminal work of William Labov and Joshua Waletzky (1967) by analysing stories as they emerge in conversation as an 'interactional achievement' among speakers and listeners (Norrick 2000, p. 2). Norrick's extremely detailed analyses reach similar conclusions to those drawn by Langellier and Peterson as well as many HCI and performance researchers discussed in this chapter, namely that conversational storytelling is much more than the repetition of a fixed text. 'Far from simply recapitulating past experience, storytellers often seem to relive, re-evaluate and reconstruct remembered experience' (Norrick 2000, p. 2).

By emphasising the performance of narrative or the interactions at the heart of conversation, these researchers underscore the importance of the dialogic relationship between performer and audience member. The audience member might be assumed to be inconsequential to the performance of a conversational story, at least if she does not actively interrupt or heckle, but this is not at all the case.

Psychologist Janet B. Bavelas et al. (2000) study the surprisingly active and influ- ential role of listeners in conversational storytelling. Even when the storyteller 'has the floor' to tell his or her story in a single turn, generic responses (such as 'mm- hm') and specific responses (such as displaying appropriate facial expressions) con- tribute significantly to the story itself, far more than previous theories of autonomous conversation or back channels would allow (2000, p. 942). A conversational story can be noticeably diminished by something as subtle as a lack of attention—as can a professional performance. Similar findings have been noted in the doctoral research of Deborah Tatar, whose contributions to HCI over the years have been substantial. These and similar findings should be brought together and built upon.

Devising

Whether a performance is classified as autobiographical or storytelling (or some- thing else entirely), it exists in the time and space shared by performer and audience members. However, while the unique performance event emerges in that time and space, its structure and/or content have almost always been planned, at least loosely, in some way. Traditional plays are often written out in advance; a director decides how the scripted words and instructions will appear to an audience, and actors embody the roles that have been written out. Plans for works in a performance art tradition might consist of an intention and a set of strategies to meet that intention, such as Third Angel and mala voadora's soliciting of stories from the public and plotting them on a map of the world drawn from their collective memory in *Story Map* (2012). An obvious exception to this idea of planning is improvised perfor- mance, but improvisation tends to take place within a tight framework, and most improvisational actors are highly trained and well practiced in their art form. This means that performances involve some degree of intention on the part of the person or people deciding to initiate them, an intention that nearly always exists prior to the performance event. This intent might be described as 'artistic' if the director, per- former, or other instigator is perceived to be an 'artist' in her own estimation or, more importantly, in the estimation of the cultural institutions involved in support- ing her career. However, loaded terms such as 'art' are not strictly necessary to describe the intention behind a given performance: interaction design and experi- ence design are not automatically excluded from these processes simply because they are not first and foremost recognised as art forms.

A common (Mermikides and Smart 2010, p. 4) approach to creating or planning a new performance is 'devising', defined by Deirdre Heddon and Jane Milling as 'a mode of work in which *no* script … exists prior to the work's creation … [although] the creation and the use of text or score often occur at different points within the devising processes' (2006, p. 3, emphasis in the original). For Allison Oddey (1994), devised theatre is 'different to conventional theatre in the sense that it explores the dynamics in the relationship between performer and spectator in the chosen space' (1994, p. 19). This exploration of performer-spectator interaction is evident in

Kitchen Show's treatment of strangers as guests in the performer's home, and in *Bubbling Tom*'s incorporation of comments and challenges to the performer's childhood recollections. Although devising is primarily thought of as a group activity and autobiography as a solitary endeavour, solo autobiographical performances are rarely created without some amount of collaboration (Heddon 2008, p. 9), and there is nothing to prevent individuals from using devising practices such as improvisation, games, physical experimentation, chance, tasks, or collage (Heddon and Milling 2006, pp. 8–11).

Autobiographical performances, by definition, are built on the life experiences of the person doing the performing, and therefore the performer would also most likely be heavily involved in the creation of the performance. While the performer of an autobiographical work might write a script, knowing that they are the only person who could perform that script, 'devising' is the term used in the very few references to the process of creating an autobiographical performance (Heddon and Kelly 2010; see also Baker 2001; Govan et al. 2007 pp. 59–68; Heddon 2008, p. 157). Similarly, storytelling performances that do not draw from a corpus of traditional tales might also require the performer to do more than interpret someone else's words. As with the fluid distinctions between representational and presentational, or conversational and aesthetic, there is no sharp dividing line between the autobiographical, the biographical, and the fictional (Heddon 2008). This is evident from the trade-offs of authorial responsibility in Robert Wilson's *The Life and Death of Marina Abramović* (2011) to the drive for a mutually understood 'truth' in the shared recollections of Third Angel's *Class of '76* (2000). The practice of devising allows performance makers to construct new performances based on personal experiences that may (or may not) be tied to a specific script.

Given the broad remit of performance studies, which is 'adjacent and related' to practices 'such as oratory' and 'folklore' (Jackson 2004, p. 11), Schechner's term 'proto-performance' can complement devising. A proto-performance 'precedes and/or gives rise to a performance … [it] might be an upcoming date that requires a performance—a birthday, Christmas party, or initiation rite' (2006, p. 225). This term is helpful for widening the scope of starting points for performance, especially in light of emerging digital media practices that initiated some recent autobiographical performances (such as *Cape Wrath*, discussed in Chap. 5). By thinking in terms of practices or events that generate or trigger performances, it is possible to incorporate these early stages into the design of performative experiences. A thoughtful, unusual approach to even the most quotidian of experiences can serve as a process for creating performance.

Participatory Performance

Finally, it is necessary to at least touch on participatory performance in the context of PED, which aims to create performative experiences that can exist outside the structure of professional performers and paying audiences. Participatory, interactive, or immersive performance and participatory art cover a vast range of practice, theory, and debate (e.g. Bishop 2012; Fensham 2012; Reason 2015) that go far beyond the scope of this initial foray into some of the most relevant aspects of performance theory and practice. These discussions are worth investigating, both within the performance studies literature and within HCI itself (e.g. Taylor et al. 2014; Holmer et al. 2015; McCarthy and Wright 2015)—McCarthy and Wright's work being far more thorough than anything I could offer in these pages. Mixed reality performances (Benford and Giannachi 2011) also rely on participants, whose contributions are planned and orchestrated by people who strive to keep their trajectories within certain bounds (2011, p. 194). In the context of this work on PED, and particularly in light of the case study in Chaps. 5 and 6, I will offer one example of participatory performance. Allan Kaprow, best known for his Happenings in New York from the late 1950s, also created presentational works he termed Activities. The Activities, which began in the 1970s, were small-scale participatory performances that 'consisted of predetermined actions based on highly structured routines derived from everyday life' (Morgan 2010, p. 11). They used instruction booklets with photographs to explain precisely how the participants—non-professionals in every case—were to carry out the Activity. Activities encouraged participants to increase their physical and mental attention to everyday activities with the aim of an 'experienced insight' to the everyday (Cull 2011, p. 86). Kaprow believed that his participants must be guided towards an experience that is partly routine and partly made unusual, 'like "Art art"' (Cull 2011, pp. 90–91). Activities aimed to put artistic performance into the hands of non-performers so that they could experience performance from the inside and come to a richer appreciation of the details of everyday life. Their performances had little to do with mimesis or representation, and everything to do with the transformation of attention and insight that came from dealing with everyday life in an intentionally unusual way. I argue that participatory performance can be a rich source of guidance and inspiration for PED, but perhaps most powerfully among those works that maintain Kaprow's focus on transforming a person's attention to the details of everyday life.

Key Performance Methodologies

Conflicting Ideas and Common Themes

Although some performance researchers use methods long established in HCI such as interviews and surveys, as for example Matthew Reason does in his work on audience research (2004), others push the boundaries of what constitutes knowledge in performance studies, and therefore how that knowledge might be pursued. As Kershaw and Nicholson state in their introduction to *Research Methods in Theatre and Performance*, 'creative approaches to research practices offer an implicit challenge to outmoded perceptions that the terms 'method' and 'methodology' imply an attempt to capture, codify and categorise knowledge' (2011a, p. 1). Some areas of research that are argued to function as performance methodologies, such as postcolonial theory (Kershaw and Nicholson 2011b) or scenography (Hannah and Harsløf 2008), would leave many HCI researchers scratching their heads. Is postcolonial theory a performance methodology that a PED researcher could recognise useful methods within?

One way of making sense of performance studies methodologies is to find common themes among them. Kershaw and Nicholson (2011a) identify two themes that reflect concerns of design-oriented research: reflexivity and unpredictability. Reflexive methodologies require researchers to account for the results of their own choices in their research process. They can then use their research as a space for reflection on the paradoxes and contradictions that may emerge (2011a, p. 5), and therefore question their own choices (2011a, p. 8). Kershaw and Nicholson describe reflexivity not as a methodology in itself but as 'a methodological key that can unpick the conundrums which plague the discipline of methods in theatre and performance research' (2011a, p. 6). The closely related concept of unpredictability refers to the fact that much performance research cannot be counted on to unfold as planned, and some of what is presented as research (or even performance) is a post-hoc construction. This is not a flaw, but rather a source of potentially 'fruitful failures' (2011a, p. 9). Fischer-Lichte (1997) agrees that while a research output might be linear, the process of engaging in performance research is circular, intuitive, and provisional, shaping the questions that it answers (1997, pp. 10–11). Along the same lines, Gilbert Cockton (2008) challenges traditional HCI principles by championing reflexivity and unpredictability in design. While there are any number of other performance methodologies that might help to orient an HCI researcher investigating PED, these 'methodological keys' provide a powerful orientation to the research process.

Applied Theatre

Another relevant methodological stance is applied theatre, which might have the effect of making strange or, conversely, of enhancing connections to distant times and places. Applied theatre refers to performances created and performed for a particular purpose or specific audience, such as performances created for dementia sufferers to explore their own memories. Jenny Hughes et al. propose an applied theatre methodology 'that privileges notions of practice' and 'support[s] the creative, social and political aims of projects' (2011, p. 188). Their methodology exemplifies the reflexivity noted by Kershaw and Nicholson (2011a) as well as the unstable nature of identity and memory uncovered by research into autobiographical performance. As Hughes et al. explain, their 'way of working challenges notions of method and methodology as epistemologically secure, finite, discrete sets of procedures fit for the purpose of discovering certain, measurable findings' (2011, p. 188). When neither the method nor the goal of research is reliably fixed, the research process becomes an iterative practice with no hierarchy between theory and practice.

Hughes et al.'s (2011) perspective on applied theatre methodology aligns well with design-oriented research within HCI in four ways. Its focus on practice mirrors the necessity of 'the bringing forth of the research prototype' in the generation of knowledge (Fällman 2003, p. 231). Second, its challenge to the fixity of methods and to the goal of 'discovering certain, measurable findings' (Hughes et al. 2011, p. 188) parallels Daniel Fällman's rejection of claims to 'a structured and linear process of moving from the abstract to the concrete' (2003, p. 229). Third, the centrality of creative practice in applied theatre research as theorised by Hughes et al. results in an aspiration to seek knowledge through 'articulations of experience' that do not respond to 'clearly defined questions' (2011, p. 194). This aspiration is shared by Fällman, who sees design-oriented research as an 'unfolding' or 'gestalt' instead of 'a process of first setting up and then solving problems' (2003, p. 230). Fourth, Hughes et al.'s work resonates with recent investigations of participatory projects within HCI, which 'requires increased attention to social and political experiences with technology, including issues of ownership, authorship, and voice' (McCarthy and Wright 2015, p. 5). The applied performance methodology foregrounds an active, creative, reflexive 'doing' that can challenge established methods and propose types of knowledge that were unpredicted at the project's outset, whether embodied, practical, contingent, emergent, or any other kind. Furthermore, some of the methods employed in applied theatre research are also commonly found in design-oriented research, such as 'focus groups, qualitative interviews, questionnaires, participant-observation, creative exercises and video recordings' (Hughes et al. 2011, p. 195). Applied theatre is also important in the context of design-oriented research because it is one of the very few types of performance that is created and/or performed by non-professionals. Clearly, the value of a performance involving elderly people with dementia exploring their own memories does not hinge on their acting skills, but rather on whether they felt themselves to have 'the opportunity to be artists in their own right, to discover their own creativity in form and content' (Oddey 1994, p. 164). There is no 'higher' set of criteria for the participants in applied theatre to meet, as either devisers or performers.

Making Strange

One of the performance methods directly applicable to PED is identified by Thecla Schiphorst in her foreword to Susan Broadhurst and Josephine Machon's book of essays on *Identity, Performance and Technology* (2012), which examines the ethical, social, and political implications of technological performance involving personal identity. This method is the practice of making the familiar strange, so that people (audiences and performers alike) become aware of their own agency in choosing how to perceive their worlds (Schiphorst 2012, p. xiv). Augusto Boal referred to this practice as 'de-mechanization' (Boal quoted in Schiphorst 2012, p.

xv), while Allan Kaprow refers to something very similar with his 'experienced insights' to everyday activities that have been made unusual (Cull 2011, p. 86). Fischer-Lichte (2008a) sees it as the aim of performance to induce a transformation in the spectator 'which alienates them from their everyday life…. Such a state can be experienced as a pleasure as well as a torment' (2008a, p. 80). As described above, experiencing the familiar from a new perspective can be central to performance practices revolving around the everyday. And as will be laid out in Chaps. 4, 5, and 6, performance analysis underpins the PED methodology by opening up performance to rigorous scrutiny, providing the basis of the new method of coded performance analysis, and shaping its approach to evaluation.

Above all, though, it is the commitment of performance studies to understanding their subject through the study and sometimes the research-driven creation of individual performances that provides the common ground with HCI, interaction design, and experience design. The methodologies and methods described here serve as examples of specific approaches that can expand and strengthen PED in its efforts to drive an understanding of performative experiences with technology.

Intermediality

This chapter on performance has almost entirely avoided a central element of PED: the involvement of technology. This is a deliberate strategy, as so much of what performance studies is uniquely positioned to offer is the nuance of shifting relationships among people as they undertake a co-creative process of engaging in live performance experiences, regardless of the types of technology involved. This section focuses on a strand of research that looks specifically at performances that involve digital technologies.

As explained in Chap. 2, I perceive any tensions between live performers and digital technologies as potentially fruitful, especially when they are directed towards the increasing degree to which these technologies are becoming accepted as extensions of the sense of self—and even more so when they recognise the vast differences in individual response to technologies in the face of emerging trends. I believe that PED is best supported by research into 'intermediality' (e.g. Nelson 2010; Chatzichristodoulou 2011) and related approaches that try to understand the relationships among people engaged with digital technologies through performance (e.g. Salter 2010). Rather than positing the digital in contrast to the live or seeking a space between the two, intermediality addresses 'this very aspect of digital culture — where devices, events, and activities are formed out of relationships, necessary interdependencies, and mutually co-relating entities' (Nelson 2010, p. 17). Therefore, many researchers of intermedial performance are interested 'in how—singularly and collectively—intermedial performances may have elicited a new cultural way of seeing, feeling and being in the contemporary world' (2010, p. 18). The inverse of this question is at the centre of Salter's investigation of technology in performance, which uncovers how technologies and 'socio-political-cultural-economic contexts' have changed how performances are created and perceived (2010, p. xiii). Intermediality looks at performances that are marked by digital technology in any way and interrogates their reciprocal relationship with their performers and audiences. This perspective allows for a rich investigation of the processes of devising, performing, and experiencing works using digital technologies, particularly emerging practices of everyday interaction with personal digital technologies.

Andy Lavender, a proponent of intermedial performance research, argues that intermediality is headed towards the immersion of the spectator—fully embodied, not limited to viewing—into events that are 'routinely intermedial' (2013, p. 9) regardless of how much of the performance uses digital technology. Lavender uses *sensibilité*, or sensibility, to reflect the move towards embodied and immersive experience demanded by intermedial performances that engage users beyond the visuals 'over there' on the stage (2013, p. 9). I argue that another aspect of this immersive intermediality is attention to the ways in which digital technology has infused not only performance technologies but the everyday lives of those people who create and constitute contemporary performance events, both as performers and as audiences, spectators, or 'immersants' (2013, p. 9). In other words, immersion happens not only in the moment of performance in terms of perceiving a digital display or sound, but also through perceiving a performance of lived experience steeped in digital technologies, where the perceiver is also entwined to some degree with digital technologies. This perspective on the effects of digital technologies on performance beyond the limits of what is presented on stage offers a way for technology to be understood in terms of Fischer-Lichte's categories of 'heightened attention' and the 'aesthetics of the event': 'conspicuousness' of the (digital media) object, an 'intensity of appearance' for the performer who is made so aware of the materiality of her digital presence, and the potential creation of a 'liminal' and 'transformational' space during the live performance of a partially digital materiality.

While personal digital media in autobiographical performance has been discussed in the literature to a limited extent (e.g. Lisa Kron's *2.5 Minute Ride* in Heddon 2008, pp. 83–85), there is as yet little sustained discussion of the role of digital media technology in creating or performing an autobiographical piece. This gap is particularly startling as digital media become more tightly integrated into the everyday lives of both performers and spectators. However, one strand of research in intermedial performance indicates that the focus on the negotiation of 'identity' and 'experience' (Heddon 2008, pp. 96–97) through memory and imagination might be supported by the incorporation of digital media. Bruce Barton (2013) argues that digital media technology does not necessarily disrupt the potential for intimate connections, but rather that it displaces intimacy from 'shared understanding' to 'shared experience' (2013, np). Because theories of autobiographical performance, autobiographical memory, and the self reject any static self to be transparently understood, the emphasis moves to the construction of a performance experience defined by relationships in a shared time and space. In addition, it has recently been argued that personal and social media technologies are:

partly responsible both for the proliferation of new forms of autobiography and for the blurring of fiction and nonfiction, as print-based, private journals and diaries yield to virtual versions featuring prose and pictures on a variety of open data platforms, such as Twitter, blog sites, YouTube, Flickr, Facebook, and, yes, Wikipedia. Social media provide the opportunity for reimaging, rewriting, and reimagining in the form of mash-ups, wikis, folksonomies, and tag clouds. (Martin 2015, p. 136)

The more that people incorporate digital technologies into their personal and social lives, the more the substance of autobiography will involve those technologies, and the more audiences will come to expect a technological element in performance. At least one performance theorist has noted that concepts of autobiography need to shift to incorporate these changes (Martin 2015, p. 136). Part of the work of PED may be to contribute to this developing definition of autobiography or 'the real' in performance by shaping the efforts of performance researchers into studying the energetic and emotional connections among co-located performers and audiences. This aligns with Lavender's observation that intermediality research has become concerned primarily with the affect, actions, and affordances created by intermedial performance (2013, p. 6). In these ways, the digital technologies involved in performance can be created and understood not as an interloper to the phenomenon of live performance but as a fundamental part of the experience of making and experiencing performance in the twenty-first century.

How Performance Underpins PED

Two examples of practice anchor this chapter. *Kitchen Show* involved a performer and audience members in an intimate, autobiographical performance set in a private space. It raises interesting and important issues of the ethics of interaction, particularly as they pertain to the 'risk in intimacy' (Baker quoted in Heathfield 1999, p. 102) that Baker pursued in this work. While Baker heightened her audience's attention to the practices of everyday life, *Kitchen Show* was interactive to only a limited degree, and the oddness of her 'actions' and 'marks' heightened 'the degree of intensity with which the performance frame operate[d]' (Bauman 1975, p. 297) in such a way as to set the event itself firmly on the 'cultural' side of the performance continuum (Wilson 2006, p. 9). *Bubbling Tom* was a 'presentational' (De Marinis 1993, pp. 48–49) performance in which storytelling, site-specificity, movement, and small audiences including friends and family members worked together to create a very personal and interactive performance event. This piece used personal analogue media—snapshots from the 1950s—as one of its structuring mechanisms, and it shared those media via a photocopied guidebook given to each audience member.

This chapter has outlined existing work in performance studies that interrogates how performers and, to some degree, spectators can shape their interactions with each other in a way that imparts meaning, emotional impact, and potentially transformational moments of liminality. Key points include:

- Performers (and spectators) whose memory and sense of self are fluid, created and re-created in relation to past experiences, present-moment relationships, and the imagined future.
- Performance as a site of 'heightened attention', 'liminality', and the potential for 'transformation' (Fischer-Lichte 2008b).
- The framing of many performance theories as a set of spectra or continua rather than ontologically fixed points, which gives HCI researchers a number of entry points for designing interactions on the more 'cultural' (Wilson 2006, p. 9) or 'Art art' (Cull 2011, p. 91) sides of those spectra.
- Attention to the ethical implications of autobiographical works.
- Close attention to everyday experience, and to attention itself, as the basis for some performance practice and theory.
- The epistemological value of practice, as evidenced by close study of particular performances and performance practices.
- Intermediality as a framework for working with emerging cultural ways of 'seeing, feeling, and being in the contemporary world' (Nelson 2010, p. 18).

Performance studies rests on a foundation of practice that parallels the design practice at the heart of experience design, interaction design, and ultimately HCI as a whole. Performance studies theorises from the work of countless practitioners who continually create new ways of presenting, representing, interrogating, and challenging the human (or posthuman) condition, while HCI theorises from the work of researchers who continually explore the boundaries of human interaction with technology. Both fields are founded on research into designed interventions in current practices of interaction involving speakers, listeners, and in many cases, digital media.

PED is driven by twin research questions: how can HCI, interaction design, and experience design contribute to the understanding and development of intermedial performance? And how can theories and practices of performance contribute to the understanding and development of digital technologies whose interactions include performative elements? Although arguments can be made for the relevance of a wide range of performance theories and practices, this text focuses on those that deal directly with an individual's performance of herself, and on those that range from the fully 'cultural' (Wilson 2006, p. 9) or 'aesthetic' (Fischer-Lichte 2008b) to the everyday. By understanding how performance can 'make special' (Dissanayake 2003) everyday life experiences, it is possible to formulate a practice within which people who do not identify as artists can perform their experiences with digital technologies, particularly technologies for sharing personal digital media such as photographs. In return, a deeper understanding of how people engage with technology can illuminate the creation and perception of intermedial performances, particularly intermedial autobiographical performances. PED involves a holistic approach to performances, or performative experiences, involving digital media technology. It responds to the call for a 'performative view' (Bardzell et al. 2010) with Pearson's impassioned call 'to get rid of the theatre "object", the play, the "well-made show"', and to replace it with 'a "special world" where extra-daily occurrences and experiences and changes in status are possible' (1998, pp. 39–40). I believe that PED's combination of performance and design can create Pearson's 'special world', a 'making strange' that 'engages and re-engages the audience with material which is intimately familiar and infinitely other' (Pearson 2003, p. 175). It will do so not by embedding fragments of performance theory or practice into unchanged HCI or design processes, but by combining the complementary perspectives of both disciplines to create a way of working more closely attuned to the relationships between self, technology, and others.

References

Andres J, Joyce S, Love B, Raussert W, Wait AR (2010) Introduction. In: Raussert W et al (eds) Remembering and forgetting: memory in images and texts. Aisthesis Verlag, Bielefeld, pp 7–20

Aston E (2000) 'Transforming' women's lives: Bobby Baker's performances of 'Daily Life'. New Theatre Q 16(01):17–25

Baker B (2001) Performance artist Bobby Baker. In: Allen P (ed) Art, not chance: nine artists diaries. Calouste Gulbenkian Foundation, London, pp 31–42

Balabanović M, Chu L, Wolff G (2000) Storytelling with digital photographs. In: Proceedings of the SIGCHI conference on human factors in computing systems. ACM Press, New York, pp 564–571

Baldwyn L (1996) Blending in: the immaterial art of Bobby Baker's culinary events. TDR 40(4):37–55

Barclay CR (1994) Composing protoselves through improvisation. In: Neisser U, Fivush R (eds) The remembering self: construction and agency in self narrative. Cambridge University Press, Cambridge, pp 55–77

Bardzell J, Bolter J, Löwgren J (2010) Interaction criticism: three readings of an interaction design, and what they get us. Interactions 17(2):32–37

Barrett M (2007) The armature of reason. In: Barrett M, Baker B (eds) Bobby Baker: redeeming features of daily life. Routledge, London/New York, pp 224–229

Barton B (2013) New betrayals: intimacy in mediatised performance. E&I 3: np

Bauman R (1975) Verbal art as performance. Am Anthropol 77(2):290–311

Bavelas JB, Coates L, Johnson T (2000) Listeners as co-narrators. J Pers Soc Psychol 79(6):941–952

Bean A (2006) Anne Bean: autobituary: shadow deeds. Matt's Gallery, London/Manchester

Benford S, Giannachi G (2011) Performing mixed reality. MIT Press, Cambridge, MA/London

Benford S, Crabtree A, Reeves S, Sheridan J, Dix A, Flintham M, Drozd A (2006) The frame of the game: blurring the boundary between fiction and reality in mobile experiences. In: Proceedings of the SIGCHI conference on human factors in computing systems. ACM Press, New York, pp 427–436

Benjamin W (2006) The storyteller. In: Hale D (ed) The novel: an anthology of criticism and theory 1900–2000. Blackwell Publishing, Malden, pp 361–378

Bishop C (2012) Artificial hells: participatory art and the politics of spectatorship. Verso Books, London/New York

Blažević M, Jablanovec B (2012) Mandić? What the fuck is Mandić? In: Performance Research. 17(3):133–135

Bowers J, Taylor R, Hook J, Freeman D, Bramley C, Newell C (2014) HCI: human-computer improvisation. In: Proceedings of the 2014 companion publication on Designing interactive systems. ACM Press, New York, pp 203–206

Broadhurst S, Machon J (2012) Identity, performance and technology: practices of empowerment, embodiment and technicity. Palgrave Macmillan, Basingstoke/New York

Brown G (1993) Right off her trolley: Bobby Baker's latest daffy domestic drama checks out the supermarket. The Independent, 9 June 1993, np

Bruner J (1994) The "remembered" self. In: Neisser U, Fivush R (eds) The remembering self: construction and agency in self narrative. Cambridge University Press, Cambridge, pp 41–54

Butler J (2002) Gender trouble: feminism and the subversion of identity. Routledge, New York

Chatzichristodoulou M (2009) How to kidnap your audiences: an interview with Matt Adams from Blast theory. In: Chatzichristodoulou M et al (eds) Interfaces of performance. Ashgate, Farnham/Burlington, pp 107–118

Chatzichristodoulou M (2011) Mapping intermediality in performance. Contemp Theatr Rev 21(2):230–231

Cockton G (2008) Revisiting usability's three key principles. In: CHI '08 extended abstracts on human factors in computing systems. ACM Press, New York, pp 2473–2484

Corness G, Schiphorst T (2013) Performing with a system's intention: embodied cues in performer-system interaction. In: Proceedings of the 9th ACM conference on creativity & cognition. ACM Press, New York, pp 156–164

Corness G, Carlson K, Schiphorst T (2011) Audience empathy: a phenomenological method for mediated performance. In: Proceedings of the 8th ACM conference on creativity and cognition. ACM Press, New York, pp 127–136

Cull L (2011) Attention training immanence and ontological participation in Kaprow, Deleuze and Bergson. Perform Res 16(4):80–91

Dalsgaard P, Hansen LK (2008) Performing perception: staging aesthetics of interaction. ACM TOCHI 15(3):1–33

Darby K (2010) My twenty-five. [online] Available at: https://remapthemap.wordpress.com/my-twenty-five-2010/. Accessed 24 Oct 2014

De Marinis M (1993) The semiotics of performance. Translated by A. O'Healy. Indiana University Press: Bloomington/Indianapolis

Devendorf L, Rosner DK (2015) Reimagining digital fabrication as performance art. In: Proceedings of the 33rd annual ACM conference extended abstracts on human factors in computing systems. ACM Press, New York, pp 555–566

Dewey J (2005) Art as experience. Perigee Books, New York

Dissanayake E (2003) The core of art: making special. J Can Assoc Curric Stud 1(2):13–38

Dix A, Sheridan J, Reeves S, Benford S, O'Malley C (2006) Formalising performative interaction. In: Proceedings of the 12th international conference on interactive systems: design, specification, and verification. Springer, Berlin/Heidelberg, pp 15–25

Dolan J (2005) Utopia in performance: finding hope at the theater. University of Michigan Press, Ann Arbor

Edmonds E (2010) The art of interaction. Digit Creat 21(4):257–264

England D, Edmonds E, Sheridan JG, Pobiner S, Bryan-Kinns N, Wright P, Twidale M, Diana C (2011) Digital arts and interaction (invited). In: Proceedings of the 2011 annual conference extended abstracts on human factors in computing systems. ACM Press, New York, pp 609–612

England D, Spence J, Latulipe C, Edmonds E, Candy L, Schiphorst T, Bryan-Kinns N, Woolford K (2014) Curating the digital: spaces for art and interaction. In: CHI'14 extended abstracts on human factors in computing systems. ACM Press, New York, pp 21–4

Fällman D (2003) Design-oriented human-computer interaction. In: Proceedings of the SIGCHI conference on human factors in computing systems. ACM Press, New York, pp 225–232

Fdili Alaoui S, Jacquemin C, Bevilacqua F (2013) Chiseling bodies: an augmented dance performance. In: CHI '13 extended abstracts on human factors in computing systems. ACM Press, New York, pp 2915–2918

Fensham R (2012) Postdramatic spectatorship: participate or else. Crit Stages 7:1–8

Ferris L (2005) Cooking up the self: Bobby Baker and Blondell Cummings do the kitchen. In: Smith S, Watson J (eds) Interfaces: women, autobiography, image, performance. University of Michigan Press, Ann Arbor, pp 186–210

Fischer-Lichte E (1997) The show and the gaze of theatre: a European perspective. University of Iowa Press, Iowa City

Fischer-Lichte E (2008a) Sense and sensation: exploring the interplay between the semiotic and performative dimensions of theatre. J Dram Theor Crit 22(2):69–81

Fischer-Lichte E (2008) The transformative power of performance: a new aesthetics. Routledge, London

Geigel J, Schweppe M (2004) Theatrical storytelling in a virtual space. In: Proceedings of the 1st ACM workshop on story representation, mechanism and context. ACM Press, New York, pp 39–46

Goffman E (1959) The presentation of self in everyday life. Doubleday, Garden City

Goldberg RL (2011) Performance art: from futurism to the present, 3rd edn. Thames & Hudson, New York

Gorman S (2008) Theatre for a media-saturated age. In: Holdsworth N, Luckhurst M (eds) A concise companion to contemporary British and Irish drama. Oxford/Wiley-Blackwell, Malden/Carlton, pp 263–282

Govan E, Nicholson H, Normington K (2007) Making a performance: devising histories and contemporary practices. Routledge, London

Hannah D, Harsløf O (2008) Performance design. Museum Tusculanum Press, Copenhagen

Hansen LK, Rico J, Jacucci G, Brewster S, Ashbrook D (2011) Performative interaction in public space. In: CHI '11 extended abstracts on human factors in computing systems. ACM Press, New York, pp 49–52

Harris G, Aston E (2007) Integrity: the essential ingredient. In: Barrett M, Baker B (eds) Bobby Baker: redeeming features of daily life. Routledge, London/New York, pp 109–115

Heathfield A (1999) Risk in intimacy: an interview with Bobby Baker. Perform Res Cooking 4(1):97–106

Heddon D (2002) Performing the archive: following in the footsteps. Perform Res 7(4):64–77

Heddon D (2008) Autobiography and performance. Palgrave Macmillan, Basingstoke

Heddon D, Howells A (2011) From talking to silence: a confessional journey. J Perform Art PAJ 97 33(1):1–12

Heddon D, Kelly A (2010) Distance dramaturgy. Perform Res 20(2):214–220

Heddon D, Milling J (2006) Devising performance: a critical history. Palgrave Macmillan, Basingstoke

Heddon D, Iball H, Zerihan R (2012) Come closer: confessions of intimate spectators in one to one performance. Contemp Theatr Rev 22(1):120–133

Hoffmann J, Jonas J (2005) Perform. Thames & Hudson, New York

Holland AC, Kensinger EA (2010) Emotion and autobiographical memory. Phys Life Rev 7(1):88–131

Holmer HB, DiSalvo C, Sengers P, Lodato T (2015) Constructing and constraining participation in participatory arts and HCI. Int J Hum Comput Stud 74:107–123

Hook J, Schofield G, Taylor R, Bartindale T, McCarthy J, Wright P (2012) Exploring HCI's relationship with liveness. In: CHI '12 extended abstracts on human factors in computing systems. ACM Press, New York, pp 2771–2774

Hughes J, Kidd J, McNamara C (2011) The usefulness of mess: artistry, improvisation and decomposition in the practice of research in applied theatre. In: Kershaw B, Nicholson H (eds) Research methods in theatre and performance. Edinburgh University Press, Edinburgh, pp 186–209

Iball H (2007) Kitchen Show. In: Barrett M, Baker B (eds) Bobby Baker: redeeming features of daily life. Routledge, London/New York, pp 185–187

Jackson S (2004) Professing performance: theatre in the academy from philology to performativity. Cambridge University Press, Cambridge

Jacucci G (2004) Interaction as performance: cases of configuring physical interfaces in mixed media. PhD thesis, University of Oulu

Jacucci C, Jacucci G, Wagner I, Psik T (2005) A manifesto for the performative development of ubiquitous media. In: Proceedings of the 4th decennial conference on critical computing: between sense and sensibility. ACM Press, New York, pp 19–28

Johnson D (2012) Introduction: the what, when and where of live art. Contemp Theatr Rev 22(1):4–16

Kershaw B, Nicholson H (2011a) Introduction: doing methods creatively. In: Kershaw B, Nicholson H (eds) Research methods in theatre and performance. Edinburgh University Press, Edinburgh, pp 1–15

Kershaw B, Nicholson H (2011b) Research methods in theatre and performance. Edinburgh University Press, Edinburgh

Kuhn A (2007) Photography and cultural memory: a methodological exploration. Vis Stud 22(3):283–292

Labov W, Waletzky J (1967) Narrative analysis. In: Helm J (ed) Essays on the verbal and visual arts. University of Washington Press, Seattle, pp 12–44

Langellier KM, Peterson E (2004) Storytelling in daily life: performing narrative. Temple University Press, Philadelphia

Laurel B (1993) Computers as theatre. Addison-Wesley, Reading

Lavender A (2013) Feeling engaged: intermedial *mise en sensibilité*. In: FIRT/IFTR conference, Barcelona, 22–26 July 2013

Lawson J (2009) Food confessions: disclosing the self through the performance of food. M/C J 12(5):np

Lehmann H-T (2006) Postdramatic theatre. Routledge, London/New York

Leong TW, Wright P (2013) Understanding 'tingle' in opera performances. In: Proceedings of the 25th Australian computer-human interaction conference: augmentation, application, innovation, collaboration. ACM Press, New York, pp 43–52

Leong T, Gaye L, Tanaka A, Taylor R, Wright P (2011) The user in flux: bringing HCI and digital arts together to interrogate shifting roles in interactive media. In: Proceedings of the 2011 annual conference extended abstracts on human factors in computing systems. ACM Press, New York, pp 45–48

Light A (2011) HCI as heterodoxy: technologies of identity and the queering of interaction with computers. Interact Comput 23:430–439

Maguire T (2015) Performing story on the contemporary stage. Palgrave Macmillan, Basingstoke/New York

Marranca B (1979) The self as text: uses of autobiography in theatre (animations as model). PAJ J Perform Art 4(1–2):85–105

Martin C (2015) The real and its outliers (review). Theatr J 67(1):135–146

McCarthy J, Wright P (2004) Technology as experience. MIT Press, Cambridge, MA

McCarthy J, Wright P (2015) Taking [a]part: the politics and aesthetics of participation in experience-centered design. MIT Press, Cambridge/London

Mehto K, Kantola V, Tiitta S, Kankainen T (2006) Interacting with user data: theory and examples of drama and dramaturgy as methods of exploration and evaluation in user-centered design. Interact Comput 18(5):977–995

Mermikides A, Smart J (2010) Introduction. In: Mermikides A, Smart J (eds) Devising in process. Palgrave Macmillan, Basingstoke/New York, pp 1–29

Mock R (2009) Tohu-bohu: Rachel Rosenthal's performances of diasporic cultural memory. In: Counsell C, Mock R (eds) Performance, embodiment and cultural memory. Cambridge Scholars Publishing, Newcastle Upon Tyne, pp 59–79

Morgan RC (2010) Thoughts on re-performance, experience, and archivism. PAJ J Perform Art 32(3):1–15

Nam HY, Nitsche M (2014) Interactive installations as performance: inspiration for HCI. In: Proceedings of the 8th international conference on tangible, embedded and embodied interaction. ACM Press, New York, pp 189–196

Nelson R (2010) Introduction: prospective mapping. In: Bay-Cheng S et al (eds) Mapping intermediality in performance. Amsterdam University Press, Amsterdam, pp 13–23

Norrick NR (2000) Conversational narrative: storytelling in everyday talk. John Benjamins Publishing Company, Amsterdam/Philadelphia

O'Bryan J (2011) Ontology and autobiographical performance: Joanna Frueh's Aesthetics of Orgasm. TDR 55(2):126–136

Oddey A (1994) Devising theatre: a practical and theoretical handbook. Routledge, London

Pearson M (1998) My balls/your chin. Perform Res 3(2):35–41

Pearson M (2003) Bubbling Tom. In: Heathfield A (ed) Small acts: performance, the millennium and the marking of time. Black Dog Publishing Ltd, London, pp 172–185

Pearson M (2007) 'In Comes I': performance, memory and landscape. University of Exeter Press, Exeter

Pearson M, Shanks M (2001) Theatre/archaeology: disciplinary dialogues, 1st edn. Routledge, London/New York

Phelan P (2004) Marina Abramović: witnessing shadows. Theatr J 56(4):569–577

Phillips Á (2009) Live autobiography: an investigation of autobiographical performance practice. PhD thesis, National College of Art and Design, Dublin

Reason M (2004) Theatre audiences and perceptions of 'liveness' in performance. Particip@tions 1(2):1–24

Reason M (2015) Participations on participation: researching the active theatre audience. Particip J Audien Recep Stud 12(1):271–280

Redström J (2006) Towards user design? On the shift from object to user as the subject of design. Des Stud 27(2):123–139

Reeves S, Benford S, O'Malley C, Fraser M (2005) Designing the spectator experience. In: Proceedings of the SIGCHI conference on human factors in computing systems. ACM Press, New York, pp 741–750

Rico J, Jacucci G, Reeves S, Hansen LK, Brewster S (2010) Designing for performative interactions in public spaces. In: Proceedings of the 12th ACM international conference adjunct papers on ubiquitous computing. ACM Press, New York, pp 519–522

Roms H, Edwards R (2012) Towards a prehistory of live art in the UK. Contemp Theatr Rev 22(1):17–31

Salter C (2010) Entangled: technology and the transformation of performance. MIT Press, Cambridge, MA

Schechner R (2000) Post post-structuralism? TDR 44(3):4–7

Schechner R (2002) My art in life: interviewing Spalding Gray. TDR 46(4):154–174

Schechner R (2006) Performance studies: an introduction, 2nd edn. Routledge, New York

Schiphorst T (2012) Foreword. In: Broadhurst S, Machon J (eds) Identity, performance and technology: practices of empowerment, embodiment and technicity. Palgrave Macmillan, Basingstoke/New York, pp xi–xvi

Sheridan JG, Bryan-Kinns N, Bayliss A (2007) Encouraging witting participation and performance in digital live art. In: Proceedings of the 21st British HCI group annual conference on people and computers: HCI...but not as we know it. British Computer Society, Swinton, pp 13–23

Spence J (2015) Performing digital media design. In: Proceedings of the 2015 ACM SIGCHI conference on creativity and cognition. ACM Press, New York, pp 401–402

Spence J, Frohlich DM, Andrews S (2013) Performative experience design. In: CHI '13 extended abstracts on human factors in computing systems. ACM Press, New York, pp 2049–2058

States BO (1996) Performance as metaphor. Theatr J 48(1):1–26

Stephenson J (2013) Performing autobiography: contemporary Canadian drama. University of Toronto Press, Toronto

Taylor R, Schofield G, Shearer J, Wright P, Boulanger P, Olivier P (2014) Nightingallery: theatrical framing and orchestration in participatory performance. Pers Ubiquit Comput 18(7):1583–1600

van Doorn M, de Vries AP (2006) Co-creation in ambient narratives. In: Cai Y, Abascal J (eds) Ambient intelligence in everyday life. Springer, Berlin/Heidelberg, pp 103–129

van Doorn M, van Loenen E, de Vries AP (2008) Deconstructing ambient intelligence into ambient narratives: the intelligent shop window. In: Proceedings of the 1st international conference on ambient media and systems. ICST, Brussels, pp 1–8

Wagner I, Broll W, Jacucci G, Kuutti K, McCall R, Morrison A, Schmalstieg D, Terrin JJ (2009) On the role of presence in mixed reality. Presen Teleoper Virt Environ 18(4):249–276

Wakkary R, Schiphorst T, Budd J (2004) Cross-dressing and border crossing: exploring experience methods across disciplines. In: CHI '04 extended abstracts on human factors in computing systems. ACM Press, New York, pp 1709–1710

Wilkie F (2004) Out of place: the negotiation of place in site-specific performance. PhD thesis, University of Surrey

Williamson J, Hansen LK (2012) Designing performative interactions in public spaces. In: Proceedings of the designing interactive systems conference. ACM Press, New York, pp 791–792

Wilson M (2006) Storytelling and theatre: contemporary storytellers and their art. Palgrave Macmillan, Basingstoke

Wright P, McCarthy J (2010) Experience-centered design: designers, users, and communities in dialogue. Synth Lect Hum Cent Informat 3:1–123

Chapter 4
The Performative Experience Design Methodology

Abstract This chapter begins with an overview of the unit of analysis, experience, as it is understood in both performance studies and HCI and design. It then presents an overview the PED methodology and how it can be applied to any experience design project involving an element of performance. In Step 1, designer/researchers explore their areas of interest to *develop a line of enquiry*. Step 2 is the process of *selecting which performances to view* in order to shed light on the line of enquiry, depending on the genres, approaches, or theories with most promise. Step 3 is the *performance analyses* of a small number of these performances, arriving at a set of properties that can be designed for. Step 4 is the *design exploration*, an ideation process that leads to a mapping of the design space and the creation of a prototype that can be put into service. Step 5 is the *performed experience,* in which the prototype is used in the closest possible approximation to its intended context, on multiple occasions where possible, gathering as much external and subjective data on the performance as is reasonable. Step 6 is a set of interlocking *analyses* of the prototype in use: thematic analysis, interaction analysis, and a hybrid form known as 'coded performance analysis'. The findings can lead to frameworks, theories, guidelines, and other useful tools for research and practice.

The Unit of Analysis: Experience

When discussing methodologies, it is worthwhile to specify their object—in other words, the unit of analysis, or the type of phenomenon being studied. This might be a particular run of performances as exemplified by one or more iterations viewed by a critic or researcher—or, in the case of practice-as-research, the entire process of developing and performing. Some genres are expected to unfold with little variation between individual performances, such as West End musicals or other traditional big-budget productions, while participatory and some experimental works depend to a large degree on unpredictable contributions. In the former case, the description of a single performance might be assumed to apply to most or all viewings of that show. In the latter case, it is more obvious that each 'viewing' is likely to be very different. However, there is still a significant consistency between individual instances of a given performance—and yet each performance can only be accessed by one individual at a time, in one unique time and place. This conundrum is

© Springer International Publishing Switzerland 2016
J. Spence, *Performative Experience Design*, Springer Series on Cultural
Computing, DOI 10.1007/978-3-319-28395-1_4

particularly evident in immersive performances such as Punchdrunk's *The Drowned Man*, in which spectators move through a large space at will. Each spectator has a unique experience, as no one can view all of the simultaneous elements of the show in one night, not to mention the spontaneous interactions among spectators as they navigate the space. In terms of analysing and designing for anything like a performance, then, what exactly do we mean? Is it a scripted and staged series of words and movements intended to be repeated as closely as possible, night after night? Or does it focus on the unique contours of a particular incidence? Or, to apply a term from HCI, is it bound to the 'trajectory' (Benford and Giannachi 2011) of a single person making perhaps unrepeatable choices throughout the event?

Increasingly, the response seems to include the term 'experience', drawing attention to an individual's unique, embodied perception of a given performance—whether that individual is a performer or a spectator. (This is in contrast to research that uses the term 'experience' to address groups of people presumed to share certain perspectives and receive certain responses from a wider community, such as articles about 'the Jewish experience' or 'the *Zainichi* Korean-Japanese experience'.) Much like the taxonomy developed to categorise the uses of performance in HCI, some of these performance texts interpret the specifics of experience as addressing the embodied nature of perception, while others expand that understanding into a multi-sensory and multi-level approach to engagement. Phillip B. Zarrilli turns to Merleau-Ponty's phenomenology in his investigation of the embodied experience of an actor, viewing the performer's body not as a tool to be manipulated by his mind but 'as the very means and medium through which the world comes into being and is experienced' (2004, p. 655). Similarly, in 'Place in the performance experience', Gay McAuley (2003) uses the term to signify a felt, embodied perception. This perception can be performative, and in that sense constitutes performance: 'the performative experience of place necessarily involves being there, and this fact distinguishes performance from all the other art forms. Spectators must be with the performers, *in* the place rather than looking *at* it or at representations of it' (2003, p. 610). Leaving aside the challenge that McAuley's view poses to many types of digital or telematic performance, these examples indicate the use of 'experience' in performance studies to refer to an internally perceived state of being, whether limited to an individual or referring to those states of being shared by a group of people.

Expanding beyond embodiment, Jennifer Radbourne et al.'s book on the relatively new field of audience experience research (2013) aims to accurately identify and measure the 'engagement' that audiences have (or fail to have) with performances of various sorts. This perspective is presented more acutely by Robert C. Morgan, who uses a slightly abstracted version of 'experience' in discussing re-performance. He refers to 'experience in art' as that which 'used to be called aesthetics' (2010, p. 2), and 'art' as 'the repository of experience' (2010, p. 15), using the term 'experience' to refer to a felt moment in the present, in contrast with the documentation of past performances. Reason goes so far as to 'directly interrogat[e] the fundamental question of what it means to experience art' by carefully tracing the relationship between a person's immediate experience and their ability to reflect on or 'externalise' their experience at a later time (2010, p. 15). These examples do not form a homogeneous picture of 'experience' across the fields of performance and HCI, but they do indicate an increasing attention to a deeply personal and multi-sensory encounter with a designed event, which can apply equally to an aesthetic performance or to an interaction with technology.

Many of the concerns of user experience (UX) and experience design align with these emerging uses of 'experience' and audience experience research in performance studies. They share an emphasis on the way that products (theatrical performances or technological devices) are perceived by their audiences/consumers/recipients/users. Researchers strive to understand this perception as thoroughly as possible, looking for 'engagement' through opinions and behaviours. As leading experience design researchers have warned, a shallow approach to this task can lead to the understanding of 'experience' as a marketing exercise, determining whether audiences believe that the time and/or financial investment in the given performance or product has been worthwhile (Blythe et al. 2006). Along these lines, Kari Kuutti offers an almost tongue-in-cheek definition of user experience: 'something that can be measured and used in predicting how well does a product sell' (Kuutti 2010, p. 717). Even when a richer definition of experience is sought, as by Law et al. (2009), the result is a diagram that sets 'art' alongside 'brand' and 'event', and entirely outside the box containing 'user experience'—in their terms, anything for which one might design. Forlizzi's observation pushes researchers towards a more thorough examination of the relationships among types of experience: 'our every-day, moment-to-moment experience, understanding the world by comparing it with what we find familiar, and understanding changes in people and contexts of product use over longer periods of time—even a lifetime' (2010, p. 61). In both performance and experience design, the push is towards an ever more complex understanding of what it means to have an experience and therefore how those experiences might be shaped.

One common reference point for researchers in both fields is Dewey (see McCarthy and Wright 2004), who defines experience as 'the result, the sign, and the reward of that interaction of organism and environment which, when it is carried to the full, is a transformation of interaction into participation and communication' (2005, p. 23). A key distinction for him is between experience, which is a continuous process of an often dulled or routinised perception, and '*an* experience', which occurs 'when the material experienced runs its course to fulfillment. Then and then only is it integrated within and demarcated in the general stream of experience from other experiences' (2005, pp. 36–37). Dewey believes that everyday life is made up of a stream of undifferentiated experience punctuated by individual, complete, 'integrated' and 'demarcated' experiences that he terms '*an* experience' (2005, pp. 36–37, emphasis in the original). For him, the experience of art is always *an* experience. It possesses different degrees of organisation and integration, with emotion (though not discrete emotions) at the heart of this integration. An aesthetic experience has a 'heightened vitality' that:

signifies active and alert commerce with the world; at its height it signifies complete inter-penetration of self and the world of objects and events… it affords our sole demonstration of a stability that is not stagnation but is rhythmic and developing… it is art in germ. (2005, pp. 18–19)

Dewey's view on the relationship between art and experience underscores the fundamental role of experience in interactions with technology, especially those that include an element of performance or invite an aesthetic response. The idea of an aesthetic experience does not depend on any of the official trappings of the art world or of theatrical performance. Instead, it is located in the felt experience of each uniquely situated person—who is likely influenced by those around him in any number of roles—in dialogical relation to all the elements of her surroundings, as well as her own past experiences and expectations. Based on Dewey's conception of aesthetic experience, Wright et al. are able to set forward a framework of 'the aesthetics of human-computer interaction and interaction design' which is 'holistic', 'constructivist', and 'dialogical' (2008, p. 1). Dewey's notions of experience are a basis for Reason's work within performance studies, as well: he uses Dewey (though not without reservations) to build his concept of experience as existing not within but in relation to a performance, and not only in the moments that the performance takes place, but also in the spectator's subsequent meaning-making processes (2010, pp. 23–24). PED operates from these overlapping and complex understandings of experience.

The Methodology of Performative Experience Design

The PED methodology capitalises on the fact that both HCI and performance studies are oriented towards practice: HCI by creating and studying novel interactions, and performance studies by studying (and sometimes also creating) novel productions. It leads to the creation of a unique design/performance that could be studied using the lenses of both fields. I stress that the methodology presented in this chapter is a guideline for future research based on initial work on a particular strand of PED research, that of co-located personal digital media sharing. I offer this 'how-to' chapter in the spirit that other researchers may make any number of alterations to the methodology as it is set out here. I trust that others will develop and improve upon this early work, especially as it will apply to other topics of research.

The PED methodology incorporates performance theory and practice into the user research process of assessing current practices in light of future possibilities, creating prototypes, and analysing those prototypes in use (Frohlich 2004, p. 9). This results in a number of significant alterations to existing design methods. Finding a way to articulate and design for properties of performance calls for the adoption of the method known as 'performance analysis' into the design cycle. Analysing the results then requires the creation of a hybrid method of analysis, which I have termed 'coded performance analysis'. The complete methodology consists of developing a line of enquiry, selecting performances to watch,

Fig. 4.1 PED
methodology

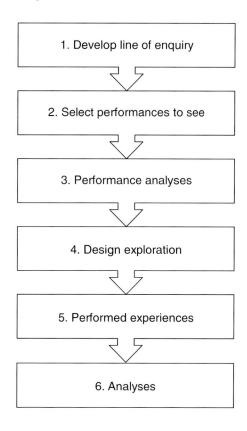

performance analyses, design exploration, performed experiences, and analyses (see Fig. 4.1).

Step 1: Develop Line of Enquiry

Developing a line of enquiry differs from establishing a fixed research question at the outset, especially one that seeks a simple answer to a closed question. Exploratory approaches suit the goals of much of the work in interaction and experience research that is aimed at 'exploring possibilities outside of current paradigms', as Fällman puts it (2007, p. 197), or the traditions of research through design (Frayling 1993; Zimmerman et al. 2007; Gaver 2012). The 'design-oriented research' that Fällman identifies is in this way very similar to performance research that embraces the 'reflexivity' and 'unpredictability' identified by Kershaw and Nicholson (2011), which allow for research questions to emerge through open-ended and inclusive investigations. Both fields are well represented in this first step of the PED methodology.

The development process may begin from insights or questions raised in the HCI literature: for example, one might be intrigued by how dinner party guests responded to the dynamic, interactive display of photos from their Facebook accounts in 4Photos (ten Bhömer et al. 2010), and wonder what the effect would be of formalising their storytelling participation. It may also begin from more overtly artistic inspiration, such as the ongoing aesthetic experimentations undertaken by Blast Theory and the Mixed Reality Lab at the University of Nottingham (Benford and Giannachi 2011). The line of enquiry must, of course, include some element of performance or performativity, though that can range from large-scale participation in open spaces (e.g. Taylor et al. 2014) to the private sense that one's behaviour may be—or has been—observed (e.g. Blast Theory's *Ulrike and Eamonn Compliant*, described in Benford and Giannachi 2011, pp. 194–200; Dalsgaard and Hansen 2008). The diagram of the PED space (see Fig. 1.3) can help to frame relevant questions: if the line of enquiry being considered lies closer to one end of the performance or experience design axis, what might happen if it were moved in the other direction?

The process of investigating potential lines of enquiry for PED should involve serious deliberation over at least the following three elements of the type of experience intended by the researcher: performative participation, content, and scenarios of use. 'Performative participation' refers to the degree and type of performance that the experiencers might be expected to undertake. This is an enormously fluid and wide-ranging category that includes such examples as learning and displaying new physical and aesthetic skills at a festival (iPoi, Sheridan et al. 2007); manipulating a touch screen to influence a live music performance (Humanaquarium, Taylor et al. 2011); or reacting spontaneously to friends' photos in a private setting (4Photos, ten Bhömer et al. 2010). Questions to ask regarding performative participation might include whether the participation must be 'witting' (Sheridan et al. 2007); whether bystanders can contribute in some way; whether the participation is primarily physical, verbal, musical, or other; whether their participation could be overlooked as ordinary behaviour or would make the participant a spectacle for others (e.g. Huggard et al. 2013)—or whether the participant's identity could be at least temporarily obscured (e.g. Osmose, discussed in Reeves et al. 2005, p. 747). If the performative participation involves physical movements, dance, and/or musical contributions, what level of skill or basic ability is involved (Loke and Robertson 2010), and how might the design accommodate potential participants with different skills or abilities? If the performative participation is primarily verbal, what kind of verbal contribution is expected? Will participants be answering questions, telling stories, engaging in reminiscence, or co-telling with others? What participation might be desirable from an audience member watching others interact? Will participation take place in part in a virtual reality, and if so, how will both the embodied and the virtual experience be treated? Or will participation be limited to performers or 'orchestrators' (Benford et al. 2006), and if so, what is the relationship between designer and performer? Such questions do not need to be answered at this stage, but it is important to explore them early on in order to clarify precisely what the line of enquiry will be. By articulating which types of performative participation are of interest—or even articulating confusion or ambiguity in the attempt to identify interesting types of performative participation—the researcher will be well equipped to make substantial inroads into PED.

The second element to consider at this stage is 'content', or the type of data with which participants will interact. These might be representations of biometric data, digital media such as photos or music, or any output or feedback from a technological device. Examples include representations of the potential participant's physical body in an interactive artwork (Glitching, Hood 2015); the changes to an emerging performance based on their interaction with a touchscreen (Humanaquarium, Taylor et al. 2011); personal photos (4Photos, ten Böhmer et al. 2010); and a game jointly controlled by squeezing a pillow (Musical Embrace, Huggard et al. 2013). If the project at hand is seeking to explore a particular type of content, then this would seem to be a tickbox exercise. However, it may be worth spending time considering whether alternative or additional types of data might illuminate the problem space.

The final element is 'scenarios of use', which is simply a process of imagining potential real-life situations or contexts of use (Suchman 1987, 2007; Wright 2011). This might seem to be a strange thing to explore before settling on a line of enquiry, much less a potential prototype. However, in the case of PED, context is utterly critical in deciding on a line of enquiry, and might even generate a previously unimagined line of enquiry. Performance itself is extremely dependent on its context, particularly performances that involve a level of physical and emotional intimacy between performers and audience members. For example, Leslie Hill and Helen Paris of the performance group Curious found that increasing the number of audience members from 24 to 48 in *the moment I saw you I knew I could love you* (2010) nearly destroyed the experience for both spectators and performers (2014, p. 85). The physicality of the audience experience was also key to the performance's emotional and aesthetic power: the audience perched on three inflatable life rafts placed on the stage, so that any one person's movement would force fellow audience members to physically rebalance themselves (pp. 82–83). A context for use might be as straightforward, in HCI terms, as an interactive demonstration at a conference, but it would ideally be more grounded in the ultimate real-world situations of its use. Although the designers of 4Photos and Humanaquarium did not use the PED methodology, they both created projects with very specific contexts of use: 4Photos at a small dinner party with the device placed in the centre of the table (ten Böhmer et al. 2010), and Humanaquarium in a variety of public environments where the designers could witness firsthand, or even address in real time, the changes in audience interaction from one situation to another (Taylor et al. 2011). Similarly, a recent surge of interest in experience design for museums has offered a way into imagining scenarios of use for small groups in museums (e.g. Clarke et al. 2015; Taylor et al. 2015). Concrete scenarios of use can drive the development of a line of enquiry in unexpected directions at this earliest stage of the process, where those changes can have the most impact.

The performative participations, content, and scenarios of use can be flexible and fluid. Indeed, different lines of enquiry might entail their own categories, in addition to or replacing these three. The examples above come from the HCI literature, but inspiration for these categories can come directly from performance or any other life experience. There can be long lists of candidates for each category, barring specific project requirements. It is less important to decide on the best performative participation, content, and scenario of use than to begin exploring how they might shape and be shaped by the precise line of enquiry that is eventually decided on.

Step 2: Select Performances to Watch

The second step is an exploration of which performances would illuminate the line of enquiry. This could be a series of works by a particular group or a style, genre, movement, technique, theme, set of practices—anything that might address or provide a perspective on the line of enquiry. A line of enquiry focused on wearable technology might suit a series of dance performances that explore costume, while a line of enquiry looking at emotional reactions might suit a series of performances with expert sound designers on the creative team. There is at this stage no assumption as to what those performances might reveal or what design direction they might provide.

There is also no need to be overly selective, other than the financial and practical limitations on identifying and travelling to appropriate performances. As with any other human endeavour, performances can offer a very different experience from what their description would lead one to believe. Observations made in one performance can help guide the selection of further ones, and performances that end up contributing little to the research at hand do not need to be analysed in full. There are no hard and fast rules for how many performances are required for the PED methodology to be successful. Choosing only one or two risks missing important and possibly contradictory factors that would radically alter the analysis, while one or two dozen might take an inordinate amount of time and energy to produce diminishing returns. It is also important to remember the purpose of the analyses, which is to generate a set of properties that can guide the design exploration and serve as benchmarks for the analysis of the prototype in use. There is no expectation that the analyses will constitute any sort of 'proof' or definition, or that the properties arrived at must apply unfailingly to every instance of that type of performance. In other words, keep the line of enquiry in mind, and go out to see what you judge to be the most potentially relevant performances.

Finally, there is the question of whether all of the performances for Steps 2 and 3 of the PED methodology must be seen live, as some performance researchers would contend (Pavis 2003, pp. 20–21). Bearing in mind that the purpose of seeing them is to search for insights into the interactions between performers and audiences (and possibly also with technologies), live performance will offer the fullest opportunity to arrive at these insights. The researcher will be part of the live interaction and able to feel for herself how the event develops, possibly by paying more attention to audience interactions than to what is happening on stage—a luxury not afforded to many who watch video recordings or performances created for the camera. However, documentation can reveal actions or interactions that were missed in the live experience of a performance, especially in immersive or mixed reality performances whose scope reaches far beyond what one individual can take in. Repeated viewings of video recordings, perhaps focusing on different aspects of the performance, can complement or in some cases supplant the live experience. Video documentation is inferior to live performance in some ways and yet offers benefits of its own, as Denise Varney and Rachel Fensham explain (2000), and written documentation often offers a spectator's perspective on how the performance was received as well as what it consisted of. It is best to go to live performances whenever possible, in order to get the fullest sense of the experience as it unfolds, and for these live performances to be well represented in the performance analyses. However, in PED there is no principle dictating that one should avoid performances that can be known only through documentation.

Step 3: Performance Analyses

The third step is performance analyses conducted on several aesthetic or 'cultural' performances (Wilson 2006, p. 9) chosen for their potential to illuminate the line of enquiry, for example through techniques, thematic concerns, or devising practices. Performance analysis, a common method in performance studies, offers a systematic approach to understanding the meaning, structure, and effects of a performance (McAuley 1998). There is no single agreed method for performance analysis, but most approaches began with the search for the meanings of different performances, using theories of semiotics (e.g. States 1985; McAuley 1998, p. 1; Pavis 2003, p. 24; Fischer-Lichte 2008a, p. 69; Rozik 2010). Over time, it became generally accepted that mapping meanings to theatrical elements does not adequately account for the full emotional and aesthetic impact of many performances. In response, many theorists have over time incorporated phenomenology into their approaches in an attempt to include the feelings experienced by a spectator engaged with a performance (e.g. Pavis as described in Rozik 2010, p. 5; States 1985; Fischer-Lichte 1997, 2008a, p. 69). Using this combination of approaches, performance analysis does not aspire to the postpositivist aim of quantifying, defining, or standardising a performance, but rather to explore the meanings, emotions, and 'poetic' (Langellier and Peterson 2004, p. 54) aspects of perceiving a performance. Performance analysis takes each performance event on its own terms, allowing the analyst to be both rigorous and open-minded, detailed and holistic, in understanding the situated, contextualised 'how' of how a particular person communicates his or her lived experience to an audience (Fischer-Lichte 2008b, pp. 70–71). The analyses are necessarily subjective, and no two analysts would arrive at precisely the same conclusions. However, an evidence-based performance analysis can provide a unique insight into the meanings, emotions, and potentially transformational insights that are made special (Dissanayake 2003) through performance.

Performance analysis could be seen in HCI terms as a form of interaction criticism (Bardzell et al. 2010) undertaking the inductive analysis of performance data. The analysis of these data addresses intangible or holistic concepts such as rhythmic and energetic relationships and their emotional effects on the spectator. Performance analysis could also be understood as addressing what Harold G. Nelson and Erik Stolterman (2012) might agree to call the 'ultimate particular' (2012, p. 31) of one performance (perhaps witnessed in multiple iterations), experienced by one unabashedly subjective audience member in one unique spatio-temporal, social, and intrapersonal context. Nelson and Stolterman's 'ultimate particular is a singular and unique composition or assembly' from which universal abstractions cannot be made, although 'patterns of accurate descriptions, and explanations, through controlled observation' can provide the basis for valid guidelines and theories (2012, p. 31). Performance analysis could be described in just such terms, though perhaps lacking the emphasis on control.

As McAuley puts it, 'There is no single way to do performance analysis, and indeed the nature of the performances impact upon the analytical method' (1998, p. 8). One might approach a long-running musical differently from an experimental work of physical theatre at a festival, for example (1998, p. 8). One might focus on the process of generating the performance, or on the social context of its reception (1998, p. 2). It is possible to do an analysis based on a single viewing, though multiple encounters are almost always preferable, and as I have already argued, a video of a particular production (if it is available) can be useful even if it cannot capture the entirety of the felt experience of forming part of a live audience. At least for the purposes of the PED methodology, performance analysis can be described as the act of carefully considering all of the relevant aspects of a given performance in order to arrive at conclusions about the meanings or effects achieved. This is a more complex and drawn-out process than simply deciding whether a performance was 'good' or 'bad', although of course these types of value judgements are part of virtually any immediate response to a performance. To quote McAuley again: 'Meaning is created in a dynamic process by the spectator in his/her experience… always shifting, ready to be modified in light of later experiences, other people's perceptions, etc' (1998, p. 10). Performance analysis is the attempt to pin down the meanings or effects achieved by a performance, with 'the added responsibility of making clear the process whereby the meanings have been reached' (1998, p. 10).

McAuley offers a template for conducting a performance analysis that some may find a helpful starting point, directing an analyst's attention to the physical elements of the performance, the narrative or structural elements, the 'paradigms' or repeated patterns of related elements, and what the performance is 'saying' overall (1998, pp. 4–5). Patrice Pavis has created a slightly different template that countless theatre graduates will recognise (Pavis 2005), and I would argue that Fischer-Lichte's components of aesthetic performance could provide a similarly useful starting point for analysis, particularly for works that do not emphasise narrative: corporeality, spatiality, tonality, temporality, meaning, and effect (Fischer-Lichte 2008b). However, if these options sound more daunting than helpful, there is no need to give up. Simply go to a performance, pay as close attention as possible, take thorough notes immediately afterwards, and write up what struck you as interesting with as much supporting detail as you can muster. This might not earn you a space in the world's leading performance journals, but it will put you well on your way to an interesting, practical, and generative design exploration.

Step 4: Design Exploration

The design exploration begins with the generation of design ideas that are fed by both HCI and performance studies: the performative participations, content, and scenarios of use that guided that development of the line of enquiry, alongside memorable elements of the performances that were viewed and the insights gained from the findings of the performance analyses. While there may be any number of ways of combining these elements from across HCI and performance, I suggest listing each element on a separate card labelled with its category: (A) performative participations, (B) content, (C) scenarios of use, (D) performance elements, and (E) insights from findings. Draw one or two cards at random from each category and look at them in combination, conjuring possible situations in which most or all of the cards could be addressed within the same experience. Note or sketch ideas that arise along with the combination of elements (A–E) that gave rise to those ideas, and pursue them as warranted. Cards will need to be dealt a great number of times to cover a fair range of permutations, but the process is extremely valuable in terms of the range of possibilities that arise. These ideas should be developed, reshaped, abandoned, and renewed with one overriding driver: an image of the performance that would be likely to result from their implementation. Again, the specific categories may change based on the line of enquiry and/or the specific research questions being addressed.

This card technique is a modified example of the 'insight combination' method described by Jon Kolko (2010). For him, design is a process of synthesis, or 'an abductive sensemaking process' (2010, p. 19) similar to induction but allowing for insights from outside the problem space.[1] Where many designers in both industry and academia gloss over the step between the beginning of the design process and the birth of potential prototypes, Kolko uses a discussion of synthesis to reveal something of the 'informal', 'implicit', but 'critical' early stages of design (2010, pp. 16–17). Synthesis methods are therefore 'the keys for relating research to design—synthesis methods are the ways in which ethnographic insights lead to new, innovative, appropriate, or compelling ideas' (2010, p. 17). Kolko describes three methods: reframing, concept mapping, and insight combination. Insight combination pairs insights from gathered data—in this case, theories and practices of performance—with design patterns in the 'core domain'—interaction and experience design; with a slight shift of perspective, this same practice could be read as

---

[1] Like Kolko, Pelle Ehn points to Charles Sanders Peirce's treatment of 'abduction' as key to design logic (Ehn 1988, p. 213).

pairing gathered data from relevant fields in HCI with design patterns in the core domain of performance. The fact that PED is a design practice lends more weight to the former, while the fact that its uses are received and analysed as performances gives weight to the latter. I do not recommend the one-to-one mapping of insight to pattern advocated by Kolko because that stage is most applicable to clearly defined problems in need of a solution rather than the fundamentally exploratory (and often non-commercial) purpose of PED research. Instead, the combinations should be allowed to launch the process of 'creative design' (Wolf et al. 2006, p. 521) and 'design exploration' (Fällman 2008, pp. 7–8) that can lead to a number of germinal ideas.

It is important not to impose artificial constraints in this early stage. An overly optimistic idea might be adapted at a later point. More importantly, the goal of this step is just as much to explore the possibilities and implications of the various combinations of HCI and performance elements as it is to advance towards the best possible design. Instead, continue generating ideas and pay attention as they 'talk[] back' (Fällman 2003, p. 230) through recurring motifs and tendencies towards particular approaches. I interpret this process in light of Wolf et al.'s argument that creative design explores an uncharted design space at the same time as it generates practical solutions (2006, p. 521). Fällman draws the same conclusion, that 'design is just as much about finding a problem as it is about developing a solution' (2003, p. 229).[2] Moreover, I understand the problem-setting goals described by Wolf et al. (2006) and Fällman (2008) to be coterminal with the articulation of the project's 'design space' as discussed by Bill Gaver (2011, 2012) in the context of design workbooks. The result of this problem-setting initial design exploration is a collection of design ideas that map the design space. These ideas can be effectively brought into conversation with each other through the creation of a design workbook, defined as a methodological tool for allowing ideas to develop over time, among multiple members of a design team, or out of a productive juxtaposition (Gaver 2011, p. 1551). Gaver, whose work is nothing if not 'creative design', sees the role of workbooks in the design process as involving:

> not just the description of a design space but its creation: through the multiplicity of design ideas they contain they implicitly suggest important issues, approaches and options that might be considered in designing for a given situation, and in their provisional nature show those ideas, approaches and options in the making and still malleable to change. (Gaver 2011, p. 1551)

The design workbook functions as 'a fulcrum in the transition from initial background research to the generation of designs to be developed' (2011, p. 1552), a process that 'may emerge slowly over time' (2011, p. 1551). The map of the design space emerges from the application of what Stolterman (2008) refers to as 'a *designerly way* of thinking' (2008, p. 55, emphasis in the original) or a 'designerly approach' (2008, p. 61) to analyses of performance. Because the PED methodology draws primarily from Fällman's view that the creation of a prototype is 'a vital part

---

[2] Fällman cites Schön (1983) *The Reflective Practitioner* in his argument.

of the research process' (2003, p. 231), it does not use the design process as the sole research method, as Gaver argues (2012). However, Gaver's tools for conceptualising and mapping a design space are extremely useful in such a novel and open-ended activity.

While the process of charting the design space is extremely important in PED, it is also necessary to decide on one design to be taken forward for prototyping in order to observe the performative experiences brought about by its use. As Edmonds points out, '[o]bservation, in some sense, of an interactive system in action is the only way to understand it' (2010, p. 260). In other words, as I have argued, the 'ultimate particular' (Nelson and Stolterman 2012, p. 31) is not the designed artefact but each individual performance engendered by its use. The prototype itself may be physical or ephemeral, aesthetic in its own right or instrumental. The PED methodology does not hinge on the technology in the prototype, but rather on the experiences that the prototype can trigger. Again, this perspective is in line with the work of Fällman. He critiques the expectations that many HCI researchers place on a prototype, which is the tendency noted by Stephanie Houde and Charles Hill (1997) to focus on its level of fidelity rather than the attributes of the design being prototyped (discussed in Fällman 2003, p. 230). Houde and Hill propose a triangular model with vertices representing the role, look and feel, and implementation that a prototype would strive to convey (1997, p. 369). Any prototype will emphasise one or more of these functions. A prototype intended to prompt performance would most likely excel at conveying the role the prototype would play in the user's experience—and Houde and Hill (1997) demonstrate that even paper storyboards can be convincing prototypes when role is the key concern (1997, p. 372). As Fällman notes, the only significant requirement of a prototype is that it be 'the means to get at knowledge' (2007, p. 197).

Getting from the wide-open design space to a single prototype can be a straightforward case of selecting the obvious best option or a quagmire of contradictions and doubt. In this sense, PED is no different from any other design discipline. Design critiques, or 'crits', are extremely valuable, all the more so if the people delivering the critiques include performance theorists and/or practitioners. In my own experience, HCI and performance professionals may come equipped with no knowledge whatsoever of the other's field, yet they will often converge on the strongest ideas for entirely different reasons. Many of the most interesting and beneficial discussions come from putting together the perceived strengths and weaknesses of an idea from the two disciplinary perspectives and deciding how to reconcile any disagreements. Regardless of the backgrounds of the people involved, it is critical that they focus their attention on the possible intra- and interpersonal interactions that could emerge from using each design in a particular context. For this reason, it can be helpful to keep track of the design elements [(A) performative participations, (B) content, (C) scenarios of use, (D) performance elements, and (E) insights from findings] that gave rise to each design, though of course these can be altered as necessary as each design idea evolves.

The entirety of the design exploration process can be understood as a parallel to processes of devising a new performance. The ideas generated may vary in terms of feasibility, degree of development, and potential to respond to the project's artistic intent. For example, in a diary of her creative process in developing six proposed or commissioned works involving autobiographical material, Bobby Baker says that '[o]ne idea and image lead to another, and at one point … I am so excited that I nearly ride under a bus' (2001, p. 37). Less than 3 weeks later, she sees three elderly women talking to each other on a street corner. That familiar, ordinary sight is made strange for Baker, who then has the idea of 'stationing three old ladies on the corner of every street in a given area.… There's a lot missing to the idea and the pragmatics are somewhat daunting. Never mind!' (2001, p. 38). Three weeks after that, Baker is '[c]ompletely stuck. Can't get on…' (2001, p. 38). Her creative process is highly unpredictable, but much if not all of her work succeeds in its aim of getting 'her audience to question social and political assumptions about social roles and identity categories' (Harris and Aston 2007, p. 109). As with the process of generating design ideas to map a design space and create a prototype, less compelling ideas are discarded and one is selected for development and eventual use *in situ*.

Step 5: Performed Experience

At this point, you will have a prototype of a high enough fidelity to generate the types of experiences you envision. It is time to test the prototype by putting it into use in the context for which it was intended, or as close to that context as is practical. This requires paying careful attention to the people being invited to use it. Depending on the scenario of use, different factors will be relevant, from demographics to personality to physical ability to performance skills and any number of other factors besides, all of them entirely dependent on the type of performative experience that is aimed for. It also requires effort in terms of creating an appropriate context, including but not at all limited to the time of day and day of the week (for example, the difference between Tuesday at 10:00 am and Saturday at 10:00 pm), the physical location, the ambiance of the space, the ways in which participants will be viewed by the public or perhaps perceive a risk that they will be viewed by the public, noise levels, lighting levels, access to and reliability of technological infrastructure, how the technology is introduced and explained, how the performative experience is structured or guided, and what cues are given to constrain or liberate the participants' expressivity.

It is also extremely worthwhile to create several different performances with the prototype involving as many individuals as possible and practical. Performances are highly subjective experiences, and a single jarring element—a disruptive participant, a technical malfunction, a trapped bird flying through the space at the most inopportune moment—can disrupt perceptions of the event as a whole. All of the variations that emerge (hopefully not caused by any of these extreme situations!) will be opportunities for discussion during analysis. If at all possible, the researchers should observe these performances as they occur, taking care not to draw attention to themselves (unless this attention is part of the performative experience being generated or addresses one of the project's research questions).

Researchers should make extensive notes of each performance as soon as possible afterwards. The advice on conducting performance analysis in Step 3 can also be used to guide the type of content to be covered in the note-taking process, though of course the researcher is in the best position to know what he or she most needs to stay alert for. Each performance should also be video recorded as thoroughly as possible, again without drawing undue attention to the fact of the recording (and with the same caveats). Whatever data that the participants are working with should be captured as well. Finally, it can be very useful to elicit reactions from participants and/or audiences immediately after the event through interviews, questionnaires, or other ethnographic methods; biometrics and other such data gathered during the performance are another alternative depending on the project aims. The case study in this text generated four separate performances of nearly an hour in length, while other PED projects may generate many more performances of a much shorter (or greater) length, so it is important to consider the specific needs of both researchers and participants in each performance context. In the end, the best guide to Step 5 is your own intention in combination with the methods and findings from previous work identified during Step 1.

Step 6: Analyses

The sixth and final step of the PED methodology is a series of analyses of the prototype in use. Three methods of analysis are combined in this step: thematic analysis, interaction analysis, and a novel method called 'coded performance analysis'. The first two are commonly used in HCI, while the third applies HCI methods to the performance analysis method used on the 'cultural' performances in Step 3. Data for these analyses are taken from the researcher's memory, written notes, video records, the data the participants worked with, and any reactions gathered from them during or after each performance. Depending on the project requirements, these methods of data collection and analysis may be altered or extended, though I would advise careful consideration of all three of the analysis methods described below.

These three forms of analysis—thematic, interaction, and coded performance—result in a set of findings on the types of experience triggered by the use of the prototype. In traditional HCI, a designed device or system would be evaluated based on the success of these experiences. However, this emphasis on evaluation is starting to shift for some experience design research. Phoebe Sengers et al. undertook a project similar to PED in that it sought to create a particular type of experience 'obliquely: not by engineering it in, but by providing opportunities where it may emerge' (2008, p. 347). While they did not abandon the idea of evaluation, they found that their 'shifts in principles also shift the central evaluation question from "does it work?" to "how is the system made to work?" and "what does 'working' mean in the shifting context of this particular system for this particular dyad?"'

(2008, p. 352). Wright and McCarthy take this shift one step further: 'If the key to good usability engineering is evaluation, then the key to good aesthetic interaction design is understanding how the user makes sense of the artifact and his/her interactions with it at emotional, sensual, and intellectual levels' (2008, p. 19). And while a theatre critic will evaluate a performance as more or less worthy of a reader's time and money, performance research is far more concerned with analysing *how* and *why* a performance creates particular responses among its audiences. In PED, analysis takes the place of evaluation, primarily because there is no easily identified phenomenon to be unambiguously evaluated for its degree of success or failure, and any evaluation would need to be based on two very different classes of considerations—those of HCI and those of performance studies. By choosing to avoid the term 'evaluation' and its related concerns, PED does not intend to shy away from rigour or critique. All of the research plans, methods, designs, and analyses in a PED project are open to criticism for how well or poorly they further the pursuit of the research aims. However, in PED, analysis is taken as the more productive term, and the more productive perspective, for understanding the results of the complex technological, intrapersonal, interpersonal, and cultural interactions at work in performative experiences.

Thematic Analysis

Thematic analysis is an accepted practice within HCI that allows investigation of subjective accounts of the performance experiences, from both the participants' perspectives and from the researcher's. Thematic analysis allows access to participants' subjective accounts of their experiences that do not find outward expression during performance. This method of analysis also allows the researcher to work with participants' reflections on phase(s) of performance concealed from the audience, such as the devising phase.

Thematic analysis begins with a process of creating 'codes' that describe elements of interest in a data set. According to Richard E. Boyatzis, codes may compose 'a list of themes, a complex model with themes, indicators, and qualifications that are causally related; or something in between these two forms' (Boyatzis 1998, p. vii). Data collection methods for the thematic analysis employ qualitative techniques drawn from ethnography: direct observation, questionnaires, and interviews.[3] Codes can be taken from theory or be derived from the data (cf. grounded theory as developed by Barney Glaser and Anselm Strauss in the 1960s). The codes are

---

[3] In some HCI research, these techniques can be implemented in a somewhat rationalist, positivist manner, looking to gather what must be assumed to be pre-existing, non-contextualised pieces of data. In contrast, thematic analysis approaches these data in a way that takes into account the ephemerality of human performance, situated in a particular place and time, associated with feelings, memories and evocations that can never be comprehensively specified or recreated (McCarthy and Wright 2004).

subjected to an iterative process of categorising, grouping, splitting, and rejecting until the ones that remain describe all of the relevant data. Coding is commonly practiced in HCI research and is far from incompatible with much performance research.

Major themes should be taken from the properties of performance identified in the third step of the PED methodology, and specific codes created by identifying behaviours in performance that contributed to those themes. At the same time, contradictory, unexpected, and emerging behaviours should be actively sought out. This combination of inductive and deductive analysis allows for a targeted and yet holistic analysis. The coding scheme can be revised and restructured over multiple viewings of the video records, which trigger memories of the original performance events; codes can be renamed, combined, and discarded as patterns emerge. The final coding scheme will likely include multiple detectable behaviours for each of the properties of performance identified in Step 3, as well as for any emerging behaviours. Any interview, questionnaire, or other data gathered after the performance event can then be coded using these themes, to relate participants' subjective accounts of their experiences to phenomena in performance.

Interaction Analysis

Each instance of a PED performance/experience should also be subjected to a modified form of Interaction Analysis, a development from Conversation Analysis, delineated by Brigitte Jordan and Austin Henderson (1995). Interaction Analysis takes as a foundational assumption that interactions are to be construed as social (1995, p. 41). Therefore, relevant data are neither media nor transcript, but data relating to the mechanics of complex social interactions. These data, which include non-verbal elements, are best 'captured' using video in addition to field notes in an effort to minimise the 'retrospective representation' that introduces an additional and unwelcome layer of secondary interpretation and obscures the complexities of the lived experience (1995, pp. 51–52). Therefore, the data collection method for this analysis technique in the case of PED may consist of several audio-video records of each performance, taken from multiple angles.

At the heart of interaction analysis is an evidence-based focus on how a situated interaction emerges and what implications that interaction might have for the people involved. It is an inductive process, 'to the largest extent possible, free from predetermined analytic categories' (Jordan and Henderson 1995, pp. 7–8). This freedom helps researchers avoid the temptation of simply seeking evidence of what they wish to find and instead to see the complexities, contradictions, and failures in each interaction.

Interaction analysis gathers and makes sense of fine-grained empirical data such as turn-taking and the way that interactants position themselves physically (Jordan and Henderson 1995). Drawing on the work of Jean Lave and Etienne Wenger

(1991), Jordan and Henderson also point out the importance of artefacts in interaction, especially issues of ownership and of the display of nonmaterial objects (1995, p. 46). Key terms in Interaction Analysis include 'participation structures', which refer to ways in which participants indicate engagement with each other and/or towards an object of shared focus; 'trouble', which refers to any interruption in the ordinary flow of an interaction; and 'repair', the various verbal, physical, and social means of correcting interactions that have experienced 'trouble' (Jordan and Henderson 1995, pp. 37–38).

A full interaction analysis is an extraordinarily intensive procedure, involving a number of researchers going through the video material together, recording their own comments for review and analysis, and returning to the field to test emerging hypotheses. This level of intensity may be inappropriate for some smaller-scale projects, even if only for practical reasons. However, this approach still provides a framework that is well established within HCI (see e.g. Salovaara et al. 2006; Tatar et al. 2008; Tholander et al. 2008) and suitable for understanding multi-user interactions. Its main weaknesses lie in its emphasis on identifying specific causes of interactional phenomena, and its lack of strategies or categories for addressing the deeply subjective, emotional, and potentially transformational 'special world' (Pearson 1998, p. 39) of performance. It is therefore a useful component, but only one component, of an analytic strategy for PED.

Coded Performance Analysis

This third analytic method is a hybrid of thematic analysis and performance analysis called 'coded performance analysis'. The coded videos of each use of the designed system are re-examined holistically as full performances in their own right, with specific behaviours and emergent phenomena already noted. Coded performance analysis can thus address aspects of performance that interaction analysis is not equipped to investigate, such as the processes of 'making special' (Dissanayake 2003) at work in performances that might not have all the trappings of a professional show. For example, 'heightened attention' might be indicated by audience members leaning forward in their seats, which is easy to code for, but it might also be indicated by a tension in the air, an intensity of the gaze, or an unusual tone of voice, which cannot be coded to any particular word or gesture. Performance provides a language and an attunement to the ephemeral that can, of course, be productively analysed in its own right through performance analysis—but that can also be coded as in thematic analysis. This coded performance analysis can then be applied to directly observed phenomena (performances) as well as subjective data such as questionnaires and interviews. Coded performance analyses are also very similar in structure and content to the performance analyses performed in Step 3 of the PED methodology, which allows for comparison between the performances that served as inspiration and those that emerged as the result of a design process.

The power of this analytic method is its ability to incorporate subjective experiences and 'aesthetic' (Fischer-Lichte 2008b) concerns into a holistic analysis of a complete performance event. However, it soon becomes clear that this method elides the position of researcher-as-spectator with the position(s) of audience members. Therefore, it would be easy to conflate the researcher's interpretations of audience reactions with the researcher's own reactions to the performances being studied. This phenomenon puts the validity of any conclusions at risk, because it would be easy to assume that unverbalised audience reactions such as laughter or lack of attention are caused by what the researcher perceives in watching the performance. Although the researcher takes the position of spectator of the recorded performance, and may even have attended the live performance of interacting with the prototype, his or her position as researcher will at least subtly differ from those of the participant/audience members.[4] There is also every reason to believe that the researcher's reactions could be very different from the reactions of other audience members, as Heddon et al. describe so clearly in their work on one-to-one performance (2012, p. 128). Such a direct engagement with the challenges posed by coded performance analysis is in line with influential perspectives in ethnography that aim to account for possible effects of the researcher's presence on the interactions being observed (see e.g. Coffey 1999). To minimise risks to the validity of coded performance analysis, researchers should diligently differentiate between their own reactions and observable data about participants' reactions. With that caveat, though, a conscientious approach to the complexities of coded performance analysis can turn the risks in this method into worthwhile rewards.

Conclusion

This description of the PED methodology illustrates the unique place this field occupies in academic research. Neither HCI nor performance studies alone provide a satisfactory methodological approach for exploring the possibilities of PED, which embraces and intertwines the methodological premises of both disciplines. The result is a method that resembles the steps of a user-centred design process at the same time as it evokes an overarching approach to practice-led performance research. This might seem to be a surprising or even unlikely result, given the positivist roots of HCI and the arts and humanities tradition behind performance studies (described in Chap. 2). However, each field encompasses lines of enquiry that share remarkably similar perspectives and values. Design-oriented research and performance studies share a high regard for the value of practice, as both are

---

[4] In the case study discussed in Chap. 6, the difference was stark, as I watched the unfolding performance without the obligation of performing in turn. Although I avoided overt participation in the 'autopoietic feedback loop' (Fischer-Lichte 2008b, p. 165) by positioning myself outside the audience's line of sight, avoiding eye contact with the performers, and remaining still, my presence was noted (see Chaps. 6 and 7).

fundamentally oriented towards the creation and analysis of novel works in order to advance understanding in their fields. Both value the individual agency of the creator/analyst, and both favour flexibility and novelty in their approach to the research topic. With its origins in these shared priorities, the PED methodology incorporates specific methods from both HCI and performance studies into a practice-driven design cycle.

PED can provide the structure for a range of projects investigating performative, multi-user interactions with digital media technology, regardless of whether the output is construed as 'design', 'art', or something else entirely. The methodology itself should be adapted to suit the needs of particular projects, as PED can apply to any interaction with technology that has a performative element—or in other words, any interaction that exposes a user's interaction to the perception of others, particularly when the user then consciously or subconsciously alters her interaction in response to being perceived. The insights and perspectives of performance studies can inform embodied interactions with physical devices, mixed reality games played out in public spaces, online interactions using social media, the building of meaning around personal digital media, the experience of digital music, encounters with interactive artworks, participation in technologically inflected participatory artworks, and more. This wide range of application areas threatens to make the methodology seem diffuse, especially on first reading. For that reason, each step of the methodology is illustrated in the following two chapters with a case study: *Collect Yourselves!*

References

Baker B (2001) Performance artist Bobby Baker. In: Allen P (ed) Art, not chance: nine artists diaries. Calouste Gulbenkian Foundation, London, pp 31–42

Bardzell J, Bolter J, Löwgren J (2010) Interaction criticism: three readings of an interaction design, and what they get us. Interactions 17(2):32–37

Benford S, Giannachi G (2011) Performing mixed reality. MIT Press, Cambridge, MA/London

Benford S, Crabtree A, Reeves S, Sheridan J, Dix A, Flintham M, Drozd A (2006) The frame of the game: blurring the boundary between fiction and reality in mobile experiences. In: Proceedings of the SIGCHI conference on human factors in computing systems. ACM Press, New York, pp 427–436

Blythe M, Wright P, McCarthy J, Bertelsen O (2006) Theory and method for experience centered design. In: CHI '06 extended abstracts on human factors in computing systems. ACM Press, New York, pp 1691–1694

Boyatzis RE (1998) Transforming qualitative information: thematic analysis and code development. Sage, Thousand Oaks/London

Clarke R, Vines J, Wright P, Bartindale T, Shearer J, McCarthy J, Olivier P (2015) MyRun: balancing design for reflection, recounting and openness in a museum-based participatory platform. In: Proceedings of the 2015 British HCI conference. ACM Press, New York, pp 212–221

Coffey A (1999) The ethnographic self: fieldwork and the representation of identity. Sage, Thousand Oaks

Dalsgaard P, Hansen LK (2008) Performing perception: staging aesthetics of interaction. ACM Trans Comput Human Interact (TOCHI) 15(3):1–33

Dewey J (2005) Art as experience. Perigee Books, New York

Dissanayake E (2003) The core of art: making special. J Can Assoc Curric Stud 1(2):13–38

Edmonds E (2010) The art of interaction. Digit Creat 21(4):257–264

Ehn P (1988) Work-oriented design of computer artifacts. PhD thesis, Umeå University

Fällman D (2003) Design-oriented human-computer interaction. In: Proceedings of the SIGCHI conference on human factors in computing systems. ACM Press, New York, pp 225–232

Fallman D (2007) Why research-oriented design isn't design-oriented research: on the tensions between design and research in an implicit design discipline. Knowl Technol Policy 20(3):193–200

Fällman D (2008) The interaction design research triangle of design practice, design studies, and design exploration. Des Issues 24(3):4–18

Fischer-Lichte E (1997) The show and the gaze of theatre: a European perspective. University of Iowa Press, Iowa City

Fischer-Lichte E (2008a) Sense and sensation: exploring the interplay between the semiotic and performative dimensions of theatre. J Dram Theory Crit 22(2): 69–81

Fischer-Lichte E (2008) The transformative power of performance: a new aesthetics. Routledge, London

Forlizzi J (2010) All look same?: A comparison of experience design and service design. Interactions 17(5):60–62

Frayling C (1993) Research in art and design. Royal College of Art, London

Frohlich DM (2004) Audiophotography: bringing photos to life with sounds. Springer and Kluwer Academic Publishers, Dordrecht/Boston/London

Gaver W (2011) Making spaces: how design workbooks work. In: Proceedings of the SIGCHI conference on human factors in computing systems. ACM Press, New York, pp 1551–1560

Gaver W (2012) What should we expect from research through design? In: Proceedings of the SIGCHI conference on human factors in computing systems, ACM Press, New York, pp 937–946

Harris G, Aston E (2007) Integrity: the essential ingredient. In: Barrett M, Baker B (eds) Bobby Baker: redeeming features of daily life. Routledge, London/New York, pp 109–115

Heddon D, Iball H, Zerihan R (2012) Come closer: confessions of intimate spectators in one to one performance. Contemp Theatr Rev 22(1):120–133

Hill L, Paris H (2014) Performing proximity: curious intimacies. Palgrave Macmillan, New York

Hood B (2015) Glitching. In: Proceedings of the 2015 ACM SIGCHI conference on creativity and cognition. ACM Press, New York, pp 351–352

Houde S, Hill C (1997) What do prototypes prototype? In: Helander M et al (eds) Handbook of human-computer interaction, 2nd edn. Elsevier Science B.V, Amsterdam, pp 367–381

Huggard A, De Mel A, Garner J, Toprak CC, Chatham AD, Mueller F (2013) Musical embrace: facilitating engaging play experiences through social awkwardness. In: CHI'13 extended abstracts on human factors in computing systems, pp 3067–3070

Jordan B, Henderson A (1995) Interaction analysis: foundations and practice. J Learn Sci 4(1):39–103

Kershaw B, Nicholson H (2011) Introduction: doing methods creatively. In: Kershaw B, Nicholson H (eds) Research methods in theatre and performance. Edinburgh University Press, Edinburgh, pp 1–15

Kolko J (2010) Abductive thinking and sensemaking: the drivers of design synthesis. Design Issues 26(1):15–28

Kuutti K (2010) Where are the Ionians of user experience research? In: Proceedings of the 6th Nordic conference on human-computer interaction: extending boundaries. ACM Press, New York, pp 715–718

Langellier KM, Peterson E (2004) Storytelling in daily life: performing narrative. Temple University Press, Philadelphia

Lave J, Wenger E (1991) Situated learning: Legitimate peripheral participation. Cambridge University Press, Cambridge, UK/New York

Law ELC, Roto V, Hassenzahl M, Vermeeren AP, Kort J (2009) Understanding, scoping and defin-
ing user experience: a survey approach. In: Proceedings of the SIGCHI conference on human
factors in computing systems. ACM Press, New York, pp 719–728
Loke L, Robertson T (2010) Studies of dancers: moving from experience to interaction design.
International Journal of Design 4(2):39–54
McAuley G (1998) Performance analysis: theory and practice. About Perform 4:1–12
McAuley G (2003) Place in the performance experience. Mod Drama 46(4):598–613
McCarthy J, Wright P (2004) Technology as experience. MIT Press, Cambridge, MA
Morgan RC (2010) Thoughts on re-performance, experience, and archivism. PAJ J Perform Art
32(3):1–15
Nelson HG, Stolterman E (2012) The design way: intentional change in an unpredictable world.
MIT Press, Cambridge, MA/London
Pavis P (2003) Analyzing performance: theater, dance, and film. Translated by D. Williams. Ann
Arbor: University of Michigan Press
Pavis P (2005) Analysing performance. In: Counsell C, Wolf L (eds) Performance analysis: an
introductory coursebook. Routledge, London, pp 229–232
Pearson M (1998) My balls/your chin. Perform Res 3(2):35–41
Radbourne J, Glow H, Johanson K (2013) The audience experience: a critical analysis of audiences
in the performing arts. Intellect, Bristol, UK; Chicago
Reason M (2010) Asking the audience: audience research and the experience of theatre. About
Perform 10:15–34
Reeves S, Benford S, O'Malley C, Fraser M (2005) Designing the spectator experience. In:
Proceedings of the SIGCHI conference on human factors in computing systems. ACM Press,
New York, pp 741–750
Rozik E (2010) Generating theatre meaning: a theory and methodology of performance analysis.
Sussex Academic Press, Eastbourne/Portland/Thornhill
Salovaara A, Jacucci G, Oulasvirta A, Saari T, Kanerva P, Kurvinen E, Tiitta S (2006) Collective
creation and sense-making of mobile media. In: Proceedings of the SIGCHI conference on
human factors in computing systems. ACM Press, New York, pp 1211–1220
Schön DA (1983) The reflective practitioner: how professionals think in action. Basic Books, New
York
Sengers P, Boehner K, Mateas M, Gay G (2008) The disenchantment of affect. Pers Ubiquit
Comput 12(5):347–358
Sheridan JG, Bryan-Kinns N, Bayliss A (2007) Encouraging witting participation and perfor-
mance in digital live art. In: Proceedings of the 21st British HCI group annual conference on
people and computers: HCI...but not as we know it. British Computer Society, Swinton,
pp 13–23
States BO (1985) Introduction. In: Great reckonings in little rooms: on the phenomenology of
theater. University of California Press, Berkeley, pp 1–15
Stolterman E (2008) The nature of design practice and implications for interaction design research.
Int J Des 2(1):55–65
Suchman LA (1987) Plans and situated actions: the problem of human-machine communication.
Cambridge University Press, Cambridge
Suchman L (2007) Human-machine reconfigurations: plans and situated actions. Cambridge
University Press, Cambridge
Tatar D, Lee J-S, Alaloula N (2008) Playground games: a design strategy for supporting and under-
standing coordinated activity. In: Proceedings of the 7th ACM conference on designing interac-
tive systems. ACM Press, New York, pp 68–77
Taylor R, Schofield G, Shearer J, Wallace J, Wright P, Boulanger P, Olivier P (2011) Designing
from within: humanaquarium. In: Proceedings of the 2011 annual conference on human factors
in computing systems. ACM Press, New York, pp 1855–1864

Taylor R, Schofield G, Shearer J, Wright P, Boulanger P, Olivier P (2014) Nightingallery: theatrical framing and orchestration in participatory performance. Pers Ubiquit Comput 18(7):1583–1600

Taylor R, Bowers J, Nissen B, Wood G, Chaudhry Q, Wright P, Bruce L, Glynn S, Mallinson H, Bearpark R (2015) Making magic: designing for open interactions in museum settings. In: Proceedings of the 2015 ACM SIGCHI conference on creativity and cognition, pp 313–322

ten Bhömer M, Helmes J, O'Hara K, van den Hoven E (2010) 4Photos: a collaborative photo sharing experience. In: Proceedings of the 6th Nordic conference on human-computer interaction: extending boundaries. ACM Press, New York, pp 52–61

Tholander J, Karlgren K, Ramberg R, Sökjer P (2008) Where all the interaction is: sketching in interaction design as an embodied practice. In: Proceedings of the 7th ACM conference on designing interactive systems. ACM Press, New York, pp 445–454

Varney D, Fensham R (2000) More-and-less-than: liveness, video recording, and the future of performance. New Theatr Q 16(01):88–96

Wilson M (2006) Storytelling and theatre: contemporary storytellers and their art. Palgrave Macmillan, Basingstoke

Wolf TV, Rode JA, Sussman J, Kellogg WA (2006) Dispelling design as the black art of CHI. In: Proceedings of the SIGCHI conference on human factors in computing systems. ACM Press, New York, pp 521–530

Wright P (2011) Reconsidering the H, the C, and the I: some thoughts on reading Suchman's Human-Machine Reconfigurations. Interactions 18(5):28–31

Wright P, Wallace J, McCarthy J (2008) Aesthetics and experience-centered design. ACM Trans Comput Human Interact (TOCHI) 15(4):1–21

Zarrilli PB (2004) Toward a phenomenological model of the actor's embodied modes of experience. Theatr J 56(4):653–666

Zimmerman J, Forlizzi J, Evenson S (2007) Research through design as a method for interaction design research in HCI. In: Proceedings of the SIGCHI conference on human factors in computing systems. ACM Press, New York, pp 493–502

Chapter 5
Designing *Collect Yourselves!*

Abstract Where Chap. 4 provided a generic 'how-to' for the PED methodology, this chapter details the first four steps of the methodology as it was applied in the case study for this book, a system for co-located digital photo sharing called *Collect Yourselves!* This is not meant to be a rigid or exclusive picture of what PED must do, but rather gives the reader a story to follow. Step 1 charts they way the germ of my motivations developed into an established line of enquiry through a search of the HCI literature informed by insights into performativity and performance described in Chaps. 2 and 3. Step 2 describes the process of deciding a long list of performances that I believed could contribute to the line of enquiry and how that list was shortened and refined to the four that would be subjected to analysis. Step 3 is represented by a single, full performance analysis of one of those four performances: Third Angel's *Cape Wrath*, which took place in three different versions in 2011, 2012, and 2013. The performance analyses resulted in the identification of properties of performance to be considered in the design process: self-making, heightened attention, situatedness, and the aesthetics of the event. Step 4 describes the design exploration that resulted in a map of the design space for intermedial autobiographical performance and a prototype to be performed. Steps 5 and 6 are covered in Chap. 6.

Step 1: Develop a Line of Enquiry

The general topic of interest driving this case study was what I perceived to be a weakness in the HCI literature to account for audiences in performative interactions with digital media. In my opinion, much (though not all) of this work tended to focus either on the process of selecting photos for reminiscence or on the act of sharing them, impromptu, with little regard for their eventual audience (for a similar opinion, see Cosley et al. 2012). Photographs are a familiar vernacular means of engaging on a personal level with digital technologies, which opened up possibilities for exploring performative experiences that did not need to be artist-led, though again it is worth underlining the fact that PED is relevant to any other media type or performative engagement with technology.

© Springer International Publishing Switzerland 2016
J. Spence, *Performative Experience Design*, Springer Series on Cultural
Computing, DOI 10.1007/978-3-319-28395-1_5

Because I was interested in processes of investing meaning into digital media, my line of enquiry was also shaped by questions suggested by McCarthy and Wright (2004) for determining the quality of an engagement with technology:

Do the technologies connect or fragment experience and life?
Do the technologies help to enrich our experience of what we already value, or do they impoverish it?
Do the technologies facilitate unfolding potential, critical perception, and engagement?
Specifically, does the Internet increase the potential for new relationships and new forms of communicating, or does it inhibit relating?…
Does the introduction of new technologies respect the stories we tell ourselves about what is important while also allowing us to create new stories? (2004, p. 66)

I read widely within the HCI literature on a variety of related topics that I later chose not to use, such as embodied interaction, the use of dance in HCI and design projects, and transhumanism. I went through a lengthy process of reading in different areas and gradually consolidated my line of enquiry based on my own areas of interest. I also began going to performances during the later parts of this step based on my unfolding sense of the direction my line of enquiry would take. The following section describes the line of enquiry that I decided on: co-located digital photo sharing, not unlike the conversations that emerged through use of 4Photos during a dinner party (ten Bhömer et al. 2010).

Although there are a number of media sharing projects stretching back at least to the turn of the millennium, Jarno Ojala and Sanna Malinen are accurate when they state that 'services that aim for supporting working with limited and intimate groups are still in their infancy' (2012, p. 69). Early work in creating novel interactive devices for personal viewing and small-scale display, such as StoryTrack (Balabanović et al. 2000), have been supplanted by smartphones, while online sharing has come to dominate expectations of what it means to share photos. Still, existing research provides a number of important insights, including Balabanović et al.'s observation that conversation virtually always accompanies the sharing of photographs. This conversation comes in two forms: photo-driven 'stories', which cover only one photo each, and story-driven 'stories', which are told using more than one photograph. Story-driven stories dominate for remote sharing, while the photo-driven style is used for local telling (2000, p. 570). Subsequently, Frohlich et al. coined the terms 'photo-talk' to describe 'conversation around photographs' (2002, p. 167) and 'photoware' to describe the technologies that allow for collaborative capture, archiving, and sharing of photographs in digital formats, whether the original photo was analogue or digital (2002, p. 166). These terms are complemented by David Kirk et al.'s definition of 'photowork' as the practices surrounding the capture, storage, and use of digital photographs (2006, p. 764), with implications for functions of search, browse, edit, organise, and archive.

Frohlich et al. (2002) investigate the impact of digitisation on existing practices of taking, archiving, and sharing photographs. Of their many findings, two are of particular importance to this case study. The first is the difference between storytelling and reminiscing talk, which stems from 'recipient design' (Sacks et al. 1974, p. 727), or the tendency to frame conversation to suit the expectations of the audience. Storytelling is characterised by fewer turns, dominated by the person with 'status, experience and wisdom' to communicate to those not present when the photo was taken. Responses may come in the form of 'second stories' (Frohlich 2004, p. 138) or 'response stories' (Norrick 2000, p. 112) that indicate understanding by following the themes of the story just told. Reminiscing is characterised by multiple, overlapping turns as those present when the photo was taken contribute details, 'jointly "finding" the memory together' (Frohlich et al. 2002, p. 171) and sometimes straying from the narrative. Mixed groups engage in collaborative telling (2002, p. 172). These findings indicate that co-located media sharing interactions are a complex and fluid mixture of relationships among media prompts, audience, and speakers.

The second key finding concerns the value of media sharing:

> Of all the methods of interacting around photos, sharing photos in person was described as the most common and enjoyable. Such co-present sharing was seen as a way of re-creating the past and reliving the experience with others who were there at the time. (Frohlich et al. 2002, p. 170)

The authors do not speak of conveying static information but of the *present-moment experience* of re-creating past events. They suggest that such experiences might best be fostered by technologies that would maintain the 'inefficiencies' of print-based sharing (2002, p. 174). PED suggests that many of the benefits of those 'inefficiencies' might be created through practices of performance.

Andy Crabtree et al. elaborate on the present-moment experience in terms of how stories around photos are shaped and controlled collaboratively. They also highlight recipient design in photo sharing, but they focus on the 'control centre' (2004, p. 399) that emerges around the person who owns the photo(s) being shared. Photos distribute some of the control by allowing others to interrogate, comment, or form temporary sub-groups with their own conversations. Part of the remarkable ability for groups to coordinate these activities is due to 'a host of embodied interactional *gestures* that enable persons using photographs to establish mutual orientations [and] to furnish topics' (2004, p. 401, emphasis in the original). However, Siân Lindley and Andrew Monk (2006) uncover tensions in the collaborative negotiation of digital media sharing. Participants speaking about their own photographs were frustrated with automated slideshows whose tempo they could not control, but not frustrated enough to relinquish control of photo display to their audiences. Therefore, any new design for digital media sharing should build on these observations to resolve or fruitfully heighten these tensions.

Nancy Van House et al. (2004) present a rich and nuanced analysis of what I would identify as the sharing aspects of photowork as defined by Kirk et al. (2006). Van House et al. note the importance of the precise and unique situation of each digital media sharing session in supporting the social aspects of 'memory, creating and maintaining relationships, and self-expression' (2004, p. 1; see also Stelmaszewska et al. 2008). In later work, Van House describes the value of photos as triggers to enactments of identity and relationships (2009, p. 1074). These enactments are not by-products of some other process but are key to the motivation for, and enjoyment of, the present-moment act of sharing personal photos.

As noted by both Kirk et al. and Van House, the continuing development of digital photography creates challenges to practices of photo sharing as people are 'quickly overwhelmed by the size of their collections and the opacity of computer-based storage, with indecipherable filenames' (Van House 2009, p. 1078; see also Van House 2011, pp. 128–129; Keightley and Pickering 2014, pp. 581–582). Sarvas and Frohlich (2011) identify the challenges of taking, editing, storing, and finding increasing numbers of photographs from increasing numbers of devices, as well as issues of privacy and regulation. The techniques used to navigate a few dozen physical snapshots do not translate directly to the management of multiple terabytes of digital media (2011, p. 97). Steve Whittaker et al. (2009) note that participants exhibit both poor performance and an exaggerated belief in their abilities to retrieve photos more than a year old. These difficulties in navigation and retrieval might be compounded by the observation that digital mementoes, including photographs, are sometimes perceived as less valuable than physical photographs or other mementoes. Daniela Petrelli and Steve Whittaker (2010), who discovered this phenomenon, surmise that digital archives (as folder or file names on a screen) do not spring to mind the way that physical objects do, and that digital photographs are seen as transient or ephemeral (2010, p. 166). Clearly, there is a conflict between existing practices of selecting and retrieving digital photos to share and the socially and emotionally valuable practices of co-located digital media sharing.

HCI researchers have created a number of prototypes for digital media sharing over the past decade and a half. Anything within the field of digital media sharing might qualify as what Bødker would describe as 'third-wave' because media sharing is a cultural and emotional experience that is 'non-work, non-purposeful, non-rational, etc.' (2006, pp. 1–2, 6). However, I find that existing work in media sharing can be more usefully grouped by the epistemologies implicit in the focuses they choose. First-wave thinking is seen in products that deal only with the production or offering of a media artefact, not the sharing of the experience triggered by that artefact. Examples of first-wave thinking include web-based tools such as Aisling Kelliher and Glorianna Davenport's *Confectionary*, which provides rigid structures for building narratives and promises 'an easy, risk-free and playful' environment (2007, p. 928; see also Landry and Guzdial 2006; Fono and Counts 2006). While *Confectionary* is non-work, it is certainly designed to be both purposeful and rational, and is evaluated in those terms. Their *Everyday Mediated Storytelling Model* (2007, p. 928) is, in turn, reminiscent of the standard model of production and consumption that PED challenges (see Chap. 6).

Other researchers take a second-wave HCI approach in their examination of how products impact and are impacted by the context of use. Again, a seminal example is StoryTrack (Balabanović et al. 2000), whose interface uses stories as an organisational tool, asking users to order their photos in the way that makes most sense in the telling. Other epistemologically second-wave media sharing research includes the *Personal Digital Historian* (Shen et al. 2003), an interactive tabletop system for story sharing that aims for agency on the part of all participants but runs the risk of channelling users into predetermined modes of representing their ideas and experiences; Leonard M. Ah Kun and Gary Marsden's (2007) interactive system for managing photo sharing on PDAs; *MobiPhos* (Clawson et al. 2008, 2009), an application for the capture and immediate sharing of photos within small groups of co-located users; Christian Kray et al.'s (2009) Bluetooth®-based photo sharing technique that uses spatial proximity regions to control the viewing and sharing of virtual 'stacks' of photos; Andrés Lucero et al.'s (2011) *pass-them-around* prototype that allows for both sequential and ad hoc photo sharing; and Anne Marie Piper et al.'s (2013) in-depth study of audio-enhanced paper photos designed to support reminiscence and social interaction among a very elderly user, her family, and her care staff.

   The studies I have described as epistemologically second-wave take the digital infrastructure as given: researchers input photos into a device as part of the research project, rather than designing for the full range of archive and selection activities that are an integral part of the experience of digital media sharing. These second-wave projects also tend to focus on interactions with the products themselves and frame those interactions in terms of accomplishing goals or having pleasant experiences. Framings like these can limit possibilities for the peculiar, sometimes intense, and potentially transformative interactions that can arise in some storytelling performances. These may be impromptu, conversational, and vernacular, but they remain performances in a wide range of senses, from the Butlerian performativity of the gendered self (Butler 2002) and Goffman's (1959) presentation of self to folklorist Richard Bauman's 'verbal art' (1975) and Heddon's 'performing "I"', which is 'strategically complex and layered' (2008, p. 8). A substantially third-wave approach would create triggers for people to approach their personal digital media archives critically and unconventionally, with the goal of establishing an emotional or insightful connection among people.

   A related practice that espouses this goal is digital storytelling as established by Joe Lambert, Nina Mullen, and Dana Atchley of the Center for Digital Storytelling (CDS) in California. In the early 1990s, they used emerging consumer-level video editing technology to teach people to create personal digital stories narrated over their own photographs. CDS-style digital storytelling aims to 'assist in this larger project of allowing us to coexist in a world of fluid identity' (Lambert 2002, p. 17) but instead creates a static 'mini-movie' (Meadows 2008, p. 2) for each participant, often hosted on an institutional website. Jenny Kidd (Meadows 2008) and Jo Tacchi (2009) argue that digital storytelling is reactive rather than interactive, while Jerry Watkins and Angelina Russo (2009) deny the interactivity promised by the ability of some web pages to host written comments to a fixed digital story (see also Van House 2009, p. 1085). In fact, it is the process of live, co-located storytelling over photos in the 'story circle', prior to the creation of the digital story 'mini-movie', that many hold up as the most important and most enjoyable element of digital storytelling (Lambert 2002, p. 88; Hartley and McWilliam 2009, p. 3; Lundby and Kaare 2008, pp. 118–120). Third-wave promises of a technologically mediated story circle are defeated by digital storytelling's second-wave mechanisms of production and first-wave mechanisms of consumption. However, the story circle remains a tantalising focus for the design of co-located digital media sharing technologies.

Third-wave intentions in design for media sharing can be seen in very early work such as the audioscanner and audioprint player mocked up by David Frohlich et al. (2000). These aim to give 'mood and life to the photo and trigger a richer remembering of the event' (2000, p. 1). Similarly, Frohlich et al.'s audiophoto desk offers 'a way of bringing ordinary objects to life' (2004, p. 2) by combining photos and sound through embodied interaction. Several media sharing projects, including 4Photos (ten Bhömer et al. 2010; O'Hara et al. 2012), build on these third-wave intentions. Tuck Wah Leong uses serendipity as a design driver (2009). The photo display system developed by Leong et al. (2011) 'nudges' users towards serendipitous experiences of sharing digital photos. Other examples include *Rider Spoke* (2007), a participatory performance developed by Blast Theory and the Mixed Reality Lab, in which users on bicycles engage with their location through personal storytelling; *Cueb*, a pair of interactive digital photo cubes designed actively to encourage self-disclosure between parents and their teenage children (Golsteijn and van den Hoven 2013, p. 274); David S. Kirk et al.'s *Family Archive* device, 'which offers novel *and open* interaction possibilities [that] can highlight, disrupt, change, or otherwise impact existing practices' (2010, p. 262, emphasis in the original); and the theory-rich research-through-design work of Thomas Reitmaier et al. (2013) on co-located interactions around digital media. All of these examples focus on the personal and social nature of interaction, positioning the participant as one 'who brings her entire life to the design' (Bødker 2006, p. 6).

These examples reflect not only a move towards Bødker's third wave, but also examples of what Bardzell et al. (2010) refer to as the 'performative view'. This contrasts with the 'procedural view', which would map roughly to the first and second waves in Bødker's terminology. In the performative view, which 'draws on the rich tradition of performance studies', a user is 'working through the application to communicate with an audience. ... These applications are successful precisely because they make it easier for users to reinvent their identities in the act of performance' (2010, p. 34). The authors see the performative view at work in social networking sites such as Facebook and online games. Van House also believes that sharing asynchronously does not preclude any of the identity-forming or relationship-building functions of co-located photo sharing (2011, p. 131). However, I believe that the performative view can involve much more than simply communicating with an audience or describing online interactions: performance has the potential to create transformational moments of empathy, emotion, and insight (Phelan 2004; Dolan 2005; Fischer-Lichte 2008b). Rather than assuming that relationships at a distance are as meaningful and visceral as those in a shared time and space, researchers following the 'performative view' should explore performance as directly as possible, making full use of the live interaction with a co-located audience as part of the 'rich tradition of performance studies' (Bardzell et al. 2010, p. 34). Findings from co-located interactions could then be tested or used as probes (along the lines of those described in Gaver et al. 1999) in online, asynchronous communication.

The co-located sharing of personal digital media such as photos raises the question of how autobiographical memory and reminiscence are understood within HCI. Elise van den Hoven and Barry Eggen (2007) observe that human memory does not function as a library of static memories ready to be plucked out, viewed, and returned unaltered. Instead, they argue that autobiographical memory should be understood in line with constructionist theory as a process that needs to be cued (2007, p. 435) and that results in a different recollection each time (2007, p. 434). These findings echo what van den Hoven and Eggen (2003) found in their study of the portable *Photo Browser*. Their participants spoke not about the memory triggers themselves but about the experiences behind the triggers, which indicated 'that the focus should be on how the media stored in the system can optimally trigger and set the right conditions for the experience of remembering' (2003, p. 1003). Findings regarding memory within HCI are in line with key works on memory in cultural theory and psychology described in Chap. 3, which frame memory as a performative act that can be explored and expanded through autobiographical performance (among other types).

Two key possibilities for designing 'the right conditions for the experience of remembering' have emerged in interaction design research: selectivity and context. Petrelli et al. (2009) asked participants to create a time capsule. They found that all participants were selective about their choices; none aimed for a comprehensive record. Along with selectivity, context is highly important. *Pensieve* is a system that emails daily 'memory triggers' to its users. Analysis of *Pensieve* by Dan Cosley et al. highlights the need for personalised or culture-specific triggers that reflect topical and/or temporal contexts (2012, pp. 193–195). Another important finding from work with *Pensieve* was the observation that because online social networks (specifically Facebook) orient users towards recent events, '[u]sing social media to support reminiscing may also bias people towards reminiscing about recent or easily captured events' (Peesapati et al. 2010, p. 2035). Therefore, any technologically mediated system for engaging with the past should consider selectivity and context in shaping the parameters for engagement with both memory triggers and the present-moment sharing experience.

One final issue to note in dealing with design for reminiscence and memory is the contradiction between the benefits of reminiscence, both self-reported and assessed by psychological metrics as in Isaacs et al. (2013), and the reluctance that many feel to reminisce. With *Pensieve*, participants appreciated the opportunity to reminisce but rarely did so when not directed to (Peesapati et al. 2010, p. 2034; Cosley et al. 2012, p. 180). Petrelli et al. (2008) also discovered that a significant proportion of participants' mementoes were hidden from view for a variety of reasons, and that despite the positive experience of discussing them, participants rarely did so (2008, p. 58). This situation is likely to be exacerbated by the increasing rate of accumulation of digital artefacts noted by van den Hoven et al. (2012), whereby people hoard digital media to supplement their memories and because it is easier to collect than to select (2012, p. 2; see also Frohlich et al. 2013).

An answer would be to bring more digital artefacts into easy view and increase opportunities for reminiscence. However, as Petrelli et al. (2008) warn, '[h]aving these objects in constant view would habituate people; so concealing them makes more salient the contrast between that past world and the current one' (2008, p. 60). David Frohlich and Jacqueline Fennell (2006) similarly advise that 'less' is often 'more', advocating audiophotographs in place of video to stimulate reminiscence (2006, p. 107; see also Dewey 2005, p. 108). Also, Kuhn (2010) points out that the 'value is placed on keeping—preserving family photographs and albums, even (and perhaps especially) if they are rarely looked at' (2010, p. 304). A recent design approach in this direction is to design for forgetting, as a critique of the drive to capture and store increasing amounts of data (Bannon 2006; Frohlich et al. 2013). Rather than designing for forgetting, I believe that more work can be done in designing according to current perspectives on autobiographical memory and reminiscence. Performance offers valuable practices for selecting and contextualising material in a shared, present-moment experience.

Step 2: Select Performances to Watch

The fact that photo sharing is almost invariably accompanied by conversational storytelling led to immediate parallels with autobiographical performance. Generally speaking, it involves one or more performers who represent elements of their own life experience for an audience. This genre spans a range of styles and types of content, and I initially took a very inclusive view. Even after limiting myself to UK performances (which I had the resources to see live) and the documented work of other UK artists, I had a long list of possibilities to consider. In addition to *Kitchen Show*, *Bubbling Tom*, and the four performances that I eventually chose to analyse, I attended or investigated 13 performances:

- Daniel Gosling *10.1.00> > 1 + 1?(@?):? + & + …> > 30.1.00* (2000)
- Daniel Gosling *Transformer* (2002–2003)
- Blast Theory *Rider Spoke* (2007)
- Hayley Newman *Connotations—Performance Images 1994–1998* (1998)
- Simon Pope *Waterlog* (2008)
- Polarbear *Old Me* (2011)
- Robert Wilson *The Life and Death of Abramović M* (2011)
- Marcia Farquhar's Artsadmin weekender (2012)
- Third Angel and mala voadora *Story Map* (2012)
- Martin Figura *Whistle* (2012)
- Idiot Child *I Could've Been Better* (2012)
- Chris Thorpe and Hannah Jane Walker *The Oh F*ck Moment* (2012)
- 'Hugh Hughes' *Stories from an Invisible Town* (2012)

Gosling's two works used hitchhiking as a methodology for acquiring experiences which he then shared. Gosling also framed his encounters with the drivers who gave him lifts as performances, although according to his 'manifesto of engagement' he never announced his artistic intentions to them (Merriman 2001, p. 340). His work entitled *10.1.00> > 1 + 1?(@?):? + & + …> > 30.1.00* involved three public performances of the stories he had gathered, each at a different motorway service station, and documented in the text '10.01.00 >> 30.01.00 > >><'(Gosling 2003).

Transformer[1] used the same methodology to create a website featuring still photographs, videos, sound, and text, all presented from Gosling's point of view as he hitchhiked Norway for nine days without sleeping.

Polarbear's *Old Me*[2] used anecdotes, poetry, music, and projected images to tell the story of his move from Birmingham to pursue family life as a spoken word artist in London. His small, often blurry or distorted digital media were projected against various surfaces, including a brick wall, leading them to evoke rather than detail the images associated with his performance. Martin Figura's *Whistle*[3] made far greater use of clearly indexical photographs to accompany his live performance of his autobiographical poetry.

Two of the works, presented as autobiography, were fictional in the sense that the performer's actual name and identity did not match the name and identity of the person portrayed on stage. (It is of course impossible to know the degree to which any autobiographical performances might be 'true', or how much of any work of fiction is based on the creator's own experience, but these two are avowedly works of fiction.) *I Could've Been Better*[4] told the story of an awkward man learning to swim as though from the performer's own experience. *Stories from an Invisible Town*[5] went further, presenting the performer 'Hugh Hughes' as a real person in its publicity and web presence, though 'Hugh Hughes' is a fiction performed by Hoipolloi artistic director Shôn Dale-Jones. This performance has an accompanying website, www.invisibletownstories.co.uk, populated with Hugh's stories.

The Life and Death of Marina Abramović[6] was a 'biography' initiated by and involving its subject. Abramović handed over complete control of the creative process to director Robert Wilson. The process of devising a performance based on her most 'tragic, painful, and emotional stories' was difficult but 'liberating' for Abramović, who performed the role of her own mother in this ensemble, multimodal piece (Abramović 2011). The *Waterlog* exhibitions[7] combined the 'biography' of a tree with the experiences of individual artists through a densely layered exploration of memory. The devising process involved participants committing to memory a painting of a specific tree, which had since been destroyed, then walking to the place where the tree had lived and recollecting the image. Audiences experienced the audio of these recollections played just out of reach of their associated paintings; all but one of the paintings were covered in black fabric.

---

[1] Available at www.danielgosling.com/transformer/index2.html, accessed 11 October 2014.

[2] Information at www.breakinconvention.com/events/polarbear-old-me-roundhouse, accessed 11 October 2014.

[3] Information at www.martinfigura.co.uk/whistle/, accessed 11 October 2014.

[4] Information at www.idiotchild.com/#/recent-work/4563255723, accessed 11 October 2014.

[5] Information at www.hughhughes.me/projects/stories-from-an-invisible-town/, accessed 11 October 2014.

[6] Information at www.mif.co.uk/event/robert-wilson-marina-abramovic-antony-willem-dafoe-the-life-and-death-of-marina-abramovic/, accessed 11 October 2014.

[7] Information at www.waterlog.fvu.co.uk/pope.htm, accessed 11 October 2014.

Hayley Newman's work blurs the boundary between fact and fiction; *Connotations—Performance Images 1994–1998* also blurred performance with its documentation (for a discussion of 'performance documentation' see Auslander 2006). Her 'performance' was an exhibition of photographic documentation of five years' worth of performance art. However, the actions in the photos were created solely to be documented, so although the artist did perform those actions, the stories of their timing, context, and audience reception were fictional (Newman 2004; Jalving 2005).

Three of the works solicited stories from audience members. Blast Theory's *Rider Spoke*[8] set its participants out on bicycles at night, prompting them to tell personal stories and using WiFi technology to embed recordings of these stories in the secret places they were told. *Story Map*[9] involved audience members suggesting stories that they knew to be untrue or inauthentic pertaining to every country in the world. *The Oh F*ck Moment*[10] set its two performers among their audience members around a conference table, sharing stories of sudden regret and disaster, and occasionally inviting the audience to contribute their own stories. Finally, Marcia Farquhar's Artsadmin weekender[11] brought together performance artists and scholars (including me) from across the UK to explore, create, and present works of autobiographical performance art.

After exploring some of the fringes of autobiographical practice, such as Gosling's website, Newman's performative documents or Pope's exhibition, I decided to analyse staged performances. This decision was based on a desire to focus on live performance techniques and practices as they are most directly and obviously used, before attempting to discern such practices in other contexts. I also chose not to problematise the frisson between fact and fiction any further than necessary, so I rejected overtly fictional or biographical performances. The spoken element of Figura's work was overtly poetic, and he altered many of his photos to include fanciful drawings, which made his work seem unnecessarily distant from more quotidian practices. Finally, I made the somewhat counter-intuitive decision to analyse performances that did not actively solicit stories from their audiences during performance. This decision was taken purely for reasons of scope: to fully explore mechanisms for soliciting stories, I would want to make use of the extensive literature on participatory art, which would expand the research question far beyond intermedial autobiographical performance. Therefore, I chose to focus on these four performances:

- Third Angel *Class of '76* (2000)
- Third Angel *Cape Wrath* (2011, 2012, 2013)
- Tom Marshman *Legs 11* (2011)
- Claire Morgan *Editor* (2012)

---

[8] Information at www.blasttheory.co.uk/projects/rider-spoke/, accessed 11 October 2014.

[9] Information at www.thirdangel.co.uk/archive.php?id=70, accessed 11 October 2014.

[10] Information at www.miles.surrey.ac.uk/node/145, accessed 11 October 2014.

[11] Information at www.artsadmin.co.uk/events/3031, accessed 11 October 2014.

These four performances address all of the most exciting elements of the original long list. *Class of '76* struggled with the conflict between truth and fiction, both intentional and unintentional, in the context of autobiography. *Cape Wrath* used a methodology similar to Gosling's peripatetic 'manifesto of engagement' (Merriman 2001, p. 340) and involved multiple layers of memory as reported by multiple people over a period of decades. *Legs 11* used both indexical and abstract digital media to represent the performer's past actions, accomplishments, and experiences. *Editor* explored the darkest feelings of shame and regret using a combination of poetic devices and conversational storytelling. Additionally, each performance made very different use of analogue or digital media. Taken together, they represent a thought-provoking set of practices representative of twenty-first century autobiographical performance in the UK.

All of the performers whose work is analysed here are well established as creators of live performance, particularly work dealing with autobiography and/or digital media. Alexander Kelly, based in Sheffield, has been working continuously since 1995 as part of the group Third Angel in live performance, installation, film, and other media. Third Angel have performed across the UK and in several European countries. They receive regular funding through the Arts Council England, Yorkshire, as well as ad-hoc funding from other national sources. Tom Marshman is based in Bristol and has made performances, films, and installations for over a decade. He has won support for his work from Arts Council England, has won several national awards, and has performed at numerous high-profile venues and festivals. He also leads projects that create performances out of stories gathered from members of local communities. Claire Morgan (now Claire Murphy-Morgan) is a founder member of Monkfish Productions in Gateshead, an organisation that creates multimedia spoken word performances and facilitates poetry performances in schools. Performing in her own right, Morgan has been supported by ARC, Stockton, and has performed at The Albany, London, among other venues.

One important comment must be made before moving on to the analyses. I aimed to include performances by both men and women and was open to performances dealing with any age, race, nationality, sexual orientation, religion, and the like. Given Heddon's comments about the dominance of women in autobiographical performance (2008, p. 22), I expected to struggle to find suitable male performers, but my experience was exactly the opposite. After the time frame for the design process came to an end, I encountered a number of female performances that would have made compelling inclusions to the list, such as Amy and Rosana Cade's *Sister* (2015), a live performance using these two sisters' home movies as part of an exploration of their relationships with family and sexuality. Somewhat less surprisingly, though just as regrettably, I found a dearth of non-white performers. While I am not insensitive to these imbalances, I chose to prioritise a diversity of relevant performance practices over a representative diversity of performer demographics.

Step 3: Performance Analyses

I began Step 3 with no clear idea of what autobiographical performance could offer me or what the results of my performance analyses might be. The performances I decided to analyse had much in common with conversational media sharing, which I believed would allow me to see how they differentiated themselves, both from conversational practices and from fictional, 'acted' theatre. In this way, the performance analyses shared some of the goals of grounded theory (Glaser and Strauss 1967), remaining open to emergent concepts rather than approaching the analysis with a pre-selected set of criteria. The rest of this section consists of one of the performance analyses, or rather three, as I encountered the performance of one project in three different forms. (There is no need to search for multiple incarnations of a single performance when using the PED methodology; this simply offers an example from a variety of angles.)

Cape Wrath

The germ of *Cape Wrath* was an online record of the journey on which the performance is based, when in 2011 Third Angel member Alex Kelly retraced his grandfather's 1988 trip to Cape Wrath, the most north-westerly point in the UK. I experienced that journey via social media, then saw a live performance of *Cape Wrath* on Monday, 9 April, 2012, at the Gate Theatre in London. Finally, I saw a revised version at the Edinburgh Festival Fringe on Saturday, 17 August, 2013. Comments about Kelly's decision-making process are taken from conversations on 22 November 2011 and 17 August 2013.

Cape Wrath (2011)

Third Angel works in a variety of media, and Alex Kelly is an enthusiastic user of several social media platforms. *Cape Wrath* began as a Storify project (see Fig. 5.1), an online collection of tweets (postings to the social networking site Twitter) and Instagram photos (digital photographs taken with a smartphone, then processed and archived through the Instagram smartphone application).[12] In this 'proto-performance' (Schechner 2006, p. 225), Kelly retraced his grandfather's trip to Cape Wrath as closely as he could, using nearly the same transportation methods and staying in the same hostel. Kelly experimented with video before deciding to document his travels via Twitter and Instagram and to plan a live performance. He felt that only through his live presence on stage would he be able to create a compelling

---

[12] https://storify.com/alexanderkelly/cape-wrath, accessed 7 October 2014.

Fig. 5.1 Screenshot of the beginning of the original Storify project (© Alexander Kelly, used with permission)

experience for the audience. To increase this sense of presence, he planned to use still photographs sparingly and only one video, arranged in such a way that would help bring the personality of his grandfather, Henry Ratcliffe, to life, while letting the audience experience the journey in their imaginations.

Digital media were embedded in Kelly's re-experience of his grandfather's journey. His decision to use photographs and tweets altered not only the performances he made but also the very nature of the experience that his performances were born from. Thus Kelly's digital media must be understood not only as elements to be perceived by the audience but as integral parts of the devising process, and even as integral parts of Kelly's own life experience. *Cape Wrath* was intermedial in the sense of 'how–singularly and collectively–intermedial performances may have elicited a new cultural way of seeing, feeling and being in the contemporary world' (Nelson 2010, p. 18) before Kelly ever decided to perform it.

Cape Wrath (2012)[13]

Cape Wrath was performed as a work in progress in a 70-seat black box studio at the Gate Theatre. That night, the studio was full. The stage was empty except for a small table, chair, and a projector screen at the back. The performance consisted of Kelly telling the story of his grandfather's trip to Cape Wrath as his grandfather had told it to him more than 20 years previously, interleaved with the story of Kelly's retracing of that journey and memories of other family members relating to that trip.

Sixteen photos of Kelly's journey were projected during the performance, each accompanying the relevant part of Kelly's story. Kelly appeared in none of them. They did not offer 'proof' of his journey in the manner of holiday snapshots, but rather implied his presence as the creator and documenter of his own experience (see Fig. 5.2). Many were quotidian: a shot of the bus departures board, of his porridge, or of the view from his hostel window. In terms of holiday snapshots, these photos might not have been deemed worthy of sharing, though they reflect a tendency for digital photography to include 'more images of daily life and not just special events' (Van House 2011, p. 127). However, in terms of performance, they offered a means for the audience to imagine themselves into Kelly's place, and from there into his grandfather's place. Photos taken from Kelly's own point of view, accompanied by the multi-layered story of the journey, heightened his audience's attention to the everyday details of his experience and helped them to discover his journey in much the same way as he had discovered it himself.

Kelly used a variety of techniques besides storytelling to engage his audience, most of which drew attention to the shared time and place of this particular performance. Audience members were handed programmes with an A5 photocopy of a puzzle stapled to each (see Fig. 5.3). No one that I could see wrote on the paper until Kelly invited us to, explaining that the puzzle was his grandfather's favourite and would provide an insight into his grandfather's mind. Kelly monitored our progress, offered hints, and eventually explained the answer.[14] Later in the performance, Kelly produced a bottle of Famous Grouse, his grandfather's favourite, and poured himself a drink. His grimace when tasting it underscored the difference between his grandfather's experience and Kelly's own. Then, near the end of the performance,

---

[13] A version of a short part of this section was originally published in Spence et al. 2012.

[14] Mr Kelly has requested that the puzzle be reproduced without its answer. Please contact the author for resolution.

Fig. 5.2 Kelly's photo of the lighthouse at Cape Wrath (Image © Alexander Kelly, used with permission)

Kelly stood up and gestured to the suit he was wearing. Ratcliffe had given it to the 19-year-old Kelly to wear in a play. At the time, Kelly said, he had needed to pad it out, but the extra padding was not required by the 40-something Kelly on stage. These physical elements are best understood alongside the digital rather than in contrast to them. The Famous Grouse that Kelly drank was not the same liquid that he or his grandfather had drunk on their journeys; the suit was the same, but the 19-year-old Kelly who first wore it was as absent as his deceased grandfather. The whisky, the suit, and the digital photographs all evoked ephemeral but powerful connections to Kelly's pasts and present as they co-existed on stage.

As in *Class of' 76*, Kelly was careful to acknowledge the fallibility of his memory. This heightened the audience's attention to the details of his stories, as Kelly made it clear that inconsistencies were possible. However, Kelly also shared with his audience a moment of self-discovery. While physically recreating his grandfather's journey, he realised that some parts of his grandfather's account were not true. For example, Ratcliffe had described getting a lift from a postman in a place where no roads exist. Kelly described the experience of consulting his mother, who was unable to resolve the conflict. With these acts of self-disclosure, Kelly invited his audience into an intimate connection with him and his family. His audience was now privy to the fact that his grandfather had harboured at least one secret. This position allowed audience members to join Kelly, his (deceased) grandfather, and

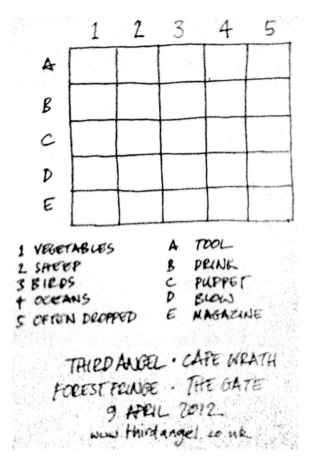

Fig. 5.3 Puzzle handed out at the beginning of *Cape Wrath* (2012) (© Alexander Kelly, used with permission)

his (absent) mother in the ethical process of negotiating competing claims to the 'truth' (Heddon 2008, p. 124).

The lies were not the only potentially uncomfortable self-disclosures of the performance. For example, Kelly forgot to pack either waterproof trousers or teabags, a situation that he found extremely distressing. He was forced to buy a pair of trousers, which were far too small for him, while fellow travellers at his hostel gave him several teabags. Then, when he arrived at Cape Wrath, he admitted to rushing around trying to see everything before remembering that his grandfather had simply sat at the edge of the cliff, thinking about his life. Kelly then tried to duplicate his grandfather's experience, but was so afraid of being blown over the edge of the cliff that he retreated to the teahouse. Only after he left did he realise that the couple running the teahouse were the same people who had served tea to his grandfather. The telling of embarrassing stories is common in conversation (Norrick 2000, p. 143), and therefore these anecdotes did not seem unusual or contrived. However, as

Fig. 5.4 The performance space for *Cape Wrath* (2013)

deeply personal admissions of thoughtlessness and regret, they made Kelly some-what vulnerable to his audience. By including embarrassing stories in his performance, Kelly helped establish a sense of intimacy with his audience.

Cape Wrath (2013)

For the Edinburgh Festival Fringe, *Cape Wrath* was rewritten and re-'staged' in a minibus parked outside of St. Stephen's church (see Fig. 5.4). Although this performance took place after my design process was complete, it reinforces many of the findings of the earlier version and presents a number of interesting variations. The small space amplified the physicality of Kelly's gestures, such as the pouring of the Famous Grouse: in fact, Kelly asked my husband to hold his glass while he poured a shot from a hip flask. Kelly further emphasised the close quarters by adding more physicality and participation to this version. For example, he moved around the van often, distributed full-size maps of Cape Wrath for his audience to use, instructed them how to refold the maps correctly, and passed around a bar of his grandfather's favourite chocolate to share. Every movement that Kelly or his audience made emphasised the audience's connections and responsibilities to each other and to the performer. Every gesture and shift of gaze was made more intense; every object was made more conspicuous; every deviation from the norms of theatrical performance (or of travelling on a minibus) was a surprise. In other words, the physicality of the performance functioned to heighten attention in all of the ways described by Fischer-Lichte (2008b) and explained in the discussion at the end of this chapter. The spoken content of the performance changed subtly, as well, to emphasise social connection. Kelly now named the people in his anecdotes and described the act of introducing himself to each one: 'She said her name was Sandy, and I said my name was Alex…. He said his name was Alan, and I said my name was Alex'. At the very end of the performance, Kelly said, 'That's us, then. I wonder if we could tell each other our names.' We all said our names in turn. Kelly replied, 'And my name is Alex'.

The 2013 version also abandoned all digital media displays. Kelly told me after the performance that until very late in the devising process, he had used a tiny projector inside the minibus, until he asked himself why he would invite people into a minibus and then treat them as if they were in a theatre. However, this lack of digital media during the performance does not 'disqualify' the 2013 performance of *Cape Wrath* as an intermedial performance. *Cape Wrath* would not have existed as a performance if not for Kelly's use of digital media from the outset, forcing him to think of his journey as a narrative as it unfolded. The effect of digital media technology on the creation of the show was also reflected in this version: Kelly explained again how he began his time at Cape Wrath rushing around, but this time he specified that he was rushing around trying to take a lot of photographs. He stopped when he realised that he was 'documenting the experience, but not having the experience'. I argue that in spite of the fact that digital media were not displayed during this performance, they were essential to Kelly's creative experience. Therefore, even this performance was intermedial, particularly in the perception of an audience member who is similarly steeped in personal digital media technology (Boenisch 2006), perhaps one who saw the story unfold on Twitter. *Cape Wrath* in all its incarnations uses performance to engage with 'a new cultural way of seeing, feeling and being in the contemporary world' (Nelson 2010, p. 18), especially as it contrasts with Kelly's grandfather's experience of simply sitting at the edge of a cliff and thinking about his life.

Step 3 Result: Properties of Autobiographical Performance

Cape Wrath was intermedial from its inception; the use of social media in its devising process made questions of 'the concrete effects of being definitively multiple and interrelational' (Nelson 2010, p. 17) central even to the version of the show that contained no digital media whatsoever. The overall feel of the performance was intimate and conversational, including the use of embarrassing anecdotes and quotidian snapshots. The images used in the 2012 version contributed to a sense of connection between Kelly and his audience as they could adopt his point of view to imagine themselves more fully into his journey. Ethical concerns about the fallibility of memory during devising led to a self-discovery that Kelly later disclosed to his audience. Physicality was key, not in an effort to reconstruct the past but rather to heighten attention to the shared time and space of the current moment of performance.

In combination with the analyses of the other three performances used for this case study, I arrived at a number of observations about what bound them together as a single style of performance as well as what helped to differentiate them from everyday conversational narrative. At first I attempted to sort them into the categories put forward by various current frameworks in the field, such as the 'five core elements' of performance (Chatzichristodoulou and Zerihan 2009, p. 2), Salter's performance epistemology (2010, p. xxiii), or Heddon's four key topics of autobiographical performance (2008). However, the findings did not sit neatly within any of these frameworks. This was particularly the case given my intention to apply the findings to the process of designing an interactive digital media sharing experience. I therefore developed my own framework that could drive the fourth step of the PED methodology in this case.

The properties of autobiographical performance, explained below, are intended to open the phenomenon of autobiographical performance to exploration by HCI researchers. They might also provide a fruitful means for performance researchers to approach autobiographical works that are not well described by other frameworks. The properties address the interactions between the performer and his or her audience members; between the performer and his or her digital media; between audience members and the performer's digital media; and among audience members. All of these relationships work together to constitute autobiographical performance.

Self-Making

The term 'self' is used with the understanding that self-making is a relational process never under the complete control of the performer (Butler 2002; McCarthy and Wright 2004, p. 106). A person engaging in autobiographical performance does not work with a unified and fixed 'self' as the 'text' of her work, but rather deals with any number of partial and shifting 'experiences of the self', called 'protoselves' (Barclay 1994, pp. 71–72). Moreover, these protoselves are formed in part by the act of creating performance (Kuhn 2007; Andres et al. 2010; Holland and Kensinger 2010). By looking at the idea of 'self' in this way, it becomes clear that the self is not simply revealed or even wholly consciously constructed for an audience. Instead, the process of creating a performance of the self involves creative and unpredictable encounters for both audience members and the performer.

Self-making is a constitutive element of autobiographical performance, where the performer also devises the performance, and where the performer's lived experience forms the material of the performance. The live presence of the performer is a necessary element of autobiographical performance, although as other performances demonstrate, the performer need not be on stage for every moment of the performance. The performer discloses selected elements of his or her experience and in at least some cases also undertakes a process of self-discovery, such as Kelly's realisation of the instability of his grandfather's story. This implicit, often hidden practice of devising in advance of the performance event is critical to autobiographical performance. This is not to say that improvised autobiographical performance would be impossible, but that it is not a key strategy in use in any of the performances I observed. Strategies for self-making range from decisions on the content of stories and the modes of performance (decided during devising), to techniques of interacting with the audience and the performer's style of speaking and moving.

Heightened Attention

Self-making takes place in every mundane interpersonal interaction. How a person speaks and moves, for example, creates an impression, or rather a variety of impressions, among different audience members. Moreover, the theoretical position informing PED asserts that performance is not a separate realm from everyday life (Dewey 2005; McCarthy and Wright 2004; Langellier and Peterson 2004; Fischer-Lichte 2008b). If performance and ordinary communication lie on a continuum, the first question is *how* the fundamentally quotidian practices of self-making can come to have so much emotional power in performance. The answer indicated by these analyses lies in the act of taking notice of the details of ordinary life. As Fischer-Lichte says, '[a]esthetic experience is not just created by exceptional events but also by perceiving the ordinary' (2008b, p. 179). Performance holds up the ordinary to attention 'and gives license to the audience to regard the act of expression and the performer with special intensity' (Bauman 1975, p. 293). Practices such as performing alongside an old photograph bring the details of both the photo and the live performer into focus. However, these practices on their own do not fully describe how autobiographical performance, which relies so heavily on the basic human act of telling stories about one's life experiences, is made special (Dissanayake 2003). To make sense of the different ways in which these performances are made 'special', I use Fischer-Lichte's three categories of 'heightened attention' (2008b, pp. 165–166). Her term refers to the processes by which performers move their audiences to invest their attention in the actions and interactions unfolding in front of them. These can result in 'an extraordinary state of permanently heightened attention' (2008b, p. 168) through which performance affects the emotions and attitudes of its audiences.

The first of Fischer-Lichte's categories is 'conspicuousness', which is the attention paid to objects (2008b, p. 166). Dewey refers to much the same process in his description of the functions of art:

> Art throws off the covers that hide the expressiveness of experienced things; it quickens us from the slackness of routine and enables us to forget ourselves by finding ourselves in the delight of experiencing the world about us in its varied qualities and forms. (2005, p. 108)

Bearing in mind that selectivity and context are two key approaches to designing technology for autobiographical memory and reminiscence, 'conspicuousness' becomes an intriguing lens through which to view performative interactions. While Fischer-Lichte denies a place for digital media in constituting the performance event (2008b, p. 100), I understand her objection to refer to fully mediatised or telematic performances that would remove human subjects from the stage. I argue instead, based on the analyses in this case study, that digital media or projections of analogue media are as much 'objects' in this sense as any physical prop. For example, the projected images in the 2012 version of *Cape Wrath* served to transport Kelly's audience into his own experiences and point of view as did the cumbersome maps and chocolate in the 2013 version staged in the minivan. These examples and others indicate not only that digital media can become conspicuous, but that they can do so in a way that contributes to the heightened attention of the live performance event.

The second category of 'heightened attention' is 'intensity of appearance', which refers to the attention paid to physically present performers (2008b, p. 165). Fischer-Lichte discusses 'intensity of appearance' in terms of three types of presence (2012). These involve distinctions that are not obviously applicable to a digital media sharing event, where exceptional acting talent is not to be expected. However, several of the practices observed in these performance analyses directly contributed to a heightened attention to the performer's physical presence, such as Kelly's repetition of the phrase, 'and my name is Alex'. I find this category useful for understanding techniques of heightening attention to a physically present performer, regardless of which type of presence he or she exemplifies.

Finally, the category of 'deviation and surprise' refers to attention paid to the structure of time in performance. Objects and people in performance are not static; the performance itself is an unfolding, multisensory, temporally bound event. For example, *Cape Wrath* (and all of the other performances analysed for this case study) comprised multiple stories, modes, and/or sections. Performers made no effort to tell a single, unified story. Each told a multiplicity of stories that built on each other over time. Even *Cape Wrath*'s overarching story of Kelly's travels to Scotland included a variety of anecdotes about the people he met along the way, as well as flashbacks to his own early years and family relationships. This observation is foundational to any proposed media-sharing experience: performance can incorporate many disparate narrative elements in any number of media. When Fischer-Lichte's three categories of heightened attention are modified to include digital or projected media and de-emphasise distinctions between types of presence, they provide a language for productively discussing the ways in which autobiographical material is made special (Dissanayake 2003) through performance.

Situatedness

Autobiographical performance attends to the shared time and space of performance as well as to the past experiences of the performer. There is no single method of doing so: while *Cape Wrath* had Kelly coaching his audiences through his grandfather's favourite puzzle, other performers used very different techniques. What was striking is that each of these performances (and many others not selected for analysis) paid such deliberate attention to the sharing of time, space, and to a certain extent experience between each unique audience and the performer of an autobiographical work. Site-specificity and site-responsiveness are important areas of interest in performance studies (see e.g. Pearson and Shanks 2001; Hill and Paris 2006), and within autobiographical performance, 'autotopography' provides a compelling theoretical lens (see e.g. Heddon 2002, 2008).[15] However, in three of the performances analysed in this chapter, the specific location was not the focus. Rather, the focus was on the spatiotemporal and perhaps personal connection between performer and audience members, wherever that connection happened to take place. In the midst of performing his or her own experience, the performer *noticed* the audience as a group of individuals. I use the term 'situatedness' to refer to this attention to the shared time and space of performance without calling undue attention to the particulars of a given location. This is not to say that such particulars might not be important: other analyses for this case study are peppered with unusual locations, such as Bobby Baker using her own kitchen as a performance space for *Kitchen Show* (1991), discussed in Chap. 3. When such particulars are used in performance, they can be explored as an element of 'situatedness'. However, it was the focus on the shared time and space of performance regardless of the unique location of the performance event that was surprising. It is also helpful regarding the purpose of these analyses to drive the design exploration for a digital media sharing system. As media technology becomes increasingly mobile and ubiquitous, the need to share media in a specific location might place an undue burden on groups who would enjoy or benefit from the sharing event (although of course the reverse could also be true, and specific locations could open a range of possibilities for media sharing—a potential area of future research). Attention to the people involved in a media sharing performance, rather than attention to the specifics of a unique location, would be likely to suit the affordances of existing personal digital media technology.

Aesthetics of the Event

Imagine an ordinary conversation between two friends in which one shares an anecdote about her experience. She has told this story before, which occasioned a self-discovery. She discloses this information in her retelling. She refers to a photo,

---

[15] The term is also used with a different meaning in HCI: see Petrelli et al. 2008.

makes her friend laugh at her figures of speech, and creates surprise with a sudden exclamation. In the middle of the story, she comments on the colour of her friend's shirt. This scenario fulfils all the themes above, yet none of them describe the emotional impact a performance can have on an audience member.

Bauman (1992) offers the possibility of identifying 'cultural performances' by the institutional framework in which they are set. Cultural performances are 'scheduled', 'temporally' and 'spatially bounded', 'programmed ... with a structured scenario or program of activity', open to the public, and 'heightened' by virtue of the fact that they represent the pinnacle of aesthetic accomplishment available within the community (1992, p. 46). The end result of these conditions is an event that is 'available for the enhancement of experience through the present enjoyment of the intrinsic qualities of the performative display' (1992, p. 46). I argue that Bauman's observations about institutional conditions for performance, while useful for pointing towards those events that a culture would deem to be 'performance', do not begin to describe the 'enhancement of experience' that he identifies. Especially from the perspective of HCI and experience design, where moving and compelling experiences with technology are developed outside of any performance frameworks, institutional markers of 'cultural performances' cannot be required for the creation of the emotional experience of watching or performing in the 'enhancement of experience' known as performance. It may be difficult to imagine why people would devote an hour of their time to Alex Kelly or other autobiographical performers without the infrastructure that Bauman refers to, but this case study is set up to explore what would happen if they did: whether something of performance can be created in the absence of most or all of Bauman's conditions. In other words, I believe that everyday conversational interaction can use strategies of performance to enhance experience, or in Walter Benjamin's terms, 'achieve an amplitude' of experience (2006, p. 366), that expands the boundaries of the quotidian. Again, I turned to Fischer-Lichte (2008b) for a starting point from which to explore what made the autobiographical performances I analysed anything more memorable than a series of informational anecdotes about a complete stranger. Fischer-Lichte's relevant topic is the 'aesthetics of the event', which has three categories: 'collapsing dichotomies'; 'liminality and transformation'; and 'autopoiesis and emergence' (2008b, p. 163).

Fischer-Lichte (2008b) identifies different types of 'collapsing dichotomies' in performance, particularly performances outside of mainstream theatre since the 1960s. Many of these erase the borderlines between politics and the aesthetic, or the social and the aesthetic (an observation also made in Heddon 2008, p. 23). Most important for autobiographical performance, and in line with Heddon's key topic, is the collapse of the dichotomy between the social and the aesthetic, which leads to the negotiation of an ethical relationship between performer and audience member, and at times among audience members (see also Heddon 2008). This can be seen in Kelly's efforts to deal transparently with the contradictions that he discovered between his grandfather's journey and the stories he told to his family about it. The collapse of dichotomies further underscores the notion that what makes a performance 'aesthetic' or extraordinary cannot be found by placing it in opposition to social interaction, but by exploring the points at which they converge.

'Autopoiesis and emergence' are key to Fischer-Lichte's argument (2008b) that performance cannot be compared to any art object. For her, the aesthetics of performance must lie wholly within the self-perpetuating and unfolding event, without ignoring the human and non-human materials that make the event possible. Autopoiesis and emergence do not seem to occupy a privileged space within autobiographical performance, yet they are fundamental to all performance. Most importantly, autopoiesis and emergence indicate that performance incorporates all of the events that take place within the audience's (and performers') perception, not only those elements that have been scripted in advance. This includes such dramatic events as a spotlight crashing onto the stage (2008b, p. 165), or the struggle to fold a large map in a small minivan in *Cape Wrath* (2013).

As explained in Chap. 3, the category of this framework that best describes the potentially powerful experience of performance is Fischer-Lichte's 'liminality and transformation' (2008b, pp. 174–180), as modified by Bauman's 'special intensity' (1975, p. 293) and Dissanayake's 'making special' (2003). The findings of these analyses indicate that 'liminality and transformation' can describe the aim or highest aspiration of autobiographical performance. I do not intend to imply a conscious intent on the part of the performers, or to claim that liminality correlates to 'success'. Rather, I see in these performances that all the other themes—self-making, all three types of 'heightened attention', situatedness, 'collapsing dichotomies', and 'autopoiesis and emergence'—can result directly or indirectly in a liminal state in which the audience member is temporarily transformed by emotional insight and a sense of connection with the performer. The potential for 'liminality and transformation' came about at moments of empathy, intimacy, or connection, such as Kelly's gently voiced regret over forgetting to ask the Cape Wrath tea shop owners about his grandfather.

These, then, are the four properties of autobiographical performance as revealed through the performance analyses conducted for this case study: self-making, heightened awareness (composed of 'conspicuousness', 'intensity of appearance', and 'deviation and surprise'), situatedness, and the 'aesthetics of the event' (composed of 'collapsing dichotomies', 'autopoiesis and emergence', and 'liminality and transformation'). The ones most closely connected to everyday experience—self-making and situatedness—are named and described based solely on these analyses, as contextualised by the relevant performance literature. Those properties that distinguish everyday experience from a more 'cultural' or 'intense' performance (Wilson 2006, p. 9) are identified using Fischer-Lichte's frameworks as a way into discussion. All four properties will form the starting point for the design process described in the rest of this chapter. The designs created through that process aim to create mechanisms or opportunities for users to engage with the properties of autobiographical performance.

Three of the four performances that I analysed used projected photos in various ways, while the fourth referred to a childhood photo without showing it. Therefore the concept of representing one's life experiences through media was a common thread, but also the heart of my line of enquiry and a necessary element of any future technological design for co-located media sharing. I therefore approached the use of photos in performance not as a property of autobiographical performance but as a technique or perspective for intertwining the mediated with the live in performance. I use intermediality as a lens through which to understand a performer's use of or reference to personal media, whether analogue or digital, because intermedial research approaches technology as part of a fabric of 'relationships, necessary inter-dependencies, and mutually co-relating entities' that create 'a new cultural way of seeing, feeling and being in the contemporary world' (Nelson 2010, pp. 17–18). This approach is generative and forward-looking, suiting analyses that will inform exploratory experience designs. From an HCI perspective, the technology would automatically be the prime area of interest, whereas these analyses allowed for an exploration of how media are integrated, perhaps even subsumed, into the broader concern of developing a performance. The four properties presented here have addressed these explorations; they do not require the addition of a separate category dedicated to the technology *per se*. These four properties name the concerns in current autobiographical performance practice, while the perspective of intermediality indicates the intention of PED to move 'beyond the tired dichotomies of digital versus analog, real versus virtual, or networked versus local' (Salter 2010, pp. xxxiii–xxiv) to approach an identity-forming, intensified, situated, ethical, and potentially transformational encounter between performers and audiences.

Step 4: Design Exploration

Mapping the Space

HCI and performance studies came together through the five categories of elements that fed my design process: the performative participations, content, and scenarios of use identified in Step 1, alongside the memorable or inspirational elements of the performances viewed in Step 2 and the insights gained from the performance analyses in Step 3. Important issues and influences, such as the theories of Butler, Bauman, Fischer-Lichte, Fällman, the Bardzells, and Dewey, were represented in these elements. For example, I maintained a focus on what Bauman identifies as the 'special intensity' with which the audience regards the performer (1975, p. 293) through instances of 'scenarios of use' such as a best man's speech where the participant would feel strongly pressured to acquit himself well. The process began with an ideation stage that resulted in a design workbook and a mapping of the design space of intermedial autobiographical performance. Each design concept demonstrated a possible route for lay audiences to perform stories of their life experiences through their personal digital media, but none engaged sufficiently with the most powerful extra-conversational elements of performance. In terms of the PED space (see Fig. 1.3), the initial designs were either too far in the top right quadrant to allow for private reflection, or too far along the left axis to offer a sufficiently complex experience. A second round of ideation resulted in a number of break-throughs in these respects, but its proposed system proved impractical. In the end, the least technologically exciting option held the most promise, because it allowed participants to engage with their digital media on their own terms, reflecting and challenging their individual habits of capture, storage, viewing, and sharing as part of a two-phase performance experience. This chapter ends with a detailed description of the prototype, titled *Collect Yourselves!*, and a discussion of the design goals that it aimed to achieve.

With the performance analyses fresh in my mind, it was difficult at first to imagine how the properties of autobiographical performance could inspire anything besides another performance, which would run the risk of sidestepping HCI altogether. In order to apply performance properties to an interaction that was not a mainly 'cultural performance' (Wilson 2006, p. 9), I began by considering those analyses in relation to a number of elements, categorised as explained in Chap. 4: (A) performative participations, (B) content, (C) scenarios of use, (D) performance elements, and (E) insights from findings. 'Performative participations' (A) were drawn from HCI research on media sharing, conversation, and related literatures on narrative. I looked individually at reminiscing, storytelling, and a mixture of the two (see e.g. Figure 3.5 in Frohlich 2004, p. 44). The 'content' category (B) was made up of the different media streams that might reflect an individual's personal life: photo, video, audio, text, GPS, and 'other' (because at this stage I had not ruled out biometric data visualisations). 'Scenarios of use' (C) was a long list of possible scenarios in which groups of people, known to each other or not, might come together to share digital media. Examples include alumni reunions, birthday celebrations, family holidays, mountain rescue teams discussing a just-completed mission, speeches made at a retirement party, conversations among walking/rambling club members on a hike, funerals, and weddings. 'Performance elements' (D) came from any and all of the performances I watched in Step 2. I allowed myself to use any image, recollection, or broader concept that sprang to mind when thinking of the performance, such as the deliberate trickery of Haley Newman's *Connotations—Performance Images 1994–1998*, the casting of Marina Abramović as her own mother in the performance of stories from her childhood (in *The Life and Death of Marina Abramović*), the conscientious search for a mutually agreeable 'truth' in *Class of '76*, and Mike Pearson's negotiation of spontaneous audience contributions in *Bubbling Tom*. The fifth and largest category, 'insights from findings, (E)' was a list of individual insights, practices, or questions raised by the performances and their analyses. (In this case study, categories D and E were not as clearly demarcated as they became after refinements to the methodology.) I wrote each of these items on cards, divided the cards into these categories, and drew a card from each category at random to start generating ideas (see Fig. 5.5).

I repeated the card-mixing exercise many dozens of times over the course of 7 months and pursued a significant percentage of those into notes and sketches of potential ideas. A few of the combinations were self-contradictory or unworkable, but most could be pursued at least some way towards a viable design, and it was from the repeated ideas and the outliers that a sense of the design space began to

Fig. 5.5 A sample combination of cards used in the initial design process. 'Here and now' refers to 'situatedness'

take shape. The most promising design ideas were subjected to regular design critiques from researchers in both interaction and experience design and performance studies. As described in Chap. 4, individuals from these two disciplines had some trouble at times understanding the tacit knowledge and unspoken assumptions embedded in each other's responses. However, with a background in both fields, I was able to parse their meanings and was often taken aback at how they would arrive at similar criticisms from entirely different starting points. When they disagreed with each other, they were kind enough to explain their reasoning so that I was able to evaluate for myself (rightly or wrongly) what the knock-on effects of their proposed changes would be in relation to their stated aims. Ultimately, we were all aiming to design a particular kind of experience for participants: whether this was framed as experience design or performance mattered less than each individual's capacity for imagination and critical thought, which was prodigious.

Eventually I selected one dozen designs that best indicated the scope of the design space of intermedial autobiographical performance for inclusion in a design workbook, which kept track of the categories of design elements (A–E) that sparked each concept. The designs ranged from subtle and passive to interactionally complex. For example, Echo is fundamentally a photo display system that extrapolates the predominant colours and shapes from several consecutive photos and presents these as a shifting, suggestive backdrop for storytelling (Fig. 5.6). Making History, on the other hand, is a dynamic game for groups of friends who are asked to remember specific photos in as much detail as possible and challenge each other over dubious recollections (Fig. 5.6). Rain Down reveals photos as though they are rained

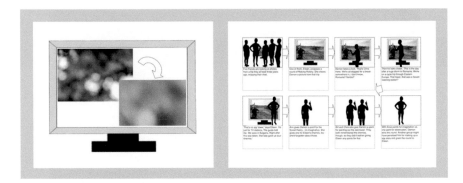

Fig. 5.6 Concept images for Echo and Making History

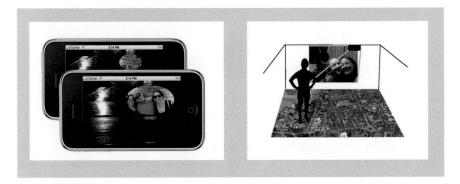

Fig. 5.7 Concept images for Rain Down and Map Mat

onto the screen one drop at a time, creating ambiguity and stretching the time it takes to recognise content, while Map Mat and Map Mat Plus place individuals or groups in an immersive environment, displaying up to five different views of the location in which a photo was taken to support reminiscence (Fig. 5.7). Tracing the Experience is an embodied interface that uses gestures to annotate and browse for photos, while Story Slider matches metadata on time and location of capture to create an interface that reflects the time that passes between the capture of each image: a slower journey between two photos is made evident by a slow transition between those photos on the slider (Fig. 5.8). In terms of the PED space (Fig. 1.3), the more visually captivating workbook designs occupied the lower left quadrant (Echo, Story Slider) and the upper left quadrant of the diagram (Rain Down, Tracing the Experience, Map Mat), while the designs that held the most promise for media sharing occupied the upper right quadrant (Making History and several others).

Together, these and six similar designs formed the outlines of the previously uncharted design space (Wolf et al. 2006, p. 526; Fällman 2003, p. 229) for intermedial autobiographical performance. Gaver uses the metaphor of the design space for its ability to 'affect designers' perceptions of possibility' (2011, p. 1554). The design possibilities for intermedial autobiographical performance at first seemed

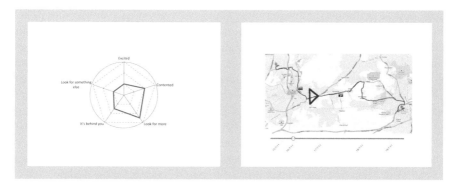

Fig. 5.8 Concept images for Tracing the Experience and Story Slider

endless, and would no doubt have been different had I selected different performances to analyse. However, the reliance on the particulars of the specific performances I selected in Step 2 and analysed in Step 3 is very much in line with the nature of design to attend to 'the unique, the particular, or even the *ultimate particular*' (Stolterman 2008, p. 59, emphasis in the original), and of 'each design research activity [to have] its own purpose and intended outcome' (Fällman and Stolterman 2010, p. 268). The design space I describe here is not an irrefutable or universally generalisable 'territory' (Gaver 2011, p. 1554), but an indicative mapping that can prove useful in further research.

The design space charted by the design workbook highlighted the following issues: the relationship between performers and audience members; the relationships among audience members; time spent dwelling with one's personal digital media; tolerance or active encouragement of ambiguous or conflicting memories; display mechanisms that allow for viewing over extended periods of time; rules or guidelines beyond the technological interface that govern interaction; making the ordinary 'strange'; engagement with a small selection of media items; metadata as a selection tool; the promotion of storytelling, reminiscence, or conversation; the use of imagination as well as memory; juxtaposition of the real with the imaginary; textual prompts to trigger memory or reaction; transparent, responsive technology; embodied interaction; dynamic attention to co-located others; the primacy of present-moment decisions and interactions. Rather than elaborating on each in turn, I will point out the gap within this space that the initial designs did not fill. Most interpreted 'performance' loosely, aligning more with the performativity of self-representation than a sustained engagement with performance practice. Most notably, none of them substantially addressed how to generate 'liminality and transformation' among their users.

The workbook designs also raised the question of how to motivate non-professionals to engage in performance practices. Mechanisms for engagement on the part of the performer are not addressed in the performance analyses simply because professional performers do not tend to expose their motivations to perform. One easy solution would have been to avoid the issue entirely and design only for professional performers. However, that would have raised an even thornier issue. Put in Kolko's terms (2010), if I were to combine insights from the gathered data on autobiographical performance with design patterns from autobiographical performance, I would be inserting design into an otherwise robust artistic process. As one goal of this research is to investigate theories and practices of autobiographical performance to understand synchronous, co-located digital media sharing, the target user group must be those whose digital media sharing would otherwise lack an overtly performative engagement: in other words, non-professional users. By the same token, an HCI-driven approach to intermedial autobiographical performance should not require professional performers to use it, as if it were merely a product to be tested. Therefore, motivation became a central concern for the design.

The most promising idea to emerge from the initial stage of the design process was the use of questions or prompts, seen in Tracing the Experience. The term 'prompt' is used to describe one of the ways in which Heddon contributed to Alex Kelly's devising process for *The Lad Lit Project* (2005), the second in Kelly's autobiographical trilogy that ended with *Cape Wrath*. Heddon and Kelly explain that Heddon's 'questions were clearly aimed at prompting Alex [Kelly] to look from other directions; Dee [Heddon] was seeking his blind spots' (Heddon and Kelly 2010, p. 219).[16] Tracing the Experience prompted users to engage with their memories and imaginations in specific ways while looking back on their photos, and this engagement with memory and imagination seemed like a possible way to generate liminality and transformation in performance. However, while the idea of prompting seemed sound, Tracing the Experience was not fully embedded in a durational performance event. Therefore, I embarked on a new design that would give participants the time and focus to engage fully with a period of imaginative reminiscing and reflecting, and later with a period of intensive interpersonal performance.

The streamlined description of the PED methodology in Chap. 4 offers a vision of the simplest possible version of events: line of enquiry leads to performances to be analysed, the results of which lead to a design exploration, from which the strongest candidate is prototyped, used, and analysed. In this case study, the design exploration was lengthier and more complex than the methodology intends. Tracing the Experience was nowhere near sufficient for the type of experience that I was aiming to create, so I took the promising idea of prompts and developed that into an entirely different design concept that I fully intended to prototype. The result was the Reunion Suitcase Game, a 'game/performance/experience' that provides a structure for people at a reunion to combine elements of their fragmented online and offline identities in a performance for their co-present friends and family. It is envisioned as an online service that extracts selections of a person's Facebook timeline, Twitter stream, Flickr account, locally stored photo collection, audio, video, blog or forum posts, comments, game characters, leaderboards, etc. Participants interact with the service in three distinct phases. In the first phase, before the reunion, participants are prompted to select and arrange six of the online items retrieved by the system. In the second phase, during the reunion, their audience draws ten cards with further questions to help shape the performance. This phase is not unlike a group

---

[16] Professor Heddon publishes under the names Dee and Deirdre.

devising process. In the third and final phase, participants perform their stories for each other. These performances are both recorded and scored. Participants gain points for incorporating the questions from phase two; audience members (who will also likely take a turn performing) gain points for contributing helpfully to the performer's story.

The Reunion Suitcase Game is a step change forward from the workbook concepts through its use of prompts in a separate devising phase. Without an opportunity to plan the upcoming performance, performers must improvise whatever they say and do, and extra-conversational improvisation is a set of skills that must be learned (Johnstone 1999). Short of forcing all participants to become adept at improvisational theatre, there would be little latitude for incorporating inspirations from professional performance. A design without a devising phase would be analogous to attempting to fully re-inhabit the past (telling a personal story triggered by a personal media artefact) without attending carefully to the present-day activities of remembering, re-judging, and perhaps coming to very different conclusions from those held at the time the media artefact was captured. The risk for the Reunion Suitcase Game was that too many game mechanics or an emphasis on winning might detract from the 'heightened attention' or 'aesthetics of the event' that the design process aimed to incorporate. This concern seems to have been well founded, as Misha Myers et al. (2014) reported an inversely proportional relationship between an emphasis on winning a board game called *Bumper Crop* and a sense of empathy for the people represented in the game. Finally, the Reunion Suitcase Game recognises that personal digital media are not simply artefacts or memory triggers but integral elements of the performer's sense of self—and sometimes integral to the shared sense of identity of a group of friends or family members. However, it proved unworkable for practical reasons. A working prototype would need to be much simpler and more elegant, ideally web-based, while maintaining the ideas of a prompt-driven devising phase, game-like motivations and structures, and immersion in the routinely intermedial. Therefore, the design was changed significantly one more time before it could be prototyped.

Collect Yourselves!

The design process concluded with the design and prototyping of *Collect Yourselves!*, a browser-based application for small groups to use in creating autobiographical performances with and for each other. It consists of two stages: devising and performing. Its participants do not need experience in theatrical performance; the application guides their interaction beyond everyday conversation and into the 'risky and dangerous' encounter of 'performing narrative' (Langellier and Peterson 2004, p. 3). In some instances, the participants are strangers to each other, while other instances are designed as social events or reunions among friends. In all cases, participants know in advance which context they will be performing in, and if performing among friends, exactly who will be present.

In the first phase, 'devising', individual participants log onto a website that offers instructions and a drag-and-drop mechanism for uploading digital photographs. Participants engage with their personal digital media archives guided by a series of carefully worded prompts. They upload one or more photographs in response to each prompt; one prompt gives the option of uploading no image at all. (Other media types were welcome in principle, but only the mechanisms for uploading and displaying photos were developed for the initial iteration.) Participants can also include text associated with a prompt, if they choose, as a reminder or scaffold for what they intend to say or do. The photos are stored along with information on the participant, the prompt with which the photo should be associated, and any text. Participants can spend as much or as little time in this part of the process as they wish.

A key differentiator between previous media sharing devices and *Collect Yourselves!* is this devising phase. *Collect Yourselves!* involves participants in the moment of performance, as *Rider Spoke* did when asking participants to deposit their stories in secret city spaces, or when 4Photos dinner party guests found their Facebook photos displayed on the centrepiece, or when the audience for Humanaquarium found themselves altering an unfolding performance by touching the 'aquarium'. Unlike those examples, though, *Collect Yourselves!* engages participants in the process of deciding the form and content of their performance, long before the performance itself takes place. Participants can reflect on any self-discoveries and shape their own self-disclosures, under the guidance of the prompts and the affordances of the system. This engagement in the devising process creates a technologically mediated encounter that is not constrained to impromptu responses demanded in the immediate moment of performance. In this, *Collect Yourselves!* goes beyond the performativity of offhand reactions and closer to the full potential of performance.

In the second phase, 'performance', five to seven participants come together in the same physical location to perform the stories behind their photos for each other. The photos are projected against a wall within the performance space. There is an interface to control the projection, of course. At least as important, though, is the performance experience as seen from multiple perspectives: performers engaged with their stories, photos, memories, and audiences; and audience members, who have no contact with the interface until it is their turn to perform. Therefore, the entire process of creating a *Collect Yourselves!* performance was mapped from four perspectives: the performer, the interface, the audience members, and the 'path' through the stories in the event as a whole (Fig. 5.9).

In the 'performance' phase, *Collect Yourselves!* makes minimal use of rules, which are largely implicit and conventional. Participants cannot respond to more than one prompt consecutively, and they cannot return to a prompt once they have finished with it. There is a time limit set for the entire group to perform the stories behind their prompts (40 min for five people, 45 min for seven), but each individual can decide for herself how long to spend on any prompt, and can select prompts in any order. The group is free to determine how their shared performance will unfold, employing what Gaver et al. refer to as 'ambiguity of context' (2003, pp. 236–237). The ambiguity of the system does not reside in the technology itself but in what

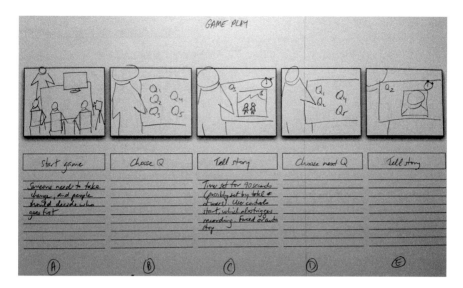

Fig. 5.9 Sample sketch of multiple elements and perspectives on the system in use

assumptions and preferences different participants bring to it. As Gaver et al. note, tactical ambiguity is more common in art than in product design (2003, p. 236); this is one more gentle way in which *Collect Yourselves!* aims to nudge its users towards performance.

Performers must stand towards the front of the room, near their projected image. However, a performer can position herself to draw attention to her own physicality and performance techniques, or she can allow the projected image to capture most of the audience's attention. In either case, *Collect Yourselves!* can be interpreted according to Salter's extension of Myron Krueger's *'responsive environments'*, which 'challeng[e] purely screen-based interaction that denied the existence of the participant's body' (2010, p. xxxix). Furthermore, individual turns can include only one photo, multiple photos, or none at all, depending on the prompt. Exchanges between individual performers can be marked by lengthy conversation or brisk silence, or anything in between. A large timer projected alongside the performer's photos counts down the time the participants spend performing.

Building the Prototype

Collect Yourselves! uses HTML5, JavaScript, CSS, PHP, MySQL, and Ajax in a simple configuration based on the two phases of interaction (see Fig. 5.10). The devising phase consists of a registration screen, where participants can select a username and password. Once registered, they see the instructions for this phase and links to the five prompts (Fig. 5.11). These instructions were written with the research context in mind; the system is not set up for public use. Clicking on a

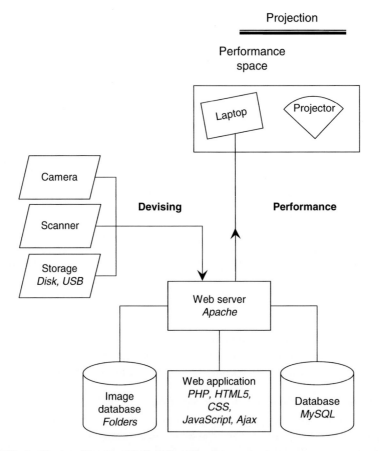

Fig. 5.10 Architecture diagram of *Collect Yourselves!*

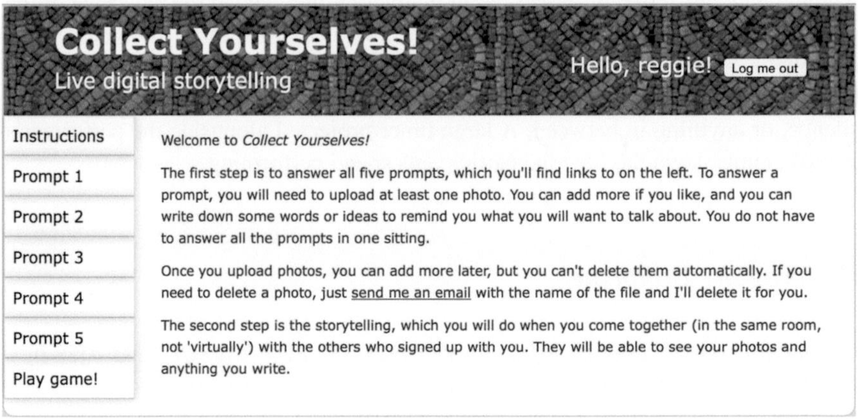

Fig. 5.11 Introductory screen for the devising phase

Fig. 5.12 Prompt 1

prompt leads to a page onto which participants can drag and drop as many photos as they like (Fig. 5.12). They are also invited, though not required, to upload text accompanying any prompt. One prompt, number five, gives them the option of uploading nothing and instead deleting their selected photo from their archives. The application is hosted online. All registration information, images, and text are uploaded into databases for later use in the performance phase.

The performance phase of the application cannot be accessed until all members of the group are present. Each must enter his or her username and password on the same iPad to access the performance interface (referred to as 'Play game!' in Fig. 5.11). Each implementation of *Collect Yourselves!* is hosted from a separate page with its own image database, which makes it easy to manage changes and to preserve participant privacy. When all participants log in on the iPad, the performance is ready to commence. The performance phase can be run online using the hosting service that handles the uploads in the devising phase. However, this places the performance phase at the mercy of the local internet connection. To minimise the risk of any interruption to this connection, a local copy of the application, databases, and image collection was made, and each performance was run on a web server hosted on a standalone computer with a local network. *Collect Yourselves!* was designed to be controlled by an iPad using a local Wi-Fi access point supplied

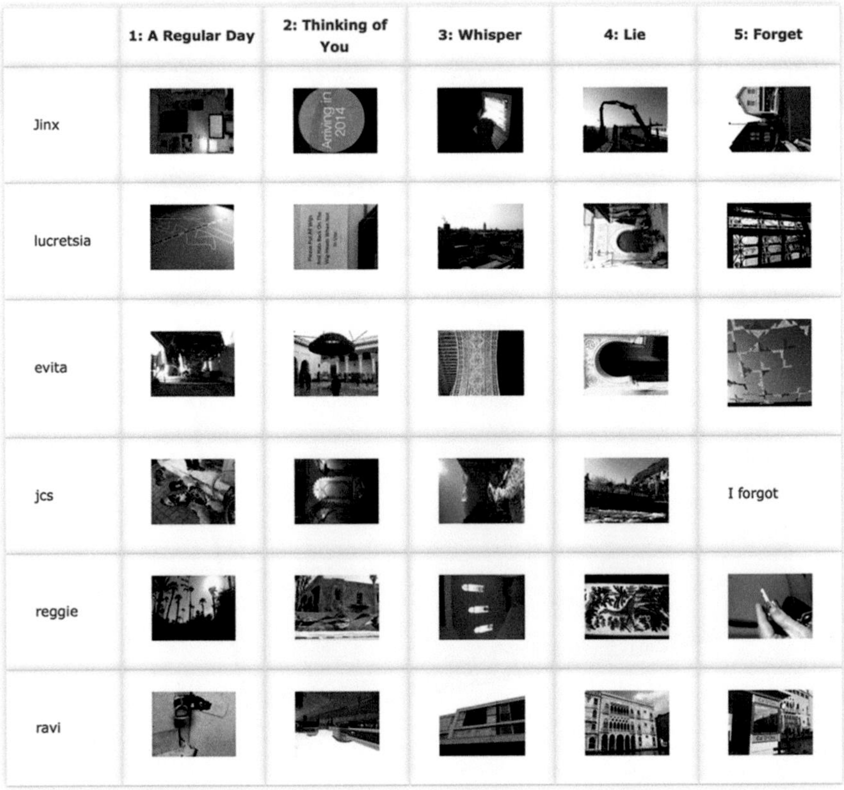

	1: A Regular Day	2: Thinking of You	3: Whisper	4: Lie	5: Forget
Jinx					
lucretsia					
evita					
jcs					I forgot
reggie					
ravi					

Fig. 5.13 Performance grid. The first column is for user names (sample data shown)

by this standalone computer, but the application can be run by any internet-connected computer.

When the performers log in, they see the main 'grid' screen on their controlling device and simultaneously projected onto the wall in front of the audience. This screen displays basic instructions above a grid of image thumbnails (Fig. 5.13). The grid is five columns wide, one for each prompt, and five to seven rows long, depending on the number of participants. Each square in the grid is a thumbnail of the first image uploaded by each person for each prompt. Participants decide among themselves who will go first. That person stands at the front of the space and clicks the thumbnail of the prompt they wish to begin with. Clicking the thumbnail starts the timer countdown and displays all the photos uploaded by that participant for that prompt (Fig. 5.14). Clicking an image enlarges it to full size (Fig. 5.15). The performer can switch among photos freely. It is worth noting that even the simple technological intervention of projecting an image in live performance is 'relatively unexplored', according to Salter (2010, p. 366). Clicking 'Finish turn' pauses the countdown timer and returns the application to the grid view. The prompt that this performer has just responded to is now blank, which prevents a performer from

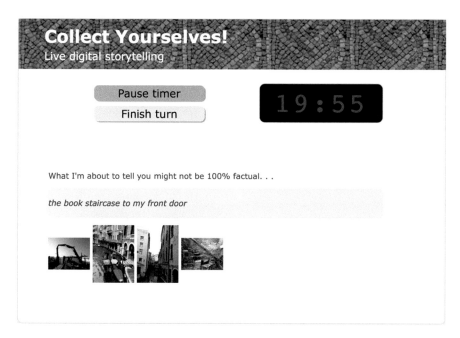

Fig. 5.14 Individual 'story' screen

returning to a prompt she has already performed. Participants decide amongst themselves who will perform next. That performer comes to the front and chooses from any of her remaining prompts; there is no need to go in order. Clicking that thumbnail re-starts the timer from where it had paused and displays that performer's photos for the prompt she has selected. The performance continues until the timer runs out or all prompts have been answered and the grid is completely blank; the aim is to get through all the stories in that time.

Prompts

The most important element of the *Collect Yourselves!* design was the least technical: the wording of the prompts, which pointed people towards specific and somewhat unusual means of engaging with their personal digital media. By engaging people in an active process of selecting particular media in the context of an upcoming performance event, the prompts created an intermedial devising process. The rationale was inspired in part by Kaprow's notion of attention:

> I scratch itches without noticing ... and now that I intentionally notice that I [scratch itches in public], the whole action looms large. It's a little strange, and my conversation about politics loses interest as itching and scratching shine brighter. In other words, attention alters what is attended. Playing with everyday life often is just paying attention to what is conventionally hidden. (2007, p. 161)

What I'm about to tell you might not be 100% factual. . .

the book staircase to my front door

Fig. 5.15 Story screen with photo expanded

The strategy behind the crafting of the prompts was to nudge participants towards a deeper process of introspection than is offered by existing media sharing technologies, such as the unguided process of sharing 'often informal and transitory' images of one's day (Van House 2009, p. 1081) or the 'considered, purposeful'—and, I would argue, unchallenged—representation of the self online (Van House 2011, p. 131). In *Collect Yourselves!*, the devising process is the primary guide to the choice of media, rather than the affordances of the technology at hand.

Prompt 1: A regular day
Where were you 6 months ago today at 2:05 p.m.? (If 2:05 p.m. 6 months ago was just a normal day and you can't remember anything in particular about it, try to imagine what it must have been like in as much detail as you can.) Find the photograph that is closest in time to that point. Describe the difference between your life in that picture and your life today. If you like, find some other photos that help make your point, too.

This prompt aimed to take participants farther back in time than online photo sharing sites tend to afford: Facebook is organised to display most recent posts first, including photos, and Van House found that half of Flickr photo views occur in the first two days an image is posted (2009, p. 1075). It also randomised the choice of photos to a certain extent, as the one closest in time to 6 months ago might be one that the participant would never choose to share, possibly because it is as forgettable as some of the snapshots in *Cape Wrath* (2012). However, the choice is always left to the discretion of the participant. Because photos are not selected automatically from a publicly accessible source, participants can always ignore the image that would technically respond best to the prompt and opt for an alternate.

> Prompt 2A (for Friend Groups): I was just thinking about you
> Think back over the time since you've all seen each other last. Try to remember a moment during this time when you thought about one of your friends (one who is part of the group that's having the reunion). Do you remember where you were, what you were doing, or what happened to make you remember your friend? Find the photo that most closely represents that moment or situation for you, and get ready to tell the story. (It's OK if the connection to the photo is loose or odd.) If you have any additional pictures that help you make your point, drop them, too.

This prompt specifically allows for groups who know each other to engage in at least a limited amount of reminiscence, where audience members might contribute to the story being told by virtue of the fact that they might recall or feel a stake in the content of the photo being shared. The prompt for Friend Groups asks participants to probe their memories rather than their archives to think of a time when one of their co-present friends came to mind. By finding a photo and story associated with this memory, participants in the devising phase reminisce about their own experience in the context of the friends they will be performing with. As one of their friends will be the subject of that memory, photo, and/or story, the live performance will create an opportunity for reminiscence among some or all of the group. At the same time, the story will maintain a fundamentally 'storytelling' structure by which the performer relates a story that only she can know, i.e., the moment when a thought of her friend crossed her mind. The intention with this prompt is to encourage reminiscence without allowing the story to collapse entirely into overlapping turns of 'collaborative question-answering' (Frohlich 2004, p. 145).

> Prompt 2B (Stranger Groups): Memorable?
> Think of the most memorable photo in your digital archive. Picture it in your mind's eye in as much detail as you can. Can you remember the photo taken immediately before it? Or the one immediately after? Find and upload all three photos and be ready to tell their stories. Be sure to write down what you were able to remember.

As with the second prompt for Friend Groups, this prompt asks participants to probe their memories before consulting their archives. Groups of strangers cannot reflect on existing relationships with each other, so this prompt asks participants to reflect on relationships among their photos. It also invites participants to spend time dwelling on their memories of these images in detail rather than picking the first photo that fulfils the prompt's criteria.

> Prompt 3: Whisper
> Find a picture of you or taken by you that isn't on any social networking site. One that you're maybe even a little bit embarrassed about. You will explain it to your friends at the reunion – in a whisper. If you have any other pictures that help your story, drop them, too.

This prompt encourages participants to disclose something embarrassing about themselves that may disturb the 'carefully curated' representation of self (Van House 2011, p. 131), or what one participant refers to as making 'another me, because I just portray … the highlights' (Conor, Stranger Group 2). This prompt was inspired by the embarrassing or even disturbing stories in all four performances analysed in Chap. 4. Again, *Collect Yourselves!* does not threaten the participant's control over her own performance. An 'embarrassing' story can be as mild or as extreme as the participant wishes. The requirement to avoid photos that have been shared on a social networking site is another effort to nudge people towards a more thoughtful and exploratory interaction with their archives in the hopes that they will surprise themselves with a fresh insight or a new meaning for an older photo (Van House 2009, p. 1082) whose meaning has not been fixed by its reception by others on a social networking site.

Prompt 4: Lie
Find a picture that you would like to show. Invent a story behind the picture. Exaggerate, embellish, or outright lie. Your goal will be to make everyone playing the game laugh out loud at least once during this turn.

Although memory and imagination are imbricated in personal storytelling, most of the prompts focus on accuracy or detail of memory. This prompt aims to emphasise imagination and explore the blurred boundaries between fact and fiction suggested by many works of autobiographical performance (Heddon 2008). Because each story must be tethered in some way to the participant's personal photo, there will be some element of 'truth' in it, which the participant can embellish or subvert as she chooses. The goal of provoking laughter is intended to make the instruction to 'lie' somewhat less threatening to participants while providing them with a socially acceptable motivation for engaging fully with the prompt.

Prompt 5: Forget
Find a picture you had forgotten all about. Try to remember what was going through your mind at the time it was taken. Now either keep it, upload it, and use your turn to describe why it's important enough to keep – or delete it completely from all your devices and backups, upload nothing, and use your turn to describe what it looked like. Drag and drop your picture here – or not. If you don't upload your picture, be sure to write a few words.

Kelly's decision to forego the projector in *Cape Wrath* (2013) inspired this prompt, as did the observation that the serendipitous discovery of forgotten photographs tends to be a very pleasurable experience (Petrelli et al. 2008, p. 58; Peesapati et al. 2010; Van House 2011, p. 130; Cosley et al. 2012; Frohlich et al. 2013). Participants are motivated to engage fully with this prompt because of the stakes: they are being asked to consider permanently deleting an element of their personal digital archive, purely for the sake of performance. While they have full control over whether to do so, and indeed whether to lie about their choice, they must still envision the effects of this small transformation.

The nomenclature for *Collect Yourselves!* posed a problem throughout the design exploration, as a balance had to be struck in guiding participants towards thinking in terms of 'game', 'performance', or 'story'. References such as 'storytelling', 'play game!', and 'perform your stories' are not a sign of inconsistency but rather an attempt to draw on commonly held expectations of what a game, performance, and story will demand of their participants where appropriate. Telling people to 'perform' without providing specific mechanics for how to do so ran the risk of creating expectations of overt theatricality and play-acting, and these might have created the exact opposite of the personal, meaningful, liminal experience of contemporary autobiographical performance. Instead we balanced the idea of performance against 'play' as defined by Roger Caillois, a 'free and voluntary activity' (2006, p. 125), situated in a particular time and place, full of 'the possibility of error or surprise' (2006, p. 126), where 'fiction…replaces and performs the same functions as do rules' (2006, p. 127). *Collect Yourselves!* is a game without a winner, a performance without a stage, and a story without an overarching narrative. The aim of *Collect Yourselves!* is to combine these elements to prompt the co-creation of a uniquely structured media sharing performance that its participants can feel is made special (Dissanayake 2003). Therefore, the focus is not on technology *per se*, but on how technology can be used to afford, prompt, or challenge perceptions and presentations of the self in relation to others. Memory and imagination are key; ambiguity, conflict, and 'making strange' are to be encouraged over efficient photowork practices. Interactions in both the devising and performance phases must allow time for participants to discover new perspectives or simply to notice details that were previously ignored.

Properties of Autobiographical Performance

The four properties of autobiographical performance identified in the third step of the PED methodology are self-making, 'heightened attention', situatedness, and the 'aesthetics of the event'. Each of these properties was translated into a corresponding design goal, which if met would manifest that property in performance. Connections between each property of autobiographical performance and its design goal were mapped, along with the specific features designed to meet that goal and the data that would indicate whether the goal has been met. This is a very detailed and apparently deterministic perspective on both 'creative design' (Wolf et al. 2006) and performance. It is not intended to imply a direct causal relationship between property, design goal, feature, and data point: this would mean that intermedial autobiographical performance is merely a problem to be solved (see e.g. 'engineering design' discussed in Wolf et al. 2006), and that human behaviour around digital media sharing is easily manipulable. It is, however, intended to indicate what Stolterman would call a rigorous approach to designing for the 'complex' (2008, p. 59) interactions that make up intermedial autobiographical performance. This mapping of properties to goals, features, and data makes my 'judgments visible and open for critique' (2008, p. 62).

All five prompts are written to provoke self-disclosure and possibly self-discovery. The fact that the application can be accessed from any location any number of times before the performance means that participants can devote as much time and energy to this process as they like, and to explore various sources of personal digital media such as forgotten external hard drives or discs stored at a parent's house. These alternative choices shape the processes of self-making as participants decide what to reveal and what to conceal in a co-located encounter with others.

'Heightened attention' is divided into the categories of 'conspicuousness', 'intensity of appearance', and 'deviation and surprise' (Fischer-Lichte 2008b). By asking participants to spend time remembering and thinking about their digital media, those photos become more conspicuous to performers during the devising phase. During performance, these details and possible dissonances should make the same media conspicuous to audience members, as well. The requirement to stand while performing, and the use of the term 'perform', should encourage participants to increase the 'intensity' and perhaps even the 'risk' in their storytelling (Wilson 2006, p. 9). Audience members, who will also be facing this pressure, should respond by recognising the 'intensity of appearance' of the performers. 'Deviation and surprise' are made possible because all participants will be aware that they are responding to the same prompts as everyone else, and so by the end of the devising phase will have some idea of the types of performances they might see. The time limit will also draw attention to the need for balance in terms of time spent holding the floor, which will make any deviations very noticeable.

The unique situated nature of each performance is woven into the process of devising as well as the process of performing, as participants know who they will be performing for (or in the case of groups of strangers, they know that they will be performing for people they do not know) as well as when and where that performance will take place. The requirement to stand while performing, which contributes to the intensity of the performer's appearance, also shapes situatedness by altering the relationships among the participants. When a participant begins a turn, she takes on the 'assumption of accountability' (Bauman 1975, p. 293) to the people who have suddenly become her 'audience' and cannot interrupt her story as easily as they would in the free flow of conversation. The use of a projector also contributes to situatedness, as performers are freed from the need to manage other people's use of their personal devices, and audiences can see all of the images without having to devote energy and attention to negotiating access to a shared screen. This is all accomplished without requiring a particular location, stage, or set.

Like 'heightened attention', the 'aesthetics of the event' is made up of three categories: 'collapsing dichotomies', 'autopoiesis and emergence', and 'liminality and transformation' (Fischer-Lichte 2008b). The collapsing of dichotomies between the social and the aesthetic should be achieved by the fact that the participants will all take the role of performer in turn. This should highlight their accountability to each other for both their 'act[s] of expression' (Bauman 1975, p. 293) and whatever real-world implications those expressions might have. 'Autopoiesis and emergence' will be achieved because each use of the system will be a temporally extended event created by people whose roles are constantly in flux, and whose media are hidden until the moment of performance. A state of 'liminality' induced by performance 'may well cause a change in the perception of reality, self, and others' (Fischer-Lichte 2008a, p. 80) for performers and audience members. Liminality can be understood in the context of the purposes or aspirations of performance as described by various practitioners and theorists: heightened attention (Bauman 1975; Fischer-Lichte 2008b), empathy (storyteller Liz Weir quoted in Wilson 2006, p. 197; Dolan 2005), and the possibility of a positive, if temporary, transformation (Phelan 2004; Fischer-Lichte 2008b). This design aims to achieve liminal and potentially transformative states in its participants through the interplay of all of the other properties of autobiographical performance—self-making, heightening attention, situatedness, collapsing dichotomies, and autopoiesis and emergence.

The aims of *Collect Yourselves!* are reflected in the observation that performance 'is not a stable state or position.… [T]he time of performance is encountered in a flow of tenses, *as* past, present and future; or memory, attention and expectation' (Giannachi et al. 2012, pp. 13–14, emphasis in the original). *Collect Yourselves!* is designed to guide participants through interaction not only with a device, and not only with other participants, but with themselves: through the traces of their past reflected in their personal digital media, with their current practices of photowork, and with their future selves as they imagine them into being during performance. Performance provides a means for people to perform the supremely human act of 'making special' (Dissanayake 2003) to an exceptionally intangible object: the digital media artefact, accompanied by a story that lasts only as long as it is remembered. It is the intention of this design to make at least a few of those photos and their stories meaningful and memorable. The next step is to analyse the design in use.

References

Abramović M (2011) Biography as material. In: Programme: the life and death of Marina Abramović. Manchester International Festival, Manchester, p 5

Ah Kun LM, Marsden G (2007) Co-present photo sharing on mobile devices. In: Proceedings of the 9th international conference on human computer interaction with mobile devices and services. ACM Press, New York, pp 277–284

Andres J, Joyce S, Love B, Raussert W, Wait AR (2010) Introduction. In: Raussert W et al (eds) Remembering and forgetting: memory in images and texts. Aisthesis Verlag, Bielefeld, pp 7–20

Auslander P (2006) The performativity of performance documentation. PAJ: J Perform Art 28(3):1–10

Balabanović M, Chu L, Wolff G (2000) Storytelling with digital photographs. In: Proceedings of the SIGCHI conference on human factors in computing systems. ACM Press, New York, pp 564–571

Bannon L (2006) Forgetting as a feature, not a bug: the duality of memory and implications for ubiquitous computing. CoDesign 2(1):3–15

Barclay CR (1994) Composing protoselves through improvisation. In: Neisser U, Fivush R (eds) The remembering self: construction and agency in self narrative. Cambridge University Press, Cambridge, pp 55–77

Bardzell J, Bolter J, Löwgren J (2010) Interaction criticism: three readings of an interaction design, and what they get us. Interactions 17(2):32–37

Bauman R (1975) Verbal art as performance. Am Anthropol 77(2):290–311

Bauman R (1992) Folklore, cultural performances, and popular entertainments: a communications-centered handbook. Oxford University Press, New York/Oxford

Benjamin W (2006) The storyteller. In: Hale D (ed) The novel: an anthology of criticism and theory 1900–2000. Blackwell Publishing, Malden, pp 361–378

Bødker S (2006) When second wave HCI meets third wave challenges. In: Proceedings of the 4th Nordic conference on human-computer interaction: changing roles. ACM Press, New York, pp 1–8

Boenisch PM (2006) Aesthetic art to aisthetic act: theatre, media, intermedial performance. In: Chapple F, Kattenbelt C (eds) Intermediality in theatre and performance. Editions Rodopi B.V, Amsterdam/New York, pp 103–116

Butler J (2002) Gender trouble: feminism and the subversion of identity. Routledge, New York

Caillois R (2006) The definition of play and the classification of games. In: Salen K, Zimmerman E (eds) The game design reader: a rules of play anthology. MIT Press, Cambridge, MA, pp 122–155

Chatzichristodoulou M, Zerihan R (2009) Introduction. In: Chatzichristodoulou M et al (eds) Interfaces of performance. Ashgate, Farnham, pp 1–5

Clawson J, Voida A, Patel N, Lyons K (2008) Mobiphos: a collocated-synchronous mobile photo sharing application. In: Proceedings of the 10th international conference on human computer interaction with mobile devices and services. ACM Press, New York, pp 187–195

Clawson J, Voida A, Patel N, Lyons K (2009) Mobiphos: a study of user engagement with a mobile collocated–synchronous photo sharing application. Int J Hum Comput Stud 67(12):1048–1059

Cosley D, Sosik VS, Schultz J, Peesapati ST, Lee S (2012) Experiences with designing tools for everyday reminiscing. Hum Comput Interact 27(1–2):175–198

Crabtree A, Rodden T, Mariani J (2004) Collaborating around collections: informing the continued development of photoware. In: Proceedings of the 2004 ACM conference on computer supported cooperative work. ACM Press, New York, pp 396–405

Dewey J (2005) Art as experience. Perigee Books, New York

Dissanayake E (2003) The core of art: making special. J Can Assoc Curr Stud 1(2):13–38

Dolan J (2005) Utopia in performance: finding hope at the theater. University of Michigan Press, Ann Arbor

Fällman D (2003) Design-oriented human-computer interaction. In: Proceedings of the SIGCHI conference on human factors in computing systems. ACM Press, New York, pp 225–232

Fällman D, Stolterman E (2010) Establishing criteria of rigour and relevance in interaction design research. Digit Creativity 21(4):265–272

Fischer-Lichte E (2008a) Sense and sensation: exploring the interplay between the semiotic and performative dimensions of theatre. J Dramat Theory Crit 22(2):69–81

Fischer-Lichte E (2008b) The transformative power of performance: a new aesthetics. Routledge, London

Fischer-Lichte E (2012) Appearing as embodied mind: defining a weak, a strong and a radical concept of presence. Archaeologies of presence: art, performance and the persistence of being, p 103

Fono D, Counts S (2006) Sandboxes: supporting social play through collaborative multimedia composition on mobile phones. In: Proceedings of the 2006 20th anniversary conference on computer supported cooperative work. ACM Press, New York, pp 163–166

Frohlich DM (2004) Audiophotography: bringing photos to life with sounds. Springer/Kluwer Academic Publishers, Dordrecht/Boston/London

Frohlich D, Fennell J (2006) Sound, paper and memorabilia: resources for a simpler digital photography. Pers Ubiquit Comput 11(2):107–116

Frohlich D, Adams G, Tallyn E (2000) Augmenting photographs with audio. Pers Ubiquit Comput 4(4):205–208

Frohlich D, Kuchinsky A, Pering C, Don A, Ariss S (2002) Requirements for photoware. In: Proceedings of the 2002 ACM conference on computer supported cooperative work. ACM Press, New York, pp 166–175

Frohlich DM, Clancy T, Robinson J, Costanza E (2004) The audiophoto desk. In: Proceedings of 2AD, second international conference on appliance design. HP, Bristol, np

Frohlich DM, Wall S, Kiddle G (2013) Rediscovery of forgotten images in domestic photo collections. Pers Ubiquit Comput 17(4):729–740

Gaver W (2011) Making spaces: how design workbooks work. In: Proceedings of the SIGCHI conference on human factors in computing systems. ACM Press, New York, pp 1551–1560

Gaver B, Dunne T, Pacenti E (1999) Design: cultural probes. Interactions 6(1):21–29

Gaver WW, Beaver J, Benford S (2003) Ambiguity as a resource for design. In: Proceedings of the SIGCHI conference on human factors in computing systems. ACM Press, New York, pp 233–240

Giannachi G, Kaye N, Shanks M (2012) Introduction: archaeologies of presence. In: Giannachi G et al (eds) Archaeologies of presence: art, performance and the persistence of being. Routledge, London, pp 1–25

Glaser BG, Strauss AL (1967) The discovery of grounded theory: strategies for qualitative research. Aldine, Chicago

Goffman E (1959) The presentation of self in everyday life. Doubleday, Garden City

Golsteijn C, van den Hoven E (2013) Facilitating parent-teenager communication through interactive photo cubes. Pers Ubiquit Comput 17(2):273–286

Gosling D (2003) 10.01.00 >> 30.01.00 > >>< In: Heathfield A (ed) Small acts: performance, the millennium and the marking of time. Black Dog Publishing Ltd, London, pp 82–91

Hartley J, McWilliam K (2009) Computational power meets human contact. In: McWilliam K, Hartley J (eds) Story circle: digital storytelling around the world. Wiley-Blackwell, Chichester, pp 3–15

Heddon D (2002) Autotopography: graffiti, landscapes & selves. Reconstruction 2(3):np

Heddon D (2008) Autobiography and performance. Palgrave Macmillan, Basingstoke

Heddon D, Kelly A (2010) Distance dramaturgy. Perform Res 20(2):214–220

Hill L, Paris H (2006) Performance and place. Palgrave Macmillan, Basingstoke

Holland AC, Kensinger EA (2010) Emotion and autobiographical memory. Phys Life Rev 7(1):88–131

Isaacs E, Konrad A, Walendowski A, Lennig T, Hollis V, Whittaker S (2013) Echoes from the past: how technology mediated reflection improves well-being. In: Proceedings of the SIGCHI conference on human factors in computing systems. ACM Press, New York, pp 1071–1080

Jalving C (2005) Inventing reality: on truth and lies in the work of Hayley Newman. In: Gade R, Jerslev A (eds) Performative realism: interdisciplinary studies in art and media. Museum Tusculanum Press, Copenhagen, p 145

Johnstone K (1999) Impro for storytellers. Routledge, New York

Kaprow A (2007) Just doing. In: Bial H (ed) The performance studies reader, 2nd edn. Routledge, London/New York, pp 159–163

Keightley E, Pickering M (2014) Technologies of memory: practices of remembering in analogue and digital photography. New Med Soc 16(4):576–593

Kelliher A, Davenport G (2007) Everyday storytelling: supporting the mediated expression of online personal testimony. In: Proceedings of the 12th international conference on human-computer interaction: applications and services. Springer-Verlag, Berlin/Heidelberg, pp 926–933

Kirk D, Sellen A, Rother C, Wood K (2006) Understanding photowork. In: Proceedings of the SIGCHI conference on human factors in computing systems. ACM Press, New York, pp 761–770

Kirk DS, Izadi S, Sellen A, Taylor S, Banks R, Hilliges O (2010) Opening up the family archive. In: Proceedings of the 2010 ACM conference on computer supported cooperative work. ACM Press, New York, pp 261–270

Kolko J (2010) Abductive thinking and sensemaking: the drivers of design synthesis. Des Issues 26(1):15–28

Kray C, Rohs M, Hook J, Kratz S (2009) Bridging the gap between the Kodak and the Flickr generations: a novel interaction technique for collocated photo sharing. Int J Hum Comput Stud 67(12):1060–1072

Kuhn A (2007) Photography and cultural memory: a methodological exploration. Vis Stud 22(3):283–292

Kuhn A (2010) Memory texts and memory work: performances of memory in and with visual media. Mem Stud 3(4):298–313

Lambert J (2002) Digital storytelling: capturing lives, creating community. Digital Diner Press, Berkeley

Landry BM, Guzdial M (2006) iTell: supporting retrospective storytelling with digital photos. In: Proceedings of the 6th conference on designing interactive systems. ACM Press, New York, pp 160–168

Langellier KM, Peterson E (2004) Storytelling in daily life: performing narrative. Temple University Press, Philadelphia

Leong TW (2009) Understanding serendipitous experiences when interacting with personal digital content. PhD thesis, University of Melbourne

Leong TW, Harper R, Regan T (2011) Nudging towards serendipity: a case with personal digital photos. In: Proceedings of the 25th BCS conference on human-computer interaction. British Computer Society, Swinton, pp 385–394

Lindley S, Monk A (2006) Designing appropriate affordances for electronic photo sharing media. In: CHI '06 extended abstracts on human factors in computing systems. ACM Press, New York, pp 1031–1036

Lucero A, Holopainen J, Jokela T (2011) Pass-them-around: collaborative use of mobile phones for photo sharing. In: Proceedings of the 2011 annual conference on human factors in computing systems. ACM Press, New York, pp 1787–1796

Lundby K, Kaare B (2008) Mediatized lives: autobiography and assumed authenticity in digital storytelling. In: Lundby K (ed) Digital storytelling, mediatized stories: self-representations in new media. Peter Lang Publishing, Inc, New York, pp 105–122

McCarthy J, Wright P (2004) Technology as experience. MIT Press, Cambridge, MA

Meadows D (2008) Introduction: about digital stories. In: BBC Capture Wales team (ed) A guide to digital storytelling. BBC Wales, p 2. http://www.bbc.co.uk/wales/audiovideo/sites/galleries/pages/digitalstorytelling.shtml

Merriman P (2001) Cultural geographies in practice: the art of hitch-hiking: Daniel Gosling's performance 10.1.00>>1+1? (@?):?+&+... >>30.1.00. Cult Geogr 8(3):340–344

Myers M, Griffiths D, Sabnani N, Joshi A, Mahapatra S (2014) Sustaining lived practices through serious play. DRHA 2014, University of Greenwich, London, 31 Aug–3 Sep 2014

Nelson R (2010) Introduction: prospective mapping. In: Bay-Cheng S et al (eds) Mapping intermediality in performance. Amsterdam University Press, Amsterdam, pp 13–23

Newman H (2004) Connotations—performance images (1994–1998). In: Heathfield A (ed) Live: art and performance. Routledge, New York, pp 166–175

Norrick NR (2000) Conversational narrative: storytelling in everyday talk. John Benjamins Publishing Company, Amsterdam/Philadelphia

O'Hara K, Helmes J, Sellen A, Harper R, ten Bhömer M, van den Hoven E (2012) Food for talk: phototalk in the context of sharing a meal. Hum Comput Interact 27(1–2):124–150

Ojala J, Malinen S (2012) Photo sharing in small groups: identifying design drivers for desired user experiences. In: Proceeding of the 16th international academic MindTrek conference. ACM Press, New York, pp 69–76

Pearson M, Shanks M (2001) Theatre/archaeology: disciplinary dialogues, 1st edn. Routledge, London/New York

Peesapati ST, Schwanda V, Schultz J, Lepage M, Jeong S, Cosley D (2010) Pensieve: supporting everyday reminiscence. In: Proceedings of the SIGCHI conference on human factors in computing systems. ACM Press, New York, pp 2027–2036

Petrelli D, Whittaker S (2010) Family memories in the home: contrasting physical and digital mementos. Pers Ubiquit Comput 14(2):153–169

Petrelli D, Whittaker S, Brockmeier J (2008) AutoTopography: what can physical mementos tell us about digital memories? In: Proceedings of the SIGCHI conference on human factors in computing systems. ACM Press, New York, pp 53–62

Petrelli D, van den Hoven E, Whittaker S (2009) Making history: intentional capture of future memories. In: Proceedings of the SIGCHI conference on human factors in computing systems. ACM Press, New York, pp 1723–1732

Phelan P (2004) Marina Abramović: witnessing shadows. Theatr J 56(4):569–577

Piper AM, Weibel N, Hollan J (2013) Audio-enhanced paper photos: encouraging social interaction at age 105. In: Proceedings of the 2013 conference on computer supported cooperative work. ACM Press, New York, pp 215–224

Reitmaier T, Benz P, Marsden G (2013) Designing and theorizing co-located interactions. In: Proceedings of the SIGCHI conference on human factors in computing systems. ACM Press, New York, pp 381–390

Sacks H, Schegloff E, Jefferson G (1974) A simplest systematics for the organization of turn-taking for conversation. Language 50(4):696–735

Salter C (2010) Entangled: technology and the transformation of performance. MIT Press, Cambridge, MA

Sarvas R, Frohlich DM (2011) From snapshots to social media: the changing picture of domestic photography. Springer-Verlag, New York

Schechner R (2006) Performance studies: an introduction, 2nd edn. Routledge, New York

Shen C, Lesh N, Vernier F (2003) Personal digital historian: story sharing around the table. Interactions 10(2):15–22

Spence J, Andrews S, Frohlich DM (2012) Now, where was I? Negotiating time in digitally augmented autobiographical performance. J Med Pract 13(3):269–284

Stelmaszewska H, Fields B, Blandford A (2008) The roles of time, place, value and relationships in collocated photo sharing with camera phones. In: Proceedings of the 22nd British HCI group annual conference on people and computers: culture, creativity, interaction. British Computer Society, Swinton, pp 141–150

Stolterman E (2008) The nature of design practice and implications for interaction design research. Int J Des 2(1):55–65

Tacchi J (2009) Finding a voice: participatory development in Southeast Asia. In: McWilliam K, Hartley J (eds) Story circle: digital storytelling around the world. Wiley-Blackwell, Chichester, pp 167–175

ten Bhömer M, Helmes J, O'Hara K, van den Hoven E (2010) 4Photos: a collaborative photo sharing experience. In: Proceedings of the 6th Nordic conference on human-computer interaction: extending boundaries. ACM Press, New York, pp 52–61

van den Hoven E, Eggen B (2003) Digital photo browsing with souvenirs. In: Proceedings of human-computer interaction (INTERACT) '03. IOS Press, Amsterdam, pp 1000–1003

van den Hoven E, Eggen B (2007) Informing augmented memory system design through autobiographical memory theory. Pers Ubiquit Comput 12(6):433–443

van den Hoven E, Sas C, Whittaker S (2012) Introduction to this special issue on designing for personal memories: past, present, and future. Hum Comput Interact 27(1–2):1–12

Van House NA (2009) Collocated photo sharing, story-telling, and the performance of self. Int J Hum Comput Stud 67(12):1073–1086

Van House NA (2011) Personal photography, digital technologies and the uses of the visual. Vis Stud 26(2):125–134

Van House NA, Davis M, Takhteyev Y, Good N, Wilhelm A, Finn M (2004) From "what?" to "why?": the social uses of personal photos. Unpublished work. Retrieved 11 May 2014 from http://www.people.ischool.berkeley.edu/~vanhouse/van%20house_et_al_2004a.pdf

Watkins J, Russo A (2009) Beyond individual expression: working with cultural institutions. In: McWilliam K, Hartley J (eds) Story circle: digital storytelling around the world. Wiley-Blackwell, Chichester, pp 269–278

Whittaker S, Bergman O, Clough P (2009) Easy on that trigger dad: a study of long term family photo retrieval. Pers Ubiquit Comput 14:31–43

Wilson M (2006) Storytelling and theatre: contemporary storytellers and their art. Palgrave Macmillan, Basingstoke

Wolf TV, Rode JA, Sussman J, Kellogg WA (2006) Dispelling design as the black art of CHI. In: Proceedings of the SIGCHI conference on human factors in computing systems. ACM Press, New York, pp 521–530

Chapter 6
Performing *Collect Yourselves!*

Abstract Continuing on from Chap. 5, this chapter presents the fifth and sixth steps of the PED methodology: the performed experience and the analyses conducted on the performed experience. Step 5 offers a description of one of the instances in which the case study for this book, *Collect Yourselves!*, was performed. It then presents the analyses conducted on this one instance: thematic analysis, modified interaction analysis, and the novel method of 'coded performance analysis'. This hybrid form, created specifically for the purposes of this work, is explained in detail so that readers can generate coded performance analyses of their own. The final section of the chapter, the findings from Step 6, begins with a brief synopsis of how the performance discussed in this chapter aligns with the other instances conducted and analysed for the project from which this case study draws. It then discusses the key findings from that project. The PED process produced new knowledge, theories, and insights that contribute to performance studies, HCI, interaction design, experience design, and PED itself. These include a new category of media sharing interaction called 'performed photos'; a new category of intermedial doubling called 'doubled indexicality'; an exploration of 'connection'; a discussion of the counterintuitive ways that liminality interacts with conversation; and a framework for understanding the investment and perception of meaning in digital media referred to as 'attending' and 'marking'.

Step 5: Performed Experience: *Collect Yourselves!*

Following insights into the effects of audiences on conversational storytelling (Bavelas et al. 2000; Frohlich et al. 2004), *Collect Yourselves!* was performed by groups that would likely exhibit different media sharing behaviours: two groups of friends and two groups of strangers. Friend Groups would be able though not required to reminisce; Stranger Groups would most likely engage only in storytelling. This required two different recruitment methods. For Friend Groups, I recruited one person who in turn recruited several of his or her friends. For Stranger Groups, I recruited individuals who were all strangers to each other. Because I was interested in everyday practices of photowork, I did not stipulate any minimum level of proficiency or particular types of devices, though I would have excluded any potential participant who never used digital photography in any way. Although the study

© Springer International Publishing Switzerland 2016   153
J. Spence, *Performative Experience Design*, Springer Series on Cultural
Computing, DOI 10.1007/978-3-319-28395-1_6

participants reflected a wide range of ages and nationalities, there was little variety in race or socioeconomic status, and only seven of the 24 participants were male. All names have been changed to preserve participant anonymity.

The participants were self-selecting to the extent that no one with a true phobia of public speaking would have volunteered, but a few informed me either before or after the performance that they were gripped by serious stage fright. Several others were clearly shy or awkward for their first turn or two, and others reported in written questionnaires that they felt a pressure to be entertaining and clever. In ordinary user-centred design, this would be a red flag that we were about to push our participants into an experience they would not enjoy. This is where the perspective of performance studies was perhaps most influential. In performance, some of the most powerful pieces are also challenging on some level. Blast Theory's *Desert Rain* (1999), a work also cited in the HCI literature, pushed audiences to reconsider their attitudes towards war, while Renato Rocha's and Keziah Serreau's *Turfed* at the 2014 LIFT festival of performance in London pushed them to rethink their attitudes and relationships to homeless youth, and Marina Abramović's *Rhythm 0* (1974) in Naples opened audience members' eyes to the inherent evil of some of their fellow spectators. Following these and other, subtler examples, such as the difficulties that audiences experienced in trying to unfold and re-fold large maps in a small van in *Cape Wrath* (2013, see Chap. 5), I did not try to mitigate the temporary discomfort that some participants expressed (see Benford et al. 2012). The intention was that by undergoing stage fright and similar pressures, a more positive and maybe even transformative experience would emerge. Of course, participants were always in complete control of what they chose to share and how they wished to interact.

The case study presented in this chapter is of Friend Group 2. Each participant was sent an email with a link to a *Collect Yourselves!* website dedicated to their group. They could register themselves and answer the prompts at their leisure over as many sessions as they wished. However, the performance could only be accessed by having all participants log in at the same time. Therefore, no one saw the layout or specific instructions for the performance phase, or each other's photos, until it was time to begin. This decision was taken to ensure the security of the personal photos and to prevent participants from 'rehearsing' their performances.

For the performance phase, the participants and I agreed on a mutually convenient time, date, and private location. The session discussed in this chapter took place from 8:00 pm on Wednesday, 19 June, 2013, among seven friends in the cosy living room of Isobel's and Quentin's home in Cambridge, UK (see Fig. 6.1). The couch was set under the staircase, contributing to a sense of being enclosed and protected. Low lighting, designed to help make the projected images more visible, contributed to a sense of relaxation and informality. Counteracting this comfort was the requirement of a slightly theatrical arrangement of seated audience and standing performer facing them. This was a design decision aiming to discourage participants from engaging in free-flowing conversation and therefore exert less control over their material. In the words of professional storyteller Daniel Morden, such constraints 'contribute to a formality which means that the story is being served by

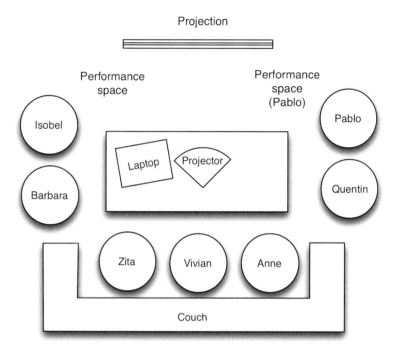

Fig. 6.1 Seating arrangements

its presentation. It's more heightened than one might have in a pub, for example' (quoted in Wilson 2006, p. 169). The performance was a balancing act: the place and time needed to be as congenial as possible so that participants would feel comfortable sharing details of their lives, while the design and rules of *Collect Yourselves!* could then nudge them into less familiar practices.

After explaining the project and obtaining informed consent, I handed out printouts of a sample performance grid and story layout. I used these to explain the interface and the rules, which were also displayed on the performance grid:

> Your whole group has 45 min to perform your stories for each other. Choose among yourselves who will go first. You can't tell more than one story in a row, and you should try to tell all your stories. The timer will count down while you're performing and pause while you're deciding who goes next. Click on a picture to start telling that story.

The controls were the thumbnails in the performance grid (click to get to that story page), the thumbnails on a story page (click to enlarge), the 'finish turn' button (click to finish turn), and the 'pause' button (which would pause the timer in case of any interruptions or problems during a turn). I also pointed out that performers should stand in the vicinity of the projection while performing. For the most part, participants understood these rules and controls right away. I remained in the room but intentionally busied myself taking notes and monitoring camera equipment so as to avoid insinuating myself into the audience or positioning myself as arbiter of any

Table 6.1 Participants

Name	M/F	Age range	Nationality	Occupational status
Isobel	F	Thirties	Spanish living in UK<5 years	Graduate student
Barbara	F	Thirties	French living in UK>5 years	Employed full-time
Zita	F	Twenties	Spanish living in UK<5 years	Employed full-time
Vivian	F	Thirties	British	Employed part-time
Anne	F	Thirties	French living in UK>5 years	Employed full-time
Quentin	M	Thirties	French living in UK<5 years	Employed full-time
Pablo	M	Thirties	Spanish living in UK<5 years	Employed full-time

negotiations. Immediately after the session ended, I elaborated on my notes to ensure nothing that stood out in the moment would be lost to my memory.

Isobel was the hostess for the evening and my contact person for the group. Only Isobel and Quentin, who are romantic partners, were good friends with each participant. All participants were friends with at least three others in the group, and the friendships overlapped: there were no isolated sub-groups who knew each other but not the others (Table 6.1). The three native Spanish speakers would occasionally make comments to each other or check that they were using the correct term in English, as did the three native French speakers. Otherwise, the session was conducted in English. While the transcriptions reveal flaws in the English spoken by non-native speakers, there were no significant failures of communication. Minor misunderstandings were easily rectified as friends quickly translated for each other when necessary.

The performance was observed and recorded on video for further examination. After the performance, participants were given a 10-min break, and the recording equipment was left running to capture their conversations. (Some participants left the room for various reasons, so the data from these conversations is not comprehensive.) The aim of this capture was to discover which elements of performance, if any, triggered further discussion. After the break, participants were asked to fill out individual questionnaires. Then they were interviewed in the style of a focus group, allowing for individual responses but not requiring each participant to answer each question separately. Other sources of data include the photos and text uploaded by each participant, permissions for which were controlled using a consent form specific to each participant's unique collection of photos.

To apply interaction analysis to the *Collect Yourselves!* case study, I also gathered the following data:

- time spent on each story, averaged by group, person, and story, with standard deviations
- story order, including the number of prompts answered per group
- whether stories became longer or shorter as the performance progressed
- time spent on each photo, averaged by group, person, and story, with standard deviations
- number of photos per prompt
- lengths of transitions, averaged by group, with standard deviations

- patterns for turn-taking (following seating order, display order, or other)
- patterns for which prompt to choose (following the previously selected prompt or not)

This combination of notes, recordings, media, and other data provided a strong indication of how the performances developed: how spectators responded to performances at various points, how and when they indicated a loss of interest, how different participants succeeded or failed at modulating their stories to fit the time constraints placed on the group, how verbal interjections helped or hindered the overall performances, etc. The performances, conversations, and interviews were transcribed for later analysis.

After the performance concluded and the participants had their 10-min break, I distributed questionnaires that asked about their subjective experience of the devising phase, the act of performing, and the act of forming an audience for others; how they would describe the experience; whether the stories they told were ones they had shared or would share in person or online; whether they would share a full or edited video of their performance. I then interviewed them as a group, asking them how they would share their photos using any technology they could imagine; how they felt the performance differed from chatting with friends; what their favourite prompt was; and which contexts they could imagine using *Collect Yourselves!* in. These questions aimed to uncover sentiments that might not be evident in performance and to indicate attitudes towards the experience of live performance.

Step 6: Analyses

Devising Phase — Thematic Analysis

'Socialising the social network'—Quentin

To gain insight into the devising phase, which I as the researcher did not have direct access to, I gathered the questionnaire and interview data described in Step 5. These were transcribed and then submitted to a process of open coding, allowing themes to emerge from the data. This analysis lays out the high-level findings from the analysis with relevant examples.

The fact that all participants had gone through the same devising process provided an immediate connection and made some participants curious to hear how others responded to these prompts that they all now had some personal investment in. Some participants found the initial devising phase (see Chap. 5) to be 'surprising', challenging, or frustrating. Several struggled to respond to the prompts in a way that they could feel satisfied by in performance, where they knew they would be 'marked as subjected to evaluation' (Bauman 1975, p. 293) for their choices. As Dewey puts it, '[a] sure thing does not arouse us emotionally' (2005, p. 69). Several participants felt intimidated by the uncertainty of the expectation to perform, and this sensation informed their devising process.

Two had a small number of photos available to them on the computers they used; Pablo later explained that most of his photos were 'at home' in Spain, so he had asked his mother to send him some. This belies the rhetoric of connectivity and easy access surrounding digital media. Another participant wished for access to older, analogue photos, and everyone was fascinated by Pablo's and Quentin's photos of themselves as children. Once an older photo had been scanned, there was no practical difference between it and the digital photos that the instructions had asked for in the unfolding of the performance. This group overwhelmingly wanted ease of access regardless of the means of capture: no one mentioned any concerns about the physicality of analogue photos or the ephemerality of digital photos. In performance, the ontologies of digital and analogue media slipped away; only the devising process was affected.

One participant found the wording of the prompts to be confusing and therefore frustrating. On the other hand, two found the devising phase experience to be 'nice' or 'interesting', and one observed that she felt 'more self confidence and trying to get closer [to] the question'. The immediate response to the question of how *Collect Yourselves!* differed from an ordinary chat was the structure provided by both phases. However, the discussion quickly turned to the intimacy generated by the photos and stories chosen during the devising phase.

> When we get together … we just talk about what we like, what we've seen, the thought of the moment, political stuff, but you don't necessarily share personal stories. At least I think it's nice to share a bit more. But you wouldn't do it if there's no structure to help you do it. (Barbara)

It would be easy to assume that these friends would be used to sharing intensely personal information with each other from time to time, and would therefore perceive *Collect Yourselves!* as a more impersonal or artificial type of interaction. However, the opposite seems to be the case. They all agreed that *Collect Yourselves!* created an experience marked by very high levels of intimacy and self-disclosure. Barbara expressed an evangelical attitude about this highly personal form of sharing: 'I think people would like this. I think they would probably feel uncomfortable at first, but I think this is needed'.

Some participants drew parallels between *Collect Yourselves!* and the norms of sharing on social networking sites, as well. Vivian noted that 'people chat anonymously about very personal things but not as much among friends'. In her experience, intimate revelations can be easier to divulge to unknown strangers online than to trusted friends in person. Quentin also noted a difference between norms of sharing intimate details online and of sharing in live interaction. He saw *Collect Yourselves!* as 'a way to bring that social network quality that usually you use in a more isolated way, on Facebook. Socialising the social network'. Isobel immediately added, 'in real life'. For these participants and those who agreed with their comments, the devising phase contributed to the intimacy that contrasted not only with regular conversation but also with communications through social networking sites.

Prompt four (lie) was the overwhelming favourite of this group in spite of the fact that it was also 'the most challenging' (Barbara). Only Anne and Vivian expressed a dislike for it. Isobel connected the fictionalising demanded by the prompt and the self-making aspect of autobiography:

> I was more excited about hearing the lies people created because it's half-true, half-lie, so it's the perfect combination of experience and creativity, because you have to invent. And what you invent says a lot about who you are, and what you did and didn't do. (Isobel)

Isobel's comment is an indication of the blurring of memory (fact) and imagination (fiction) in autobiographical performance, though in all cases, the performer is responsible for her performance. Other descriptions of prompt four (lie) include 'exciting', 'funny', 'creative', 'intriguing', and 'more of a performance' (Vivian). Other nominations for favourite prompt were prompt one (regular day), 'because it was personal' (Vivian), and prompt three (embarrassing).

Performance Phase — Interaction Analysis

'It's good to know why I keep some picture of these moments'—Pablo

Following the work of Jordan and Henderson (1995), the modified interaction analyses for *Collect Yourselves!* focus on structure, turn timing, turn-taking, participation structures, trouble and repair, spatial organisation of activity, and artefacts and documents.

Structure

There was a brief pause, after which Isobel said, 'So I go, no? It has to be by order?' I pointed out that she did not need to go first, but no one competed with her, so she began. As with Friend Group 1, the person responsible for convening the group of friends took the first turn.

Few participants chose to answer a prompt that would violate the established order (Table 6.2). This was by far the most 'chatty' performance, marked by a great deal of conversation during transitions: only eight out of 34 transitions were marked

Table 6.2 Story order

Prompt order	Percentage of prompts (%)
Prompts followed suit	68.6
Unprovoked change of order	14.3
Reverted to previous order	17.1

by silence or near silence on the part of the performer. These conversations rarely posed problems; exceptions are described below. Transitions sped up throughout the performance as the participants became accustomed to moving through the space and using the interface. Contrary to the other three *Collect Yourselves!* performances, there were no obvious 'waves' of intensity in this performance. Isobel, who began each round, was the most animated performer, and Pablo, who ended each round, was often the least dynamic. However, after his first two rounds, Pablo started to perform as entertainingly as anyone else, and Isobel's animation did not always mark a point of intensity.

Turn Timing

This group nearly completed all 35 of their stories in the 45 min allotted (see Table 6.3). Pablo had just begun the final story when the timer ran out. He completed the story without the on-screen image, and they all asked me to project it again as soon as the performance officially finished.

This group spent by far the most time on prompt two (thinking of you) and the least on prompt one (regular day), stating in interviews that they found the idea of their lives 6 months ago as not very interesting. Prompt five (forgotten) came in third for this group. Although prompt four (lie) was their favourite, many participants sped through it (Table 6.4).

Table 6.3 Turn timings

Parameter	Session plan	Session outcome
Total storytelling time (mm:ss)	45:00	44:10
Total number of stories completed	35	35
Mean time per person per prompt (mm:ss)	1:17	1:16
Mean transition time (mm:ss)	Unspecified	0:21

Note: Discrepancies between storytelling times stem from variations in counting methods

Table 6.4 Mean time per prompt (longest in *italics*)

Prompt	Mean time (mm:ss)	Ranking (longest = 1)
1 (regular day)	1:05	5
2 *(memorable)*	*1:33*	*1*
3 (embarrassing)	1:18	2
4 (lie)	1:11	4
5 (forgotten)	1:12	3

Turn-Taking

Performers took their turns in the order that their names appeared on screen: Isobel, Anne, Quentin, Barbara, Vivian, Zita, and Pablo. After Isobel's first turn, she suggested that the person sitting to her right, Barbara, go next. Barbara replied that it was Anne's turn. When Isobel protested that Anne had just taken a bite of cake, Anne offered to leave the rest of her cake for later, and proceeded to perform. Isobel seemed to want turns to follow the seating order, while Barbara seemed to want the turns to follow the order of the names on screen. When Anne finished, Quentin—whose name appeared third on screen—explicitly checked with the rest of the group that there was no need to go in seating order. This was the only extended negotiation around turn-taking or any other structural element of the performance. The turn order established in the first round was maintained throughout the session without error.

Participation Structures

Audience members signalled their participation through numerous interruptions, conversations, and direct address during performance as well as during transitions. Performers in turn signalled their participation by responding to these without losing the thread of their story or abandoning their performance until the end. The interruptions were not rude or distracting, but rather indicated strong interest in the performer's story or photo. Despite this tendency towards conversation, the performance did not splinter into subgroups or launch simultaneous conversations from audience members' own 'personal views' as some participants in Crabtree et al.'s studies did (2004, pp. 399–400). This could be in part because photos were projected on the wall rather than passed from the 'control centre' (which in this case would be the performer) to 'outlying positions' (in this case, the various audience members) (2004, p. 400). The two brief times when the performance split into multiple points of focus occurred when audience members looked at the laptop screen instead of the projection. Barbara, seeking a more detailed view of a projected photo, looked closely at the laptop screen from her 'outlying position' in the audience and then immediately began the only interaction that threatened to compete with an ongoing performance. However, the rest of the audience stayed focused on the 'control centre' of the projected image and the performance did not splinter. Similarly, Zita's habit of looking at the laptop screen rather than the projection led Isobel to look at the screen, as well, when she tried to discern the fine detail of one of Zita's images (see Fig. 6.2). The performance might have splintered in the way that Crabtree et al. describe (2004) had it not been for the overriding interest of all audience members in discerning what was in Zita's photo. It is therefore likely that projecting individual photos in sequence was important to the establishment of a single thread of performance, even when that performance was marked by conversation.

Fig. 6.2 Isobel looking at Zita's photo on screen while the others watch the projection

The other notable marker of participation was Pablo's shift from diffidence to confidence. He had a very shy and low-key manner, and usually kept his drink in his hand while performing as though he did not intend to stay at the front of the room for long or engage in anything more taxing than simple conversation. However, at the end of his second turn (prompt two, thinking of you), he paused at what would have been a natural stopping point for his story and then went on to explain the meaning of that photo:

> I mean not just a particular moment, it was just a coincidence that Vivian is here…. It's good to know why I keep some picture of these moments. (Pablo)

I understood Pablo to mean that he found the picture significant not just for the particular moment it depicts but for its relationship to the current moment of performance. The thought did not occur to him in the moment; he had already uploaded the phrase 'why I keep some picture of these moments'. However, his continuation after the pause indicated a willingness to participate more fully than necessary (and, as described below, more fully than intended). Subtle revelations like these maintained the audience's interest and signalled a level of participation at least as strong as the antics of more animated performers such as Isobel (see Figs. 6.3 and 6.10).

Trouble and Repair

Very few of the interruptions in this performance could be classed as 'trouble'. At one point, some audience members chatted while Anne was getting ready to begin prompt two (thinking of you). Anne stood silently waiting for them to finish,

Fig. 6.3 Isobel's exuberant performance of an exuberant photo (Projected photo © 'Isobel' (name withheld for reasons of confidentiality), used with permission)

indicating by her body language that she was ready to begin but showing no signs of frustration or impatience. The speakers noticed her before long and stopped speaking immediately. Barbara displayed a similar politeness. Despite the fact that she was perhaps the chattiest audience member, she was silent after three of her five turns, which prevented her stories from sparking conversations that might detract from the next performer's turn. Other than several instances of missing photos, there were no significant technical problems.

Spatial Organisation of Activity

Everyone performed from the space between Isobel's seat and the projection except Pablo, who performed from near his seat, and Zita, who stayed crouched in front of the laptop most of the time she performed. As noted above, her orientation seems to have contributed to a near collapse of the 'performance frame' (Bauman 1975, p. 297).

Artefacts and Documents

35 photos were projected for the 35 prompts. Only two prompts had multiple photos per prompt, but some participants indicated that they had attempted to upload multiples and were surprised to see only one available during performance. One participant, Anne, chose to upload nothing for prompt three (embarrassing) as well as prompt five (forgotten) (Table 6.5).

Anne wrote extensive captions; Zita wrote none. The rest wrote at least one word for at least three of their prompts. Isobel's performances consistently engaged far more in self-disclosure than her texts did, particularly as the self-disclosure related to relationships with people in the audience. For example, her prompt one (regular day) caption states that she does yoga, while her body language and word choice conveyed the relationships around her practice.

> What do I do in the morning when I wake up? I call my dear Fred, which is what we call him, he is the second man of my life here. My yoga teacher, Fred. (Isobel)

Relationships between her and Fred, and her and her partner Quentin, were all jokingly raised and explained. Barbara asked if the photo was of Quentin, and Quentin replied in the negative: 'I am the first [man of her life]'. Similarly, Isobel's text for prompt five (forgotten) states that she likes to remember Los Angeles because she dislikes the cold in England, but her performance was notable for her reminiscence about the friend whose car she and Quentin were posing with in the photo. This friend had died very young, and the entire audience was immediately curious about his story.

The other notable discrepancy between text and performance was Anne's tendency to reveal embarrassing information only in performance. Her caption for prompt one (regular day) states that she got a new job, while the performance revealed that she had already applied for it and had been turned down before trying again. Her performance for prompt two (thinking of you) also revealed something potentially embarrassing for both herself and Barbara: she had gone to Barbara's house only to find Barbara out of town, an event left out of the text.

Table 6.5 Photos uploaded

Participants	Total photos uploaded	Mean photos per prompt
Isobel	6	1.2
Barbara	5	1
Zita	6	1.2
Vivian	6	1.2
Anne	3	.6
Quentin	5	1
Pablo	5	1
Total	36	1

Note: Some participants may have intended to upload more photos than indicated

Terms such as 'energy' or 'feel' that are common in performance studies were difficult to use alongside these more tangible expressions of how participants responded to each other's photos and stories. Often, the interaction analysis provided small but concrete indications of shifts in energy that I had detected on a perceptual level during the performance; at times, the analysis challenged my subjective perceptions and led to further insights into the performance. When the ephemeral and subjective simply could not be accounted for by the events noted in the interaction analysis, a new analytic method was required.

Performance Phase — Coded Performance Analysis

'You have the same eyes'—Barbara to Vivian

The analysis that follows indicates the ways in which the four properties of performance identified in Step 3 of the PED methodology (self-making, heightened attention, situatedness, and the aesthetics of the event) manifested themselves in this performance of *Collect Yourselves!* Again, the coded performance analysis process allows for alternative themes to emerge, as group-making did. And at all times, the data were interrogated for the possibility of contradictory themes to emerge, as well. While the four properties of performance certainly did not appear in every individual story making up this performance, they did all appear in the performance taken as a whole.

Self-Making

Self-making was evidenced by self-disclosure, self-discovery, and the manner of performance. Self-making occurred not only through the selection of information to reveal through photo and story, but also through passing judgement on one's own choices and the choices of others. For example, Isobel took the haircut of her partner, Quentin, as the topic of her prompt five (forgotten). She chose a photo of herself and Quentin from several years previous for other reasons, but in performance realised how different the two of them looked. In this case, temporal dissonance led to self-discovery and then judgement. She described her own past look as 'so different' but Quentin's as 'so hot'. The implication was that she would like to see Quentin revert to his previous, shorter style. Isobel also interjected at the beginning of Quentin's prompt three (embarrassing), saying that while the photo of Quentin with a bad haircut might not be embarrassing for Quentin, it was embarrassing for her. This was clearly intended and taken as a joke, but the fact remains that Isobel felt free to pass judgement on her partner's appearance during his performance. Her own self-making was entwined with the representation of another person in the audience, speaking not only of her attitudes about herself but of her attitudes towards her partner and how she would want their relationship to be perceived.

In turn, Quentin's prompt four (lie) wove a connection to Isobel into the fabric of his story. He showed a photo of a live concert, with the bass player facing away from the audience. Quentin suavely explained that he used to be a professional bass player and pointed 'himself' out in the projected photo. He continued by saying, 'after I met Isobel I thought it was better to find a real job, stay home and we could get something together.' While the preposterousness of this statement could conceivably be read as an ironic comment on his choice to settle down with Isobel, it was delivered and received as a sincere comment. Even had Quentin been a rock star, he would have given it all up for Isobel. Quentin's reserved manner did not aim to impress his audience stylistically; therefore, there was no indication that his stated devotion to Isobel within his lie was an exaggeration.

At times, the performance served a group-making as well as a self-making function, as participants defined themselves in relation to each other. For example, the first story in this performance was Isobel's prompt one (regular day). The photo was of Isobel doing a handstand, supported by her yoga teacher, lying flat on his back with his arms and legs outstretched (see Fig. 6.4). Barbara exclaimed, 'Oh my God, I took that picture!' Isobel's photo gave Barbara the opportunity to claim a connection to Isobel through the moment they had shared 6 months previously at Isobel's yoga class, and Isobel's choice of photo reflected the richness of her social life. Barbara asked Isobel some questions about her story, which helped to set the tone for the performance: a friendly, non-competitive exchange that would maintain the performer's right to her turn while allowing space for contributions and questions from the audience. Overall, this performance was extremely relaxed, conversational, and congenial. Participants were consistently very engaged with each other's stories and with the process as a whole.

Unlike many participants in the other sessions, no one seemed uncomfortable with being seen as a good liar and all performed their prompt four (lie) without comment except Barbara, who started her story by saying that she had not been able to think of a good one. Isobel followed up her lie with an explanation of the kernel of truth behind it, though within that explanation she reverted to the lie. Quentin's lie was preposterous, but he never broke the illusion. Vivian's, Pablo's, and Anne's lies were almost as preposterous, but they also maintained the illusion. In fact, it was long after Anne had finished her deadpan story of spending nine days on a Chinese boat without a translator that Vivian exclaimed in surprise, 'Oh, that was the lie!' Vivian in turn created a well-received lie about a party where all of the guests wore pink, floppy hats, presented as though the party was just out of view of the photo she displayed—a photo of a classical sculpture in a museum (see Fig. 6.5). This group not only enjoyed the challenge of coming up with a lie, as described above, but for the most part they carried their lies off with aplomb. While of course all of the stories and 'protoselves' (Barclay 1994, pp. 71–72) created through performance were unique, self-making tended towards convergence in that they all defined themselves in relation to each other at least once during the performance, and they expressed support for each other's views and experiences.

Fig. 6.4 Isobel and Fred on a regular day (Photo © 'Isobel' (name withheld for reasons of confidentiality), used with permission)

Heightened Attention

Several of the performances in this group stood out for the tangents that the stories take compared to what seemed most obvious about the photos, a phenomenon coded as 'representation dissonance' that contributed to the 'conspicuousness' of the digital media. For example, Vivian's prompt one (regular day) was a photo of her brother and young daughter captioned in part: 'We went along to a Christmas party at the local children's centre. Here's a picture of my brother and Frances'. The photo showed a very young girl holding a stuffed rabbit and sitting on a rocking horse, with a man looking at her fondly. What Vivian chose to talk about, though, was the frog backpack that her brother gave to her daughter for Christmas. Vivian also made the 'clip-clop' horse noise that her brother taught to her daughter, and that her daughter now makes every time she sees a horse. Vivian used the performance to convey precisely those things that neither a photograph nor a caption can do

Fig. 6.5 Vivian's photo for prompt four (lie), minus the pink floppy hats (Photo © 'Vivian' (name withheld for reasons of confidentiality), used with permission)

effectively, which is to explain the enacted, embodied connections between two absent people, while giving us insight into Vivian's own feelings about the facts she was explaining. What was simply a photo of a cute child became the touchstone for a performance of Vivian's family relationships.

Another example is Zita's prompt two (thinking of you), a photograph that most of the audience had a difficult time deciphering. It showed grilled spring onions, 'a traditional meal from Catalonia' that Zita had chosen while thinking of Isobel (see Fig. 6.6). Her performance, however, punctuated by several over-the-shoulder glances back at Isobel, made it clear that Zita was 'more jealous of you than thinking of you'. Zita had missed a large family gathering for the first time, while Isobel had been back home with her own family at the same time. The onions served as a springboard for a story whose real point was homesickness. Interestingly, some of the most compelling behaviours for intensifying the performer's appearance were sudden, subtle changes, such as Zita's glance over her shoulder to indicate her jealousy. Then, on Isobel's prompting, the mood changed to joking about the 'sexual way' that people might eat the onions. Zita's performance ranged from pathos to comedy in the space of just over a minute, primarily due to the dissonance between the emotions in the story and the photo of onions.

Anne's response to prompt five (forgotten) used a lack of digital media to intensify her appearance. Anne found a photo that she had truly forgotten about and did not care about, so she did not upload it, and it seems that she actually did delete it. It was a photo of a 'very, very cute' bird that she had seen in Australia and assumed that she would never see again. The real subject of the performance, though, was

Fig. 6.6 Zita's Catalan onions, making her jealous of Isobel (Photo © 'Zita' (name withheld for reasons of confidentiality), used with permission)

Anne's surprise at having taken such a photo and her recreation of that surprise for her audience, plus the ensuing judgement that the photo 'was not interesting'. As she explained, 'I went through the different pictures, and at a certain point I just saw one and thought, what's that?' The way she crinkled her nose and turned her head indicated mild disgust at herself for having done something so silly as to take a picture of a bird simply because she would never see it again. The dissonance between the cute bird each audience member was imagining and the blank space that Anne preferred intensified Anne's appearance, not in its physicality *per se* but for how her personality might be discerned through it. Anne used a similar technique for prompt two (thinking of you). Her story described a park that she did not have a photo of, so she showed one that 'has not been taken in the same season, but this is the kind of place where I imagined Barbara, Isobel and other people I did not know yet would spend part of the afternoon together'. For Anne, this was a photographic record of her imagination that also served as a vehicle for her audience to approach Anne's memories through the exercise of their own imaginations. This intermingling of imagination with memory is frequently used in autobiography (Bruner 1994; Pearson and Shanks 2001; Govan et al. 2007; Heddon 2008, pp. 83, 99) and, I argue, serves to heighten the audience's attention to the performer as they imagine her to be.

Temporal dissonances played a particularly large role in this performance, partly because Pablo, Quentin, and Zita had few personal photos to hand and scanned in older, analogue photos instead. In Pablo's case, his audience was charmed by seeing photos of him as a very young boy in contrast to the grown man performing in front of them striking the very same pose. Temporal dissonances opened a space for performers to discover something about themselves, as well. For example, Pablo explained during his performance of prompt three (embarrassing) that he was not as embarrassed as he had thought he would be when he selected the photo (see Fig. 6.7).

Quentin, though, made use of a much more recent photo to play more intricately with performance and temporal dissonance. His photo for prompt three (embarrassing) showed him making an angry face (see Fig. 6.8). He began his story saying that he 'was really happy to go on vacation', whereupon Barbara interrupted, saying, 'You don't look very happy there'. There was laughter all around, which Quentin

Fig. 6.7 Pablo then and now (Projected photo © 'Pablo' (name withheld for reasons of confidentiality), used with permission)

Fig. 6.8 Quentin pulling a face at his bad haircut and worse holiday (Photo © 'Quentin' (name withheld for reasons of confidentiality), used with permission)

incorporated into his performance. 'I will explain why,' he said, and continued with a story of a disastrous holiday. Nothing about his story could have been inferred from the photo until he described getting a bad haircut. A quick glance confirmed that the haircut in the photo was very different from Quentin's current hairstyle. Quentin finished his story by saying, 'Robert asked me to express everything you think about Portugal'. Immediately, the photo became a piece of performance documentation (Auslander 2006). It was a photo of a performance event: Quentin's performance of his feelings during his rained-out Portuguese holiday. The Quentin of the present moment did not attempt to recreate this facial expression, but rather clenched his fists in the air to either side of his head, re-performing his past feelings in a different way and doubling, not simply repeating, the expression of those feelings. The audience could now see Quentin's frustration at his appearance and at his miserable holiday, multiply performed and displayed. This technique heightened his audience's attention to his appearance and garnered a long, loud, appreciative laugh.

Barbara followed Quentin's performance with a similar one of her own. Her photo for prompt three (embarrassing) was taken when her boyfriend asked her to show him how she would act if she were facing a dinosaur. She responded by opening her mouth very wide, and he took the photo that she now projected for her audience. Barbara did not attempt to re-enact her photo, either, but acted out the reaction of the shocked little boy who saw her at the moment the photo was taken. Barbara gave the impression that the reason she did not re-enact the photo was her true embarrassment about the size of her mouth when she opens it wide, in contrast to Quentin's nonchalance about his bad haircut, but the effect was the same. The digital media brought a slice of the past into the present moment, where the performer amplified its effect by adding further layers of detail and parallel re-enactments that complemented rather than duplicated the media. The devising phase gave performers time and guidance to select particular media and to reflect on their memories triggered by those media from two perspectives: the current time and place where they were selecting their photos, and the future performance situation as they imagined it would be. Thus the photos became 'conspicuous' to the performer first, and through the actions of the performer they became 'conspicuous' to the audience as well.

Situatedness

Situatedness was not found in every story told within a performance, and in fact some performers made only a few references to the time, place, or audience members of the performance (Barbara, Pablo, and Vivian each made five, while the others made none). However, references to others in the room were fairly common, both as topics of performance in prompt two (thinking of you) and as asides between performers and audience members. Participants made use of the spaces between stories to solidify connections among themselves. For example, Barbara asked Isobel about her yoga teacher and why he had not attended an event the previous Saturday; Isobel asked Vivian 'Is that the brother I knew?' at the end of Vivian's prompt one (regular day); Isobel interjected 'I took it' when Quentin showed a photo of himself in nothing but swimming trunks for prompt one (regular day); again, Isobel interjected 'I was the groupie,' this time in Quentin's prompt four (lie); and Barbara commented that 'you have the same eyes' to Vivian in response to Vivian's emotional disclosure of seeing her mother as a 'vulnerable old lady'. A more complex connection was made late in the performance, after Barbara told her prompt four (lie) about her brother's pig, which she said her brother had adopted like a child. When Barbara was ending her turn, Anne said, 'I'm sure Pablo understands,' referring to Pablo's recent story about the pet rabbit that his family had cooked and eaten. Pablo took up this joke: 'Yeah, this is the kind of family I want'. These brief interruptions and transitions did not detract from any performer's ability to get his or her story across. Instead, they helped to cement the relationships among the performers, giving the performance a greater sense of cohesion.

Anne also reflected the situatedness of the performance by playing with the system. She knew from experience with prompt five (forgotten) that she could fulfil the requirements of the performance without uploading a photo, so she used her tactics from prompt five on prompt three (embarrassing). Rather than find a photo that she was not actually embarrassed about, or revealing something she would rather not reveal, Anne made creative use of the explicit and implicit rules in *Collect Yourselves!* She acted within the norms and expectations of the group, gamely offering a description of a photo she would be truly embarrassed by, without violating her own boundaries or going to extreme lengths to acquire a copy of the photo from her mother in France. There is also every chance that the photo her audience imagined was more embarrassing than the actual photo she described. In either case, like storyteller Michael Parent, she 'invite [d her audience] to make their own visuals, to make their own meaning' (cited in Wilson 2006, p. 187). In refusing to show a photo, Anne successfully negotiated her personal boundaries, her own limited digital archives, the technological system, and the expectations of her fellow participants.

Aesthetics of the Event

As mentioned in Chap. 3, Fischer-Lichte lays out three phenomena that contribute to the aesthetics of the event. 'Autopoiesis and emergence' can be found in any self-sustaining and unplanned interaction, not necessarily performances towards the right side of Wilson's storytelling continuum (2006, p. 9), and therefore was not helpful in identifying or explaining the most emotionally compelling moments of performance. Similarly, 'deviation and surprise' depends on an underlying rhythm or pattern for the performance as a whole, from which a single element can deviate. However, *Collect Yourselves!* performances are made up of many individual stories, making it difficult to identify deviations or surprises other than those very few contributions that broke the rules, such as Anne's performance of prompt 3 (embarrassing) without a photo.

What emerged was the strong connection between the most interesting or moving elements and the category of 'liminality and transformation', where participants experience a transition from one emotional or attitudinal state to another. The most compelling moments came when performers took a risk and shared a personal experience that might have met with lack of interest or disapproval. These shared intimacies provided powerful moments in which both performer and audience member could find her feelings or beliefs challenged.

As noted by many participants, the value of *Collect Yourselves!* performances lay in the connections, intimacies, and insights into each other, as well as insights into their own experiences. In these liminal moments, participants could perceive each other not just through the facts of their experiences or the style of telling, but through a deeply felt sense of connection established through processes of memory and imagination. These moments did not happen unless the performer took a risk or made herself vulnerable, even slightly, to her audience. Vulnerability and risk tended to arise when performers revealed self-discoveries they had made in the course of devising or performing, or when they 'heightened attention' to themselves and/or their media in a way that revealed their 'protoselves' (Barclay 1994, pp. 71–72) in an unaccustomed light. Importantly, the converse does not hold: at no point did liminality lead to any of the other themes.

Zita embodied a combination of confidence and vulnerability that made even the least 'tellable' (Sacks 1995, p. 776) of her stories carry a slight amount of risk. She spoke quite softly and struggled more than the others with her English. She did not stand to perform but remained crouched near the laptop as though ready to stop at any moment. This also prevented her from making full use of her body, as for example Isobel often did by shifting her weight or striking a pose. However, Zita's stories nearly always contained an element of emotion or self-disclosure that not everyone would care to admit to. The onion photo (Fig. 6.6) led her to disclose her jealous homesickness (prompt two, thinking of you, described above); the photo of herself and the young boy she looks after led her to disclose her sadness over leaving her nannying job (prompt one, regular day). Prompts three (embarrassing) and five (forgotten) revealed her in oddly sexualised poses, in contradiction to her demure manner. These nuggets of emotion or self-disclosure were not embedded in a long story or hidden under layers of mannerisms, but spoken calmly and simply. Unlike Isobel, who sometimes joked about her feelings, Zita could not hide behind extravagant exaggerations or use the excuse that she was only kidding. Whatever sorrows or desires she revealed, she took the risk of revealing them directly.

Pablo's stories were sometimes not the most 'tellable' (Sacks 1995, p. 776), either: his prompt two (thinking of you) recounted a Guy Fawkes fireworks display with Isobel, Quentin, and Vivian, while his prompt one (regular day) was a description of an office car park in the snow. In these instances, he revealed very little emotion, and therefore left little room for his audience to engage with him through either memory or imagination. His performance came alive in prompt five (forgotten), a photo of him as a small boy with his pet rabbit (see Fig. 6.9). Just as placidly as before, he explained that his mother later cooked the rabbit and fed it to the family. This captured the audience's attention and they began asking questions about the experience. Pablo replied very directly: 'I think I cried, I really cried.' Like Zita, Pablo had not constructed a 'persona' to hide behind as a professional storyteller might have (storyteller Claire Mulholland cited in Wilson 2006, p. 175). Therefore, his admission rang utterly true, and the audience empathised strongly. Isobel pushed the issue further, asking if his family had forced him to eat the rabbit. 'Yeah, probably they did,' Pablo replied. 'What you can expect, 200 people living in that town, you kill the rabbit, it's just the rabbit or you.' Pablo had now hit his stride, eliciting gales of laughter from the audience on top of a moment of self-disclosure and intimacy. It was precisely Pablo's and Zita's lack of 'theatricality' in terms of a 'highly conscious approach to an audience' (Petersen 2005, p. 212) that enabled them to establish a strong emotional connection with their audience.

Risk can be seen in Barbara's prompt three (embarrassing), which shows her with her mouth wide open. Barbara was visibly embarrassed by how wide her mouth can open, due to a dislocated jaw in childhood, and her story described the 'shocked' look a small boy gave her when she opened her mouth at the moment this photo was taken. Although her audience were amused and/or sympathetic to Barbara rather than shocked or disgusted, her body language and tone of voice indicated the depth of her self-consciousness about this part of her body and therefore the risk to her self-image in revealing this vulnerability to others. The risk was located not so much in the photo of a woman with a mouth that opens wide (which, incidentally, she did not wish to see published), but in the face-to-face admission of how self-conscious she is and how negatively other people react to her. Therefore, Barbara's performance implicitly asked her audience to tread carefully around her vulnerability. Such instantaneous and emotional reactions connect performers and audience

Fig. 6.9 Pablo and his pet rabbit, which became dinner for the family (Photo © 'Pablo' (name withheld for reasons of confidentiality), used with permission)

members through acts of memory and imagination. Thinking in terms of the *punctum* (Barthes 1981, p. 27), a term used to indicate the subjective but compelling detail in a photograph that imbues it with personal significance, each of these reactions works as a performative *punctum* that sets the experience of a *Collect Yourselves!* performance apart from an everyday, undifferentiated experience (Dewey 2005).

The moment where I as an audience member, or more accurately a bystander (Benford et al. 2006), felt this 'liminality and transformation' most keenly was during Barbara's extended story for prompt two (thinking of you) about a day spent with Anne and another friend of theirs, Denis. The photo is a faux-antique snapshot of Anne standing in the middle of a field, far in the distance. Barbara described the walk they took and offered what could have been the conclusion to a short but satisfactory story: 'I really enjoyed this afternoon with Anne and Denis … because first of all it was good exercise and good company and good fun.' The 'first of all' indicated her intention to continue, which she did by taking the story in a very personal direction. 'I think the fields and all that reminded me of my childhood growing up in the countryside, and I just felt really at home in those fields'. At this point Barbara gave a quick gasp mixed with a laugh as though overwhelmed with emotion. She continued:

> This particular moment, I don't know, I really liked this vision of Anne in the field. I thought it was so poetic, almost like a fairy tale, I don't know, I'm really glad I captured that moment. She was so pretty there, I don't know, it was just really—perfect. It was a perfect kind of moment, yeah. (Barbara)

Anne giggled at the mention of her looking 'poetic', indicating pleasure and perhaps embarrassment. Barbara, meanwhile, indicated by her manner and gaze that she was entirely sincere in this description, and even paused before 'perfect' and gestured as though searching for exactly the right word (see Fig. 6.10). Towards the end of this story, she became very quiet, and her audience matched that quietness, as though aware that any sign of disapproval could cause Barbara to feel rejected or ridiculed. Finally, after she finished, an audience member softly and gently asked a follow-up question. Everyone laughed in relief, and Barbara's response came with a shift in tone that indicated the risky moment of intimate self-disclosure had passed. For me, though, this performance was condensed into Barbara's quick gasp of a laugh as she tried to perform the beauty of a perfect, fairy-tale moment, that to anyone not present that night would be nothing more meaningful than a snapshot of a far-off woman standing in the grass.

Questionnaire and Interview Responses — Thematic Analysis

'This was a live experience … it should stay that way'—Barbara

The same process of thematic analysis conducted on data relating to the devising phase was applied to data collected on the participants' subjective experiences of the entire performance process as well as their past experiences with the stories they told. Open coding was used on these data, resulting in the following.

The experience of using *Collect Yourselves!* was reported to be positive across the board. Two participants reflected on the value of the system to forge connections among both friends and friends of friends: among friends it 'deepened the bond we have', and with the others it 'made me meet new people who can become new friends'. By the end of the session, all participants felt that they knew everyone in the room. Descriptions included 'fun and intimidating', 'fun and touching', 'exciting', 'interesting', 'pleasant', and 'such a great experience'. Anne liked the 'straight path' structure of *Collect Yourselves!*, which served both to guide topics and to prevent a single story from going on for too long.

The quietest members of this group appreciated that *Collect Yourselves!* balanced the contributions of shy and talkative individuals. One of these was Pablo, who noted that the structure removes the 'leader who is driving the conversation' in regular conversation, giving quieter or shyer participants the chance to speak and 'to do the best'. This opinion was shared by the dominant performer of this group,

Fig. 6.10 Barbara trying to convey the 'perfect kind of moment' (Projected photo © 'Barbara' (name withheld for reasons of confidentiality), used with permission)

Isobel, who volunteered the comment that 'it's really good to hear the ones who are more shy'.

Zita revealed the strategies she imagined most people would use for choosing a story order. 'I was interested in why most of us except for Isobel chose the embarrassing one third,' she said. Her explanation was that 'obviously' no one would choose to perform prompt three (embarrassing) first, but that equally no one would want to leave it for last in case time ran out. This comment reveals the conscious decision-making processes at work for at least one participant.

Only one participant would be happy to share any of the photos from this session online. Most would refuse to post their 'embarrassing' photo (prompt three). Some would not share their lie (prompt four) or forgotten photo (prompt five), either. One would not show any of them, in an effort to manage the 'meaning' behind the photos and not to appear 'egocentric'. Almost all participants experienced an implicit level of control in this live experience that they do not find online.

The feeling of performing tended to include a mix of pleasure and challenge, not unlike the feeling of taking part in the devising phase. Two participants described feeling 'nervous', one of being 'a bit embarrassed', and one of being 'uncomfortable, but it was still fun as we weren't asked to talk about serious matter[s]'. This participant identified 'social pressure' as the cause of discomfort: 'Was it funny? Did I make a good choice of picture?' Half of the participants noted that feelings of nerves or discomfort passed with time.

All participants felt positive about being audience members for each other, although one participant admitted that she did not find all the stories to be interesting. Other responses include 'interested', 'amused', 'a funny and quick way to know' both friends and strangers, and 'curious about the others' choices'. Anne noted the importance of sharing time and space with performers, rather than simply looking at their photos or hearing their stories:

> I think we can learn a lot about people by how they react, rather than through biographical stories. But I think they are quite complementary. It's true there is one face we very often don't see. (Anne)

This interest in seeing the 'one face we very often don't see' describes the importance of live performance in a dynamic, reciprocal environment where the audience can challenge the performer to see their reaction. Vivian described the experience of being an audience member in different terms but arrived at a similar conclusion. She called it 'empathetic' and said that 'it's more intimate as an experience than a usual drinks party or a Facebook browse'. Intimacy is also implicated in participants' attitudes towards sharing the video record of their performances to others. All would be reluctant to show the full video or would refuse outright, primarily because it is too 'private' or 'personal' to be shared. Interestingly, though, two participants cite the liveness of the performance experience as a reason not to share a video of the performance online. Barbara admits that she might show an edited version to friends but would not be inclined to do so because she 'like[d] that this was a live experience and felt it should stay that way'. Similarly, Vivian would refuse to share any version of the video because the value lay in the moment of experience, and the performance would not 'be as entertaining as a video as it was as an experience'. In my interpretation, these responses raise the issue of liveness, not in pursuit of its ontology, but as a key component of the phenomenological experience of self-disclosure, risk, and intimacy. Live and recorded versions of a performance do not have to be posited as hopelessly irreconcilable in order for an individual to prefer one type of experience over another. For at least these two participants, their personal digital media have been bound up in an ephemeral, intimate experience that they wish to preserve only in memory.

Step 6 Result: Findings

Findings Across the Four Performances

Although only one *Collect Yourselves!* performance has been analysed in detail in this text, a total of four performances were analysed, two among groups of friends and two among groups of strangers. The results across the four performances were broadly similar, with a few notable exceptions. This section lists the headline similarities and differences, in part to indicate how individual analyses can be combined in PED, and in part to ground the examples from the other three groups that will be used throughout the rest of this text.

The experience of using *Collect Yourselves!* resulted in a number of effects across all four groups:

- participants made an honest effort to fulfil the 'spirit' of the requirements of the prompts and of the performance situation, even in the rare instances where they violated the 'letter' of those requirements;
- those efforts led many to frustration, challenge, discomfort, and risk;
- many who initially felt uncomfortable came to enjoy the experience;
- the most enjoyable parts were often perceived as the most challenging;
- challenging situations created the space for self-discovery, surprise, connection, and shared intimacy which was stronger and more frequent than would be expected in a corresponding period of regular conversation or media sharing;
- these connections were highly valued, as were the more frequent but less intense insights into other people's lives;
- these connections would not have been created without the experience of the devising phase;
- the overall experience was improved for those who engaged with reminiscence in either or both phases;
- and all groups envisioned *Collect Yourselves!* being used by both groups of friends and groups of strangers.

There were also contrasts in use between the two types of groups. The Friend Groups tended to demonstrate more of the following qualities than did the Stranger Groups:

- conventional and unified approaches to the negotiated act of group performance
- coherence in style, tone, and timing
- 'success' in performing all stories in the allotted time
- acceptance and enjoyment of each other's stories
- positivity about the experience as a whole
- self-discovery, intimacy, and risk
- reluctance to be seen as a good liar.

In comparison to what would be expected of conversational photo sharing according to the literature, the *Collect Yourselves!* performances elicited a much more even distribution of time spent speaking; much greater and richer engagement with digital media; multiple instances of self-disclosure and self-discovery; several moments of connection, intimacy, vulnerability, and risk; and behaviours that contribute to all categories of 'heightened attention' and the 'aesthetics of the event' (Fischer-Lichte 2008). Friends performing with *Collect Yourselves!* found themselves learning more about each other and feeling more intimately connected than they had imagined, primarily through meeting the challenge of a two-phase performance experience.

This case study sought to generate a performative experience with the properties of autobiographical performance using a technological system as the primary instigator. The findings across all four performances indicate that those performative experiences, which I have termed intermedial autobiographical performance, did in fact possess the properties of autobiographical performance: self-making, heightened attention, situatedness, and the aesthetics of the event. Each performance had moments of emotional and aesthetic power as perceived during the performance by audience members and as reported after the fact by audience members and performers. As an example of PED, intermedial autobiographical performances generated by the use of *Collect Yourselves!* reveal both the external structures and the internally felt experiences of a performance event as it invites participants into a deeper, more reflective, and potentially transformative relationship with each other, and with their own life experiences. Intermedial autobiographical performance frames media sharing as a meeting place, where performers and audiences can come together in a challenging and risky space that brings them to insights about themselves and each other through memory and imagination. In this space, it is possible to design parameters within which 'everyone experiences themselves as involved and responsible for a situation nobody single-handedly created' (Fischer-Lichte 2008, p. 165), least of all the designer.

New Knowledge, Theories, and Insights

The process of analysing the four *Collect Yourselves!* performances, along with the knowledge-generating processes of performance analysis (Step 3 in the PED methodology) and design exploration (Step 4 in the PED methodology), resulted in the production of new knowledge, theories, and insights. These are offered as an example of how the results of a PED process can contribute to the disciplines of HCI, interaction and experience design, and performance studies, and to round out discussion of the case study. I define 'performed photos' as a new category of photos in the context of media sharing, extending the work of Balabanović et al. (2000) within the HCI literature. I then define 'doubled indexicality' as an important extension of Dixon's categories of 'digital doubles' in performance (2007), of particular relevance to intermedial studies and PED. These are followed by discussions of the workings of connection and liminality in conversational performance. The final discussion, 'attending and marking', draws from the entire process of conceptualising, designing, and analysing *Collect Yourselves!* It posits a way of understanding engagement with digital media that focuses on the construction of meaning through performance rather than the 'production' or 'consumption' of the media artefact.

Performed Photos

Previous research in media sharing has allowed users to offer the most simplistic of descriptions unchallenged, noting that comments such as 'This is my parents at home' are related to efforts 'to preserve memory and aid recall' (Balabanović et al. 2000, p. 570). I do not dispute the value of recalling facts, but I suggest that there is at least as much value in seeking out new contexts in which to remember and recollect past experiences. Previous research revealed two main categories of story-telling for media sharing: 'story-driven', in which users source photos to support a particular narrative, and 'photo-driven', in which users describe a series of photos in often simplistic terms (Balabanović et al. 2000, p. 570). Balabanović et al. note that media sharing that is prompted by the appearance of a photo rather than the desire to tell a particular story tends to be limited to identifying information such as 'this is my wife' (2000, p. 570). However, some of the *Collect Yourselves!* prompts, particularly prompts one (regular day) and five (forgotten), ask participants to share media based on the characteristics of the photo, regardless of what story might or might not be associated with it. Such information might be felt not to 'count' as a story, much less as 'party pieces', as Marta in Stranger Group 1 phrased it. In spite of this restriction, there was often no obvious difference between 'photo-driven' and 'story-driven' stories in terms of length, the 'tellability' or worthiness of being told (Sacks 1995, p. 776), or engagement with the properties of autobiographical perfor-mance. Stories for prompts one (regular day), two (memorable), and five (forgot-ten), which asked users to choose a photo regardless of the 'tellability' of the story behind it, were nearly always indistinguishable from the others in terms of narra-tive, detail, and their engagement with the properties of autobiographical perfor-mance. Some of these even formed high points of 'heightened attention' and 'liminality and transformation'.

'Performed photos' emerged as a new category of storytelling around one or more photos that develops a fleshed-out and/or narrativised description of a photo in response to a prompt. These occupy a crossroads between the 'photo-driven' and the 'story-driven' (Balabanović et al. 2000, p. 570). Performed photos are those that participants might not consider candidates for sharing in the absence of the prompt, but these stories can open up performers as well as audiences to previously unfore-seen self-discovery, insight, and connection. The new stories were 'photo-driven' in terms of the motivation for telling them, but performers almost always provided significant description and narrative instead of the simple identifiers noted by Balabanović et al. (2000, p. 570), and usually performed them using at least one behaviour that indicated 'heightened attention' or the 'aesthetics of the event'. 'Performed photos' include Isobel's self-disclosure about a deceased friend that captured her audience's attention so strongly, and Pablo's story of being fed his pet rabbit for dinner. The devising phase, perhaps in combination with a pressure to perform in an extra-conversational scenario, contributed to the emergence of this category of 'performed photos' that is at the heart of what Quentin calls 'socialising the social network'. It demonstrates the potential for even the most forgettable of digital media to become meaningful and 'tellable' (Sacks 1995, p. 776) through practices of performance.

PED may also extend these categories further using Reeves et al.'s taxonomy of interactions in terms of manipulations and effects, and their observations about the ways in which spectators can interact with an experience or performance (2005). For example, the few *Collect Yourselves!* participants who struggled to use the trackpad immediately adopted the 'expressive' approach, making a show of their ineptitude and folding their difficulties into the persona that they performed for their audiences (2005, p. 745). Future work in this area could explore the effects on liminality and transformation of adding layers of complexity to the ways in which participants can hide or exaggerate their interactions and transitions in small and private performances, or use these strategies to imagine how to open up such performances to a larger audience. There is a responsibility inherent in any effort to guide users, particularly when that guidance might temporarily misdirect or deceive. Moreover, the assumption that designers can or should decide what is beneficial, and for whom, is a fraught concept. Still, the responsibility must be taken seriously, as performed photos have many of the same ethical implications identified by Heddon (2008) in autobiographical performance such as the need to take account of the feelings of people involved or implied in the material being performed.

Doubled Indexicality

Many have argued about the nature of digital media in a performance context, as discussed in Chap. 2. After analysing *Legs 11* (2011) by Tom Marshman, and in light of the topics of interest in the design exploration that resulted in *Collect Yourselves!*, a new way of conceptualising the effects of media in performance emerged.

In *Legs 11*, Marshman used professional and amateur video, photos, music, dance, storytelling, and participatory elements to conjure for his audience some of his experience of suffering and then recovering from varicose veins. This includes entering a competition to become a model and spokesperson for Pretty Polly, a major brand of stockings, a competition that was implicitly but clearly aimed at women rather than male performance artists. (He made the finals and featured in some of their promotional material.) The audience was exposed to dissonance on many levels: between photos of Marshman's varicose veins and the healthy legs he displayed for them in live performance; between the male Marshman and the other, female contestants for the Pretty Polly competition; between the professionally produced broadcast videos and Marshman's easygoing live presence next to them; and between the medical, commercial, and artistic contexts in which he displayed his legs.

Marshman projected two photographs of his ankles and legs taken before surgery. The flat lighting and a stark white backdrop suggested they might have been taken by Marshman's doctors for their own purposes and only later shared with Marshman. While they were being projected, Marshman described his surgery in an easy, conversational manner, a performance of the 'everyday' in comparison to his stylised dances. Similarly, Marshman screened a section of a television programme in which he featured as a patient, asking the show's doctor for advice on his varicose veins. Another was a professionally produced video for the Pretty Polly company, which had run a nationwide competition looking for a (presumed female) model to represent their tights and stockings. Marshman entered this competition and reached the finals, which were recorded for Pretty Polly's marketing purposes; Marshman then used Pretty Polly's video in his own performance, for his own purposes.

Marshman also displayed the photograph he submitted for the Pretty Polly competition, first on its own and then in the context of the web page of his competition entry. Finally, Marshman showed an amateur video taken by friends in which he ran a half-marathon with a pair of artificial legs propped over his shoulders, as a publicity stunt to gain favour with Pretty Polly's decision-makers. The contrast in style between the starkly clinical or marketing-driven images and Marshman's very personal and matter-of-fact storytelling added dissonant perspectives to Marshman's story and invited his audiences to imagine themselves into the times and places he described.

One might interpret Marshman's photos of his diseased legs as an example of the 'digital double', a well-known concept within the study of digital performance set out by Dixon. He describes a digital double as having the potential to 'reflect upon the changing nature and understanding of the body and self, spirit, technology, and theater' (2007, p. 244). Marshman certainly explored body and self using digital representations. However, Dixon's notion of the digital double cannot be easily applied. One type of digital double, the 'double as reflection' (2007, p. 245), addresses Marshman's themes of body and self, but for Dixon it should do so 'as a digital image that mirrors the identical visual form and real-time movement of the performer or interactive user' (2007, p. 246). Marshman's media failed this test. Dixon's second type of digital double, the 'double as alter-ego', is a 'shadow double … an alternate, and invariably darker embodiment' (2007, p. 250). While Marshman's diseased legs could be seen as a 'darker embodiment' of his healthy self, his playful and triumphant representations as a Pretty Polly finalist could not. Neither can his digital images be construed as 'spiritual emanation' (2007, p. 253) or 'manipulable mannequin' (2007, p. 259), Dixon's two remaining categories. Examples of digital doubling chosen by Dixon also depend on interactive technological manipulations during the performance, such as live motion capture (2007, p. 260), or the 'careful rehearsal' required to play opposite a recording (2007, p. 246). Marshman's digital representations did not call for manipulation or skill. Some other operation was at work.

This other operation comes from the fact that Marshman's media were grounded in the practices of everyday life, including vernacular practices of photowork (Kirk et al. 2006) and the easy transfer of digital images from one 'owner' and context to another (Van House 2011, p. 128). These practices stand in contrast to the 'digital artistic aspiration' (Dixon 2007, p. 254) that Dixon sees in performances using digital images of the performer. Marshman did not use these media (aside from an initial film) for their visual aesthetics but instead to provide a visual trace of his experience as it appeared from another perspective. In combination with Marshman's presence, this trace created a representational dissonance.

The closest description of this dissonance is 'contiguity' as defined by Batchen (2001) in his work relating to reminiscence. Contiguity is based on Roland Barthes's 'having-been-there' of an analogue photograph created by light reflecting off of the object onto the photographic plate (1977, p. 44). For Batchen, this not only refers to the photographed object's visual representation but also provides a 'carnal' or empathic connection between the object and the viewer (Batchen 2001, p. 21).

Contiguity is the 'magic' force that offers 'the possibility of a direct emotional empathy across an otherwise insurmountable abyss of space and time' (2001, p. 21). Contiguity is defined in work relating to reminiscence, but it cannot be limited strictly to reminiscence. The viewer cannot know, remember, or take the subject position of every object in every photograph she owns; the 'direct emotional empathy' must be in some way a potential supplement to the limits of subjectivity and human memory. It is also clear that photographs can offer 'direct emotional empathy' for those not present at the taking of the photograph, through acts of memory and imagination (Kuhn 2010; Frohlich et al. 2013). The reaction of Marshman's audience to the photos of his legs is evidence of this empathy at work, outside the bounds of personal reminiscence.

Furthermore, Batchen presents his analysis as part of an argument differentiating analogue from digital photography. He posits that digital photography robs people of this sense of physical connection: 'it is precisely a capacity for visual continguity [sic] that is now under threat as the photographic image is irresistibly transformed into a continuous flow of data' (2001, p. 22). Finally, Batchen suggests that the image must not only be analogue, it must be perceived as analogue, to have contiguity: '[c]ontiguity depends on the knowledge of that difference [between analogue and digital].... If we don't bring that knowledge, then there is no contiguity effect' (2001, p. 23). Clearly, Batchen's theory addresses a common phenomenon, that of using a photograph to connect immediately, viscerally, and empathetically to a past experience, which is reconstructed rather than retrieved through varying degrees of personal recollection and imagination. However, this phenomenon has not stopped since the advent of digital photography (Van House 2011; Sarvas and Frohlich 2011). Contiguity is an important basis for understanding how Marshman's digital media created a sense of connection in his audience, but if the photos were not announced and believed to be analogue, where did this contiguity come from?

I argue that contiguity comes from the relationship between the photo, whether digital or analogue, and the live presence of the performer. The relation between photograph and physical presence is argued in Batchen's later book, *Forget Me Not: Photography and Remembrance* (2004). Batchen describes the historical practice of keeping a loved one's lock of hair together with their photographic portrait. People engaging in this practice tended to overlook the physicality of the photograph (and therefore the contiguity effect that Batchen originally posited), and saw instead 'a sort of window' to the person photographed. Batchen wonders, 'Could the addition of a tactile portion of the human body to a photograph be an effort to bridge the distance, temporal and otherwise, between viewer and person viewed as well as between likeness and subject?' (2004, p. 74). He suggests that it can, and that the mechanism for this action is presence. 'Truth to presence is joined by the actual presence of a part of the body being signified' (2004, p. 75). I suggest that the physical body of the performer functions in much the same way as the lock of hair, using presence to create not Dixon's 'digital double' but a 'doubled indexicality' (Batchen 2004, p. 75). I use Batchen's term to extend Dixon's range of the potential for digital doubling into intermedial performance, particularly in autobiographical performance and other 'presentational' performances (De Marinis 1993) that reflect on the performer's identity.

'Doubled indexicality' serves to reinforce the presence of what is actually absent—in this case, Marshman's varicose veins—and to transform Barthes's '*studium* of mere resemblance … into the *punctum* of the subject-as-ghost' (2004, p. 76, emphasis in the original). In other words, it is the physical presence of the performer that permits the full measure of the audience's sense of connection to the performer. Fischer-Lichte can also be read as supporting at least part of this argument; her analysis of Frank Castorf's production of *The Idiot* (2002) argues that the use of video to interrupt a live performance 'brought about the apotheosis of the bodily co-presence of actors and spectators' (Fischer-Lichte 2008, p. 73), causing in the audience an experience of 'transcendence' (2008, p. 73). The intriguing dissonance between the performer and his representation heightens the audience's attention to both image and performer and contributes to the sense of connection that the audience can make to the performer through acts of memory and imagination.

'Doubled indexicality' also bridges the gap between analogue and digital. The presence of the performer frees the image from the burden of physical manifestation. In fact, Batchen writes of 'a desire for pure opticality' (2004, p. 73) which is even better served by digital than by analogue photography. These ephemeral, projected images of Marshman's legs, released from any 'haptic purchase on history' (Batchen 2001, p. 23) that they might have had as analogue photographs, represented a medical condition that had since vanished. Thus in this case, digital photographs underscore rather than contradict Phelan's assertion that '[p]erformance's only life is in the present' (1993, p. 146). 'Doubled indexicality' can connect audiences to the past alongside the present, and the distant alongside the immediate.

Doubled indexicality can be seen throughout the *Collect Yourselves!* performances. It serves to heighten attention that oscillates between 'conspicuousness' and 'intensity of appearance'. Vivian's prompt five (forgotten) is an example, where the story of a forgotten snapshot of her mother on a family holiday transformed into a story about mutability and loss. Vivian's mother had been badgering her to settle down when the photo was taken, but from the vantage point of the devising phase, Vivian saw her mother as a 'quite vulnerable old lady'. Vivian's performance of this photo simultaneously invited the audience to view her mother as vulnerable and old ('conspicuousness') and to witness her own change of perspective, which Vivian admitted 'made me a bit sad' ('intensity of appearance'). This effect was intensified when Barbara interjected that Vivian has her mother's eyes. Doubled indexicality heightens attention to live performers and to their media through highlighting the gap or disparity between the two.

Connection

By 'connection' I refer to the fact that 'the *experience* of sharing images and stories, especially face-to-face, enacts the relationships between owner and viewer' (Van House 2009, p. 1083, emphasis in the original). 'Connection' is the present-moment sensation of that experience whereby relationships are enacted and therefore in some way altered (for the most part, strengthened). Many would be reluctant to share a video of the event online or would refuse outright, often citing the ephemerality and 'event'-ness of the performance as the key reasons. I understand this reluctance to indicate that it was more important for these participants to forge connections than to share information. The digital media artefacts served the performance, rather than the other way around.

Before conducting these studies, it had seemed reasonable to assume that Friend Groups would feel confident enough in their relationships with each other to strike out with individualistic performances, extravagant lies, and outright reminiscence, whereas individuals in Stranger Groups would strive to converge as much as possible. In fact, the opposite was true. Friend Groups tended to perform their connections to each other, not just in their responses to prompt two (thinking of you) but in their interactions throughout the performance, in both performer and audience member roles. Stranger Groups, on the other hand, performed their differentiations from each other and were notably less even in their distribution of time and attention. It had also seemed plausible that groups of friends might have found the artificiality of the performance structure to be a hindrance to intimacy, but again, the opposite proved to be true. Friends tightened their bonds with each other and made discoveries about each other—and themselves—that they might never otherwise have made. Strangers had a similar though less intense experience, connecting with each other because of, not in spite of, the constraints against ordinary conversational interaction.

Performers adapted to the unique situation of performance through the structure as well as the content of their performances. Participants shaped their interactions with the technology to suit their priorities: Friend Groups tended to prioritise group cohesion and harmony when negotiating turn-taking and story length, while Stranger Groups tended to prioritise ways of distinguishing themselves from each other, even at the expense of taking their turns in order or allowing their fellow participants the chance to tell all of their stories as intended. However, these differences between Friend Groups and Stranger Groups pale in comparison to the perceived balancing effect that *Collect Yourselves!* had on all its participants. All groups distributed the time among themselves far more evenly than would be expected from conversational storytelling, where as one participant put it, 'undoubtedly a few people would dominate' (Terese). Three groups made the unsolicited comment that they appreciated the opportunity for quieter participants to feel able to assert themselves. This impression of equality offered by *Collect Yourselves!* is taken as a positive aspect of the performance experience and a further indication of the possibly subconscious yet very clear way in which participants formed connections with each other.

Liminality in Conversational Performance

The *Collect Yourselves!* analyses establish that 'liminality and transformation' is the most important element of intermedial autobiographical performance, not the overall 'aesthetics of the event' that Fischer-Lichte (2008) subordinates them to. Moreover, the potential for 'liminality and transformation' does not necessarily increase the more 'professional' or 'theatrical' a performance seems. In many instances the opposite is true. Gestures, manipulations of the voice, and short periods of 'acting out' another character are all commonly found in the most quotidian of conversational narratives (Langellier and Peterson 2004), and an increase in these techniques does not necessarily lead to an increase in liminality or transformation. Conversely, the more conversational performances, particularly in the group analysed here, marked by interruption, questioning, and co-telling, had a coherence in terms of energy and attention against which moments of 'liminality and transformation' could more easily appear. So, for example, the sudden drop in Isobel's tone when she mentioned her friend who had passed away was instantly paralleled by an increase of attention from her audience, who could then follow up with questions and entice Isobel to extend her story in this new direction. The subsequent insight into Isobel's and Quentin's relationship with this friend generated an empathy among audience members that added a note of sincerity and gravity to all of the reminiscences that followed. This situation corresponds to the most powerful moments in two of the other professional autobiographical performances analysed for this case study, *Legs 11* and *Editor*, which came not from the most 'artistic' or 'theatrical' elements but in the quiet, personal stories told directly to the audience. In sum, *Collect Yourselves!* has revealed the limitations of the framework of the 'aesthetics of the event' in the context of intermedial autobiographical performance, one that a focus on 'liminality and transformation' can address.

The design process for *Collect Yourselves!* took on a challenge in attempting to embed performance aesthetics into an interactive technology. Perhaps the most important finding from this attempt was that, to the extent that it succeeded in meeting those design goals, it did so indirectly. Connection, intimacy, challenge, risk, and transformation emerged through the devising and performance processes despite the fact that neither the prompts nor the rules directly solicited those feelings or behaviours. Where *Collect Yourselves!* stands apart from much of the other work in design is that it allows participants to create these potent experiences as part of an emergent performance event that includes a discrete devising phase. At no point are intimacy or risk presented as goals, and as the analyses have revealed, not all performers engaged with those behaviours. However, the overall positive reaction to the experience, especially those reactions that reflect a sense of challenge or discomfort mixed with the positive feelings, indicate that this oblique approach is successful to at least some degree.

'Attending' and 'Marking' in Performance

One question that has been evoked but not answered through this discussion is whether the performance phase of *Collect Yourselves!* generated what would be generally accepted as a performance. As one of the Stranger Group participants said, her stories were hardly 'party pieces', much less something she would expect to see performed on a stage. There was also no clapping in any of the performances, even after another Stranger Group participant commented that she felt the audience should clap for a fellow performer. This reluctance to clap could indicate that they did not perceive their actions as a performance, or it could be due at least in part to the fact that they were all performers as well as audience members. However, I argue that the performances differed from ordinary, purely conversational digital media sharing sessions in a more fundamental way, through two functions that I have termed 'attending' and 'marking'.

'Attending' is associated with 'heightened attention' and refers to the act of perceiving that an audience member undertakes in response to 'license' that is 'given… to the audience to regard the act of expression and the performer with special intensity' (Bauman 1975, p. 293). Attention is more than the direction in which an audience member points their visual field. It can encompass all senses, including the proprioceptive, as the spectator becomes increasingly or decreasingly involved with what he or she is paying attention to. It also includes an individual spectator's memories and imagination as they are triggered by elements of the performance, leading to unique cognitive and emotional responses from each one that are nevertheless linked by those elements that they attend to. When performance theorists speak of 'energy' within a performance, this act of attending is a large part of what they are referring to.

The other main element of the function of 'energy' in performance is 'marking', the process by which a performer invests meaning in an otherwise insignificant-seeming performance element. Marking is particularly key for the use of digital media in performance, as digital media are sometimes seen as lacking essential properties of live performance or even as functioning in opposition to the aims of live performance (see e.g. Phelan 1993; Fischer-Lichte 2008, p. 165). For example, Barbara's photo of a person in the far distance of an empty green field is utterly unremarkable on its own to anyone unfamiliar with the situation in which it was taken or the deep feelings it represents for Barbara. Annotating the photo 'Anne dans le champs' ('Anne in the field') informs the audience that the person-shaped mark in the far distance is their fellow audience member Anne, but the annotation gives no context for this information, and the photo does not allow spectators to compare the Anne in the photo to the Anne in the room. It is only Barbara's animated and deeply heartfelt performance of trying to convey the 'perfect kind of moment' that invests the photo with meaning for someone beyond Barbara herself. Her performance of this photo transforms it from an everyday snapshot to an integral part of an aesthetic performance, which audiences might then attend to with a greater investment of their own personal memories, imaginations, and emotional energy. Audiences shift their attention as the performance progresses and thereby change the 'energy' or 'feeling' of the performance. Marking and attending work in tandem to integrate otherwise quotidian objects, words, gestures, sounds, and the like—including digital media—into a performance experience that can change people's emotions and challenge their attitudes.

An experience can be 'marked' more or less strongly without implying a hard distinction between aesthetic and non-aesthetic performance. Rather, 'marking' and 'attending' move a performance along the spectrum towards the 'cultural', 'intense', 'risky', and 'rewarding' (Wilson 2006, p. 9), making the event 'special' (Dissanayake 2003). As Benford commented at the CHI 2013 Digital Arts panel question and answer session, HCI looks at moments of interaction at the expense of understanding consumption and production—particularly production—and does not account for value or meaning in experience. One way in which performance can provide the missing focus on value and meaning is to reframe 'consumption' and 'production' in terms of the 'attending' and 'marking', respectively, of an interactive event. 'Attending' is one way in which a spectator engages with a performance beyond sitting passively. The performance is not 'consumed' as one might consume a commodity, or even as one might process the information contained within a media artefact. Rather, an audience member actively engages with the performance through memory and imagination, thereby making it 'special' (Dissanayake 2003). 'Marking' is how one 'produces' a performance rather than an unremarkable fragment of conversation. The performer invests something of the self through self-discovery, self-disclosure, choices of how others are represented, manipulation of energy levels, risk, vulnerability, connection, and intimacy. 'Attending' and 'marking' work together, as in Fischer-Lichte's 'autopoietic feedback loop' (2008, p. 165), one feeding off the other as the performance develops. Together, they indicate those moments when interactions with personal digital media become charged with emotion and insight through a vulnerable co-presence. Because performance can be understood as attending to and marking everyday practices, such as the taking and sharing of digital photographs, 'the potential for performance is always present' (Bauman 1992, p. 44). Anyone can create an intermedial autobiographical performance, given the right triggers and parameters. Through the extended, two-phase interaction with their own digital photos guided by the *Collect Yourselves!* system, participants surprised themselves and others with forgotten or unrealised attitudes, relationships, and memories. By their own accounts, their time spent engaged with each other through the *Collect Yourselves!* framework was more insightful, connected, intimate, and potentially transformational than ordinary media sharing or conversation.

References

Auslander P (2006) The performativity of performance documentation. PAJ: A J Perform Art 28(3):1–10

Balabanović M, Chu L, Wolff G (2000) Storytelling with digital photographs. In: Proceedings of the SIGCHI conference on human factors in computing systems. ACM Press, New York, pp 564–571

Barclay CR (1994) Composing protoselves through improvisation. In: Neisser U, Fivush R (eds) The remembering self: construction and agency in self narrative. Cambridge University Press, Cambridge, pp 55–77

Barthes R (1977) Image, music, text. Fontana, London

Barthes R (1981) Camera lucida. Hill and Wang, New York

Batchen G (2001) Carnal knowledge. pp. 21–23. In: Jones A et al The body and technology. Art J 60(1):20–39

Batchen G (2004) Forget me not: photography and remembrance. Princeton Architectural Press, New York

Bauman R (1975) Verbal art as performance. Am Anthropol 77(2):290–311

Bauman R (1992) Folklore, cultural performances, and popular entertainments: a communications-centered handbook. Oxford University Press, New York/Oxford

Bavelas JB, Coates L, Johnson T (2000) Listeners as co-narrators. J Pers Soc Psychol 79(6):941–952

Benford S, Crabtree A, Reeves S, Sheridan J, Dix A, Flintham M, Drozd A (2006) The frame of the game: blurring the boundary between fiction and reality in mobile experiences. In: Proceedings of the SIGCHI conference on human factors in computing systems. ACM Press, New York, pp 427–436

Benford S, Greenhalgh C, Giannachi G, Walker B, Marshall J, Rodden T (2012) Uncomfortable interactions. In: Proceedings of the SIGCHI conference on human factors in computing systems. ACM Press, New York, pp 2005–2014

Bruner J (1994) The "remembered" self. In: Neisser U, Fivush R (eds) The remembering self: construction and agency in self narrative. Cambridge University Press, Cambridge, pp 41–54

Crabtree A, Rodden T, Mariani J (2004) Collaborating around collections: informing the continued development of photoware. In: Proceedings of the 2004 ACM conference on computer supported cooperative work. ACM Press, New York, pp 396–405

De Marinis M (1993) The semiotics of performance. Translated by O'Healy A. Indiana University Press, Bloomington/Indianapolis

Dewey J (2005) Art as experience. Perigee Books, New York

Dissanayake E (2003) The core of art: making special. J Can Assoc Curr Stud 1(2):13–38

Dixon S (2007) Digital performance: a history of new media in theater, dance, performance art, and installation. MIT Press, Cambridge, MA/London

Fischer-Lichte E (2008) The transformative power of performance: a new aesthetics. Routledge, London

Frohlich DM, Clancy T, Robinson J, Costanza E (2004) The audiophoto desk. In: Proceedings of 2AD, second international conference on appliance design. HP, Bristol, np

Frohlich DM, Wall S, Kiddle G (2013) Rediscovery of forgotten images in domestic photo collections. Pers Ubiquit Comput 17(4):729–740

Govan E, Nicholson H, Normington K (2007) Making a performance: devising histories and contemporary practices. Routledge, London

Heddon D (2008) Autobiography and performance. Palgrave Macmillan, Basingstoke

Jordan B, Henderson A (1995) Interaction analysis: foundations and practice. J Learn Sci 4(1):39–103

Kirk D, Sellen A, Rother C, Wood K (2006) Understanding photowork. In: Proceedings of the SIGCHI conference on human factors in computing systems. ACM Press, New York, pp 761–770

Kuhn A (2010) Memory texts and memory work: performances of memory in and with visual media. Mem Stud 3(4):298–313

Langellier KM, Peterson E (2004) Storytelling in daily life: performing narrative. Temple University Press, Philadelphia

Pearson M, Shanks M (2001) Theatre/archaeology: disciplinary dialogues, 1st edn. Routledge, London/New York

Petersen AR (2005) Between image and stage: the theatricality and performativity of installation art. In: Jerslev A, Gade R (eds) Performative realism: interdisciplinary studies in art and media. Museum Tusculanum Press, Copenhagen, pp 209–234

Phelan P (1993) Unmarked: the politics of performance. Routledge, London

Reeves S, Benford S, O'Malley C, Fraser M (2005) Designing the spectator experience. In: Proceedings of the SIGCHI conference on human factors in computing systems. ACM Press, New York, pp 741–750

Sacks H (1995) Lectures on conversation. Blackwell Publishing, Cambridge, MA/Oxford

Sarvas R, Frohlich DM (2011) From snapshots to social media: the changing picture of domestic photography. Springer, New York

Van House NA (2009) Collocated photo sharing, story-telling, and the performance of self. Int J Hum Comput Stud 67(12):1073–1086

Van House NA (2011) Personal photography, digital technologies and the uses of the visual. Vis Stud 26(2):125–134

Wilson M (2006) Storytelling and theatre: contemporary storytellers and their art. Palgrave Macmillan, Basingstoke

Chapter 7
Guidelines for Designer/Researchers

Abstract This chapter presents guidelines for designer/researchers who want to explore the possibilities of Performative Experience Design in their own work. These guidelines arise in large part from the work done with *Collect Yourselves!* as well as other existing projects whose aims and methods coincide with those of PED such as mixed reality performances and Humanaquarium. They are contextualised with many of the theories raised throughout the book and illustrated with examples from all of the *Collect Yourselves!* performances. The guidelines cover key ideas of designing for opportunity, emergence, possible new forms of interaction, and an alteration of meaning; considering the idiosyncrasies of each audience and audience member; allowing for large variations in practices and attitudes; challenging users to take risks and make themselves vulnerable; considering a devising phase, dissonance, and processes of meaning-making in the designed experience; and exploring performance analysis and coded performance analysis to work with elements of interaction that cannot be detected by existing HCI methods.

Guidelines for Design: In Summary

The case study presented in the previous two chapters stands as an example of how PED can be implemented in the context of personal digital media sharing. That case study deals with photographs and storytelling as the primary means of engagement that are re-imagined through the lens of performance and designed for as a 'performative experience' that incorporates all of the properties of autobiographical performance identified in Step 3 of the methodology. This current chapter returns to the focus of Chaps. 1, 2, 3, and 4, which is to say of PED as a whole, where photos and stories may or may not be relevant areas for engagement.

As explained earlier, PED can be used as a framework for designing experiences that are performative in any number of ways, including other senses besides the visual, other means of performance besides narrative, and other types of technology besides the storage and display of photography. The following guidelines point out what PED can offer to designers interested in working with ideas of performance, performativity, meaningful interpersonal interactions, and the experience of the self in relation to digital technologies. Each provides examples drawn from the case study and/or the relevant literature to illustrate its point.

© Springer International Publishing Switzerland 2016   193
J. Spence, *Performative Experience Design*, Springer Series on Cultural
Computing, DOI 10.1007/978-3-319-28395-1_7

- Guideline 1: Design for the *opportunity* for people to perform in the ways you envision.
- Guideline 2: Consider audiences—in all of their idiosyncrasies—as a key contributor to performance.
- Guideline 3: Design for performance as an emergent, shifting, co-creative process of heightening attention that develops felt connections among performers and audience members.
- Guideline 4: Consider a devising phase as an important component of the overall interaction.
- Guideline 5: Consider designing performative interactions based on dissonance.
- Guideline 6: Anticipate that performance might open up new types of interaction.
- Guideline 7: Allow for large variations in practices and attitudes towards digital media technology.
- Guideline 8: Expect the possibility for performance to alter the meanings that people invest in digital media.
- Guideline 9: Use performance to challenge the user to take risks and make themselves vulnerable.
- Guideline 10: Consider processes of individual and/or group meaning-making after the conclusion of a specific performance.
- Guideline 11: Explore performance analysis and coded performance analysis as means of analysing elements of interaction that cannot be detected by existing methods in HCI.

Guidelines for Design: In Detail

Guideline 1: Design for the *opportunity* for people to perform in the ways you envision.

Attempting to force any of the emotional or aesthetic conditions generated by the performative experience could easily result in refusal or half-hearted compliance. Even interactions devoid of any significant emotional or aesthetic element, such as basic conversation or interaction with a museum exhibit, can be loaded with an expectation to 'perform' that can put people off. Designing indirect means of encouraging a desired type of interaction can be far more powerful than providing direct instructions or unyielding affordances.

It may be impossible to prove a negative statement, but I suspect that any attempts to directly instruct people to 'perform' in the sense of generating a liminal and transformational moment of exchange between performers and audience members would fail. The existing literature in both HCI and performance studies, the design space charted for intermedial autobiographical performance, and personal experience all indicate that ephemeral, contingent states such as the liminal cannot be directed any more than a person can be directed to be happy at a moment's notice. Risk, intimacy, dissonance, liminality, transformation—all of these are fragile conditions. Even the solitary devising phase of *Collect Yourselves!* risked desensitising its participants to their personal digital media, as researchers have already noted the danger of engaging too frequently in reminiscence (Frohlich and Fennell 2006, p. 107; Petrelli et al. 2008, p. 60; Kuhn 2010, p. 304). Prompts that participants can reinterpret as they please, rules they can break—under these conditions, one can design fertile environments in which performance *may* take hold.

The prompts used in *Collect Yourselves!* exemplify the kind of oblique instruction that can arrive at emotionally and aesthetically pleasing performances. Because prompts are based on language instead of novel technologies, they might seem unexciting or inappropriate for engagement with digital technologies. I argue instead that they provide a rich means of gently guiding participants to engage with digital technologies in new ways. One Friend Group participant, Xiu, originally wrote, 'It's great as I used photos to share life experiences', then crossed out the 'I' and wrote 'we'. This comment is a performative reflection of the possibility for a designed technological intervention to create the conditions in which participants feel a positive sense of human connection.

The very loose rules in *Collect Yourselves!* functioned in a similar way, guiding participants towards types of interaction that would not ordinarily be afforded or constrained by digital media technology without trying to impose a single correct way to perform. Designs should balance rules that cannot be broken due to the way the technology is developed with rules that can easily be broken, such as the decision taken by Conor in Stranger Group 2 to click the 'Finish Turn' button at the beginning of one of his turns. This action removed his photo from the projection and turned off the timer for the duration of his story. While his disregard for the rules could have resulted in a complete loss of structure had the other participants followed his lead, it instead contributed strongly to the self that he constructed in that performance: not simply through the content he chose or how he delivered that content, but through his relationship to his fellow (rule-abiding) participants. A combination of rule types can provide fertile ground for self-making, relationship-building (or relationship-damaging), and playful approaches to performance opportunities. Also, as prompts and rules are embedded in the technology being designed, there is no reason that they cannot be combined with functionalities or interfaces that are novel or powerful in their own rights.

The process by which participants come to understand what is expected of them in a performative encounter has an enormous bearing on their perception of and engagement in the experience. This is evident in the occasional difficulties in getting participants to interact in any sustained or knowledgeable way with Humanaquarium (Taylor et al. 2011) and in the effort required to keep participants on a useful 'trajectory' in mixed reality performances (Benford and Giannachi 2011). Designers need to consider a range of existing mechanisms for guiding participants, including the creation of new mechanisms, and to balance their choices in a way that optimises opportunities for participants to co-create a meaningful performance.

Guideline 2: Consider audiences—in all of their idiosyncrasies—as a key contributor to performance.

Audiences form arguably the most important part of the unique context or situation of each set of experiences with an interactive system. Audiences must be understood not only in terms of demographics or group responses but also as a collection of individuals with the capacity for differing, even contradictory responses. PED is concerned with audiences as groups of people undergoing individual experiences, though some elements may be shared and some perceptions may overlap. The diversity of experience and response is a strength, not a weakness, of PED.

Whether considered as groups or as individuals, no two audiences are the same. And, as noted in Chap. 3, audiences can have a profound influence on unfolding performances. Designers must account for the myriad ways in which audiences might react to a performative experience—and must expect the unexpected. As Reason reminds us, 'it is necessary to talk of audiences in the plural and to be continually aware of the heterogeneous construction of empirical audiences' (2004, p. 16)—though for practical purposes I still find it helpful to speak of an audience for a specific instance of performance in the singular. For example, three of the *Collect Yourselves!* performances featured relatively quiet audiences, which might lead one to the conclusion that their polite attentiveness was critical in creating the sense of 'performance'. On the other hand, the audience discussed in Chap. 6 was far noisier, interrupting or contributing often throughout the performance. It would be easy to imagine that this would detract from the intensity of the performance and give it instead the air of a regular conversation. The opposite was true. As described in Chap. 6, audience interactions formed a hugely significant part of this performance. They drew performers out into unplanned narratives, instilled confidence, established or reinforced interpersonal connections, and created a space where performers felt happy to reveal their vulnerabilities. Had this audience been more hostile or attention-seeking in their contributions, the performance as a whole would undoubtedly have taken on a different tone. Yet controlling the audience is not the answer, at least not in cases like the one presented here. If *Collect Yourselves!* had been designed to prevent all conversations or interjections, this performance would have emerged very differently and, I suspect, in a far less emotionally and aesthetically engaging way.

Guideline 3: Design for performance as an emergent, shifting, co-creative process of heightening attention that develops felt connections among performers and audience members.

It is a subtle but critical imperative of PED that the designer keeps in mind the many different self-generating, interpersonal, meaningful performances that may emerge as a consequence of the design; this is a very different focus from designing a device or system and then imagining how the user is likely to react to it. No matter what form a design might take, the live performative experience that emerges from it is a separate entity. It can be triggered and to a certain extent controlled by the design, but the emerging relationship between performers and audience members will be a major contributor to the felt experience of using the design.

This guideline refers to the centrality of the 'autopoietic feedback loop' (Fischer-Lichte 2008, p. 165) discussed in Chaps. 1 and 3. The coded performance analyses of *Collect Yourselves!* trace the development of the autopoietic feedback loops through shifts in attention and the responding changes in energy. For example, in Stranger Group 1, Joanna often gave very energetic, even frantic performances, but her audience rarely matched her energy levels. By contrast, most of Marta's stories were performed in an understated manner that earned a very energetic reception from her audience. Where Joanna's energy might have been expected to intensify her appearance, in fact it often pushed her audience away, as seen in the discrepancy between performer and audience energy levels during her stories. Similar violations of expectations happened in Stranger Group 2. Susan told a story that began with the audience very unimpressed but that gradually built their engagement. At the peak of her audience's investment of energy and attention, she ruptured that energy with a single phrase that made her audience feel self-conscious and uncomfortable, and the performance as a whole took some time to recover from this sudden drop. Discrepancies between a performer's high-energy attempts to capture the audience's attention and the audience's low energy levels made the performance uncomfortable or unpleasant to watch, as did a sudden misjudged comment in an otherwise engaging story. Successful build-ups of audience attention and energy levels led to what one participant called feeling 'enraptured' by performance, evidenced by leaning forward in their seats, laughing, and expressing appreciation. From the point of view of the designer of *Collect Yourselves!*, none of these outcomes was predictable, yet they accounted for some of the highest and lowest points of the performance experience.

Guideline 4: Consider a devising phase as an important component of the overall interaction.

Performance consists of far more than what happens 'on stage' while events unfold. Performance also consists of the sometimes lengthy and often richly rewarding process of developing or devising the work to be performed. By introducing participants to a performative experience that has already been fully formed without their contribution, we are depriving them of the chance to take a fuller part in the experience of performing, and we are depriving ourselves as researchers of a wealth of understanding and insight into performative experiences with technology.

Most existing media sharing research views the selection of media objects as a less important part of the experience than the interaction among participants and their media (see e.g. Balabanović et al. 2000; ten Bhömer et al. 2010). Alternatively, the selection can be 'rigged' to facilitate a particular kind of sharing (see e.g. Ah Kun and Marsden 2007) or purposely left to chance (Leong et al. 2011). While these approaches have many merits, they leave open a wide space for exploring processes of selection, which can have enormous repercussions on the later media sharing session. The devising or selection process directs participants towards particular types of interaction with their digital media archives and suggests certain types of responses over others. However, this does not simply reflect the choice of one photo over another, where the audience would likely never detect the difference. Instead, the private and extended process of devising their contributions to the upcoming performance directly shapes the felt experience of the performance. Ravi in Stranger Group 1 explained the effect of the selection process in terms of its influence on the moment of performance:

> You're sort of performing it in a way … . Everyone had a performance, a way of telling the story behind the picture … . You're inviting everybody to become part of your mini-world in that picture … the smell of the place, the atmosphere, what was going on that day, the weather, the family and people around you, you became part of that setting. (Ravi)

The devising phase of *Collect Yourselves!* allowed participants to develop a full sense of the 'mini-world' of their picture long before the performance took place. Then the structure of the performance kept the participants 'on script', as another participant put it. Several people described their inclination to tell a spontaneous 'second story' (Frohlich 2004, p. 138) or 'response story' (Norrick 2000, p. 112) to establish connections with the other participants, and some even spoke in terms of discomfort with the artificiality of the requirement to tell the prepared stories rather than their spontaneously arising response stories. However, most agreed that the opportunity to select their photos in advance and the structure of keeping to these stories were ultimately enjoyable and valuable for uncovering what one participant described as the 'interesting parts of people's lives that you'd never come across if it wasn't for having done it this way'. In fact, another participant pointed out that she and her friends 'can spend a whole night, even sitting, talking, chatting, and … I wouldn't probably get into any of these stories'—stories that she enjoyed telling, and whose parallels from other participants she appreciated hearing. For *Collect Yourselves!*, it was important to understand the selection process along the same lines as the endeavour of devising a performance, rather than the simple identification of material according to the norms that already govern conversational storytelling or online media sharing practices. For PED as a whole, it is just as important to explore unusual approaches to whichever type of media, technology, or engagement is under consideration.

Guideline 5: Consider designing performative interactions based on dissonance.

Neither self nor memory is static, so why pursue media sharing strategies that treat them as if they were? Confronting people with dissonance between their personal digital media and their current perception of self can create space for self-discovery, self-disclosure, and heightened attention in ways that they could not have foreseen otherwise.

Examples of dissonance occurred throughout the four *Collect Yourselves!* performances, including a photo of a glass sculpture made from a cast of Ebba's own teeth in Stranger Group 1, or the series of photos in Friends Group 1 showing one of the participants, Wendy, in a range of different hairstyles. This guideline is a very specific instance of McCarthy and Wright's exhortation to view 'technology as experience that is open to the sensual, emotional, volitional, and dialogically imaginative aspects of felt experience' (2004, p. 184). One of these 'dialogically imaginative aspects' is the relationship among performer, projected photo, and audience in relation to photos that were particularly distant from or dissonant with the live performer. In particular, older photos tended to garner a lot of positive audience attention and energy. The reactions related to the dissonance between the live performer and his or her much younger self, as in the case of the young Pablo posing with the pet rabbit that became the family dinner, and even more so for any other forms of dissonance such as the culture shock that most audience members felt at the prospect of eating a pet for dinner. Dissonance is a necessary precursor to intimacy, risk, and vulnerability in *Collect Yourselves!* performances, and those in turn were necessary for 'liminal' and 'transformational' (Fischer-Lichte 2008) moments of performance to occur (Spence, forthcoming).

Guideline 6: Anticipate that performance might open up new types of interaction.

Adding an expectation to 'perform' during an interaction with technology can create new approaches to that interaction. There is a heightened attention and an expectation of being evaluated inherent in even the most informal performance situations. These pressures can bring about unexpected new ways of interacting with technologies, digital media, other people, and even one's own sense of self. The more that a design guides users away from their everyday habits and instinctual responses, the more opportunity there is for performance to encourage fresh types of interaction to emerge.

One of the things that *Collect Yourselves!* required participants to do was to think slightly differently about their digital photos. As described earlier, many shared Deacon's view in Stranger Group 2: 'I don't think I would have told the stories … if we didn't have the pictures to direct us'. He also made explicit reference to the importance of the prompts in arriving at those pictures: 'I'd say you could tell stories without pictures, but you'd have to be prompted to do it in a similar way. The prompts'. Fay confirmed the findings of House and Nancy (2011), saying that without the prompts, she would have selected much more recent photos that were 'prompted by what other people had been talking about'. *Collect Yourselves!* guided participants to select photos they would not ordinarily share and then to follow through in performance when they would ordinarily choose a topic that suited the emerging conversation. This led to a type of interaction that had no precedent in the HCI literature: 'performed photos', defined in Chap. 6.

This new type of photo sharing interaction not only responds to a new type of guidance, but it also caused some participants to reflect on their online media sharing practices. Conor in Stranger Group 2 contrasted the devising phase with online social networking:

There's something about choosing the photos that I found a bit odd … . In social networking sites I find that I only put the bits that I want people to see … . I create another me, because I just portray … everything's always wonderful in my life, or terrible at a moment, or just the highlights. (Conor)

I argue that even the subtlest of new types of interaction can have an effect on participants. Conor now knows the emotional, visceral, and mental effects of showing something besides the 'highlights' of his life to others. Sudden moments of questioning and insight such as Conor's might influence later decisions regarding how he presents and represents himself to others, or how he understands someone presenting or representing themselves to him. In no way would I attempt to argue that such a small novelty of interaction or the insight it brought about will change the world, but then again, neither will many of the world's serious works of performance, or art, or even technology. However, these new interactions at least have the potential to shape an experience of the world and contribute to a greater understanding of how humans can drive forward their relationships with their digital technologies in a positive way.

Guideline 7: Allow for large variations in practices and attitudes towards digital media technology.

While on the whole, digital technology has resulted in far more photos being taken than in the days of analogue photography, it does not necessarily follow that all users will have large archives at their disposal. Designers must take into account restrictions on the media available due to location (e.g. work vs. home or temporary residence vs. permanent home), storage format (e.g. portable devices, PCs, external hard drives, cloud storage, discs, or social networking sites), and personal photo-work practices (e.g. relying on others to take photos).

Conor in Stranger Group 2 is a young male professional whose peers are active online. However, he makes a point of never taking photos or posting to social networks: his partner has taken on these tasks on his behalf. (This claim seems to contradict his comments quoted above about how he portrays himself online: I took this to be shorthand for how he wants to be portrayed, and that his partner makes choices he agrees with.) For this reason, Conor felt much less personally attached to the entire process of developing and curating a digital persona, though it was clear from his performances that his sense of attachment to photos from his past was every bit as strong as the other participants'. The fact that he chose not to engage directly with digital photography or online social networking emerged as a central facet of the 'protoself' (Barclay 1994, pp. 71–72) that he put forward to his fellow performers, and the identity that he created through performance was directly shaped and constrained by his partner's choices about how he, Conor, should be represented.

Other participants described reluctance to share photos online for a variety of reasons, including security and a desire not to seem egotistical or boring, while a few relied almost entirely on social networking sites to store and manage the bulk of their personal photos. A major source of frustration was difficulty of access, especially for the international group who formed the case study for this book. Glib assurances from service providers about complete and seamless access to personal photo collections are belied by the struggles of so many participants to identify and locate desired photos from among storage options ranging from cloud services and social networking to current and previous laptops, cameras, and phones, to CDs,

DVDs, and scanned photos from before the advent of widespread consumer-level digital camera technologies. From the perspective of an HCI researcher or designer, the point of access to personal digital media is a fulcrum point full of potential to transform how people perceive, present, and perform their identities to the wider world. As PED deals with performativity from a deeply personal as well as a public perspective, it is critical to design in terms of each individual's relationship to his or her own digital media as well as the infrastructure used to access those media. Averages or trends may indicate useful conditions to bear in mind, but attention must be paid to the many outliers that even a small study can reveal.

Guideline 8: Expect the possibility for performance to alter the meanings that people invest in digital media.

Designers must bear in mind that performance can profoundly influence the meaning of a piece of digital media. Therefore, it is unwise to make assumptions about the types of content that participants might select, much less the effects their choices of digital media will have on themselves and others. The meanings that people attribute to digital media may shift, subtly or radically, through the intra- and interpersonal interactions of performance.

The stories told by Marta in Stranger Group 1 revolved around her family, and many photos represented her children and her mother. However, her high point as a performer as judged by the attentional and emotional investment of her audience came from a nondescript photo of a pink child's suitcase. The story was of Marta's thwarted attempt to sell her young daughter's beloved Trunki. Marta's audience didn't need to see a photo of Marta's daughter or the tantrum she threw when she found out about Marta's treacherous attempt to sell Trunki. After all, the power of the story was not in the daughter's tantrum but in Marta's failed attempt to dispose of a piece of pink plastic. The photo had been taken to show off the suitcase for sale online, and therefore had no obvious visual markers of the relationship between Marta and her daughter. As Marta's audience was familiar with online marketplaces, though, they could easily imagine taking a similar photograph themselves, just as they could imagine the tantrum that Marta described. This made the entire audience laugh in commiseration. Marta's performance utterly transformed the significance of her photo's content for her audience, and in turn the memory of her performance will shape her future responses to that photo (Spence et al. 2013).

Guideline 9: Use performance to challenge the user to take risks and make themselves vulnerable.

Risk and vulnerability create 'heightened attention' to the unfolding performance and can create a liminal space in which both performers and audience members must choose how to react to each other in the emerging performance. Thus, designs that challenge users to engage with risk and vulnerability can put participants into an emotionally and ethically charged relationship with each other that can lead to new ways of thinking, feeling, and interacting, allowing moments of liminality and transformation to emerge.

In terms of design, risk can be defined as creating an opportunity for others to immediately and viscerally reject what one has put on display, while vulnerability can be defined as disclosing information that another person could use maliciously if they wished. Performers take a risk when they expect that their audiences might experience a sudden negative emotional response to what they are about to perform, which might lead to a decrease in the esteem they feel for the performer. Vulnerability is a less imminently threatening situation, as an audience member who witnesses a moment of vulnerability would need to go out of her way to act in a hurtful way. The fear of speaking in public is far from uncommon (Hofmann and DiBartolo 2000), and many participants reported feeling vulnerable before performing. This phenomenon has also been described by Taylor et al. in the experiences of some participants engaging with Humanaquarium:

> They were often surprisingly forthcoming and frank in their feedback, describing how the risk-taking aspect of performing an improvisational and unknown piece of work in a public setting made them acutely aware of their relationship to the audience. Participants reported a heightened sense of vulnerability, knowing they were being watched and possibly judged by their peers, but also described feeling creatively empowered knowing that they were contributing to the execution of the performance that was being experienced by the group. (2011, p. 1858)

Collect Yourselves! indicates that risk and vulnerability can be generated even in small, private gatherings where participants have full control over what they disclose and how they disclose it. Moreover, these moments of risk and vulnerability often led to the most compelling moments across all four performances. Pablo experienced perhaps the clearest sensation of liminality and transformation reported in the interviews and questionnaires. He spoke the least of all participants in his group and preferred listening to performing. However, he surprised himself when the timer ran out during his final story: he discovered not only that his audience wanted him to continue his story, but that he wanted to continue his performance.

The challenge to engage with digital media in unfamiliar ways and then perform for others was an effort that paid off in terms of insight, pleasure, and connection. Steve Benford et al. mapped some of this territory for HCI researchers (2012) with the hope of creating experiences with at least as much value to the experiencer as discomfort. This aim can also be understood in Dewey's terms: there is no extraordinary or 'artistic' expression without some effort, or 'commotion' and 'turmoil' (2005, p. 69). While PED does not require all of its participants to feel uncomfortably vulnerable at all times, it certainly has the scope to accommodate and even encourage 'challenge' and 'risk' as key elements of a proposed design.

More importantly, why would people choose to participate in an experience that they knew would make them uncomfortable or even frightened? While the answer to this latter question is beyond the remit of this text, it is fascinating and important to note that they did. And although this is mere speculation on my part, I strongly suspect that the privacy of the *Collect Yourselves!* performances played a large role in many people's decisions to participate. I base my guess on asides from several of the participants that they would be far too frightened to perform in public or in front of a large group, as well as the reluctance that many of them expressed at the hypothetical situation of being given a video of their performance to share with others. While the exploration of performative behaviour in public spaces is clearly a worthwhile endeavour and entirely in line with the aims of PED, it is also important to investigate people's interactions on smaller scales and in different contexts.

Guideline 10: Consider processes of individual and/or group meaning-making after the conclusion of a specific performance.

Just as performance involves creative processes that begin long before the action commences 'on stage', it involves processes of meaning-making that continue well after the action concludes. The meaning of a performance for any individual shifts as they think about different aspects, recall related memories, and perceive the reactions of others. Data collection on attitudes to a performative experience should take into account processes of meaning-making undertaken by individuals and groups, possibly even designing some of this process into the overall experience.

The act of reflecting on past experiences is not often valued for its own sake within either HCI or performance studies, with the notable exception of Isaacs et al. 2013, Clarke et al. 2015, and the body of work on reminiscence (e.g. Peesapati et al. 2010; Sellen and Whittaker 2010). Reflections might be solicited for the purposes of data collection in HCI studies or, more rarely, in performance studies (see e.g. Reason 2010). However, PED is well suited to incorporate a separate phase of reflection, which would correspond to McCarthy and Wright's sense-making phases of 'reflecting' and 'appropriating' (2004, p. 126). This is not without precedent in performance, as question-and-answer or discussion sessions are not uncommon. Post-performance conversations can reflect the 'liveness' of a live performance event (Reason 2004, p. 21). And in philosophical terms, Reason articulates a need to incorporate post-performance meaning-making processes 'as a central facet of the thing [performance] itself' (2010, p. 24). For Reason, memories of a performance should not be seen as they often are within performance studies as a poor relation to the now-vanished performance experience, but rather as a related and equally valuable experience (2010, p. 26). In his experience, many spectators appreciate the opportunity to discuss what they have just seen and heard, using language that indicates an aim to construct a more complete and valid memory than they could without the process of discussion and reflection (2010, p. 27).

This was also evident with *Collect Yourselves!* performances. Immediately afterwards, groups had a 10-min break in which they talked about what they had just seen and done, and the group interviews often led to lively discussions beyond the remit of the questions I had asked. The questionnaires allowed for individual reflection, while the conversations and group interviews gave participants the chance to make sense of the novel experience they had just taken part in. It is interesting to note the tension between the traditions of the two fields: in HCI terms, these post-performance conversations are easily conceived of as *gathering data* on responses to an interaction, while in Reason's terms, they would be construed as a cognitive as well as 'embodied, kinaesthetic, intuitive' (2010, p. 28) and 'participatory' (2010, p. 31) means of *creating meaning* in relation to an aesthetic experience. While this is not an entirely unknown approach in HCI research, it is certainly one that should be further developed and encouraged in order to extend our understanding of the greater lifecycle of an experience.

Guideline 11: Explore performance analysis and coded performance analysis as means of analysing elements of interaction that cannot be detected by existing methods in HCI.

Performance analysis (taken from performance studies) and coded performance analysis (a novel adaptation of thematic analysis to performance analysis) provide rigorous yet fluid approaches to interactions and experiences in ways that traditional HCI methods are ill equipped to work with. These two methods are initial steps towards a body of techniques that can more fully address the complexities of 'what it is', the intra- and interpersonal interactions that occur through performance and the shifting, slippery meanings that we make of our experience.

The process of moving from the properties identified in the performance analyses (Step 3 of the PED methodology) to the coded performance analyses (Step 6 of the PED methodology) involved applying the standard method of thematic analysis to the content and the 'feeling' or 'sensibility' (Lavender 2013, p. 9) of performances in which the digital interactions are not simply 'over there' (2013, p. 9), on display, but embedded in the deeply personal performance of identity. Coded performance analysis was therefore able to address interactions far more subtle or 'aesthetic' than those detectable by methods such as interaction analysis. As discussed in Chap. 4, it is as important to question the purpose of evaluation in the context of performative interactions as it is to conduct those evaluations as rigorously as possible. As Pearson says of his own ways of working through performance:

> My practice is a kind of hidden knowledge articulated in a language which you will never understand. Just as I will never comprehend the baggage, more or less disguised, which you bring to my image. We must begin to deal with 'what it is', not 'what it might have been' or even 'what it resembles'. (1998, p. 41)

The branches of performance research that form the basis of PED do not pretend that there is anything ultimately stable and knowable on the part of either the performer or the audience. They seek to understand what emerges out of each unique instance of performance, through the experiences of those involved. These two methods will hopefully be complemented by further explorations into the performance literature, and into researchers' imaginations, to develop better ways of understanding 'what it is' (Pearson 1998, p. 41) and, even more importantly, what it might be.

References

Ah Kun LM, Marsden G (2007) Co-present photo sharing on mobile devices. In: Proceedings of the 9th international conference on human computer interaction with mobile devices and services. ACM Press, New York, pp 277–284

Balabanović M, Chu L, Wolff G (2000) Storytelling with digital photographs. In: Proceedings of the SIGCHI conference on human factors in computing systems. ACM Press, New York, pp 564–571

Barclay CR (1994) Composing protoselves through improvisation. In: Neisser U, Fivush R (eds) The remembering self: construction and agency in self narrative. Cambridge University Press, Cambridge, pp 55–77

Benford S, Giannachi G (2011) Performing mixed reality. MIT Press, Cambridge, MA/London

Benford S, Greenhalgh C, Giannachi G, Walker B, Marshall J, Rodden T (2012) Uncomfortable interactions. In: Proceedings of the SIGCHI conference on human factors in computing systems. ACM Press, New York, pp 2005–2014

Clarke R, Vines J, Wright P, Bartindale T, Shearer J, McCarthy J, Olivier P (2015) MyRun: balancing design for reflection, recounting and openness in a museum-based participatory platform. In: Proceedings of the 2015 British HCI conference, ACM Press, New York, pp 212–221

Crabtree A, Rodden T, Mariani J (2004) Collaborating around collections: informing the continued development of photoware. In: Proceedings of the 2004 ACM conference on computer supported cooperative work. ACM Press, New York, pp 396–405

Dewey J (2005) Art as experience. Perigee Books, New York

Fischer-Lichte E (2008) The transformative power of performance: a new aesthetics. Routledge, London

Frohlich DM (2004) Audiophotography: bringing photos to life with sounds. Springer/Kluwer Academic Publishers, Dordrecht/Boston/London

Frohlich D, Fennell J (2006) Sound, paper and memorabilia: resources for a simpler digital photography. Pers Ubiquit Comput 11(2):107–116

Hofmann SG, DiBartolo PM (2000) An instrument to assess self-statements during public speaking: scale development and preliminary psychometric properties. Behav Ther 31(3):499–515

Isaacs E, Konrad A, Walendowski A, Lennig T, Hollis V, Whittaker S (2013) Echoes from the past: how technology mediated reflection improves well-being. In: Proceedings of the SIGCHI conference on human factors in computing systems. ACM Press, New York, pp 1071–1080

Kuhn A (2010) Memory texts and memory work: performances of memory in and with visual media. Mem Stud 3(4):298–313

Lavender A (2013) Feeling engaged: intermedial *mise en sensibilité*. In: FIRT/IFTR conference. Barcelona, 22–26 July 2013

Leong TW, Harper R, Regan T (2011) Nudging towards serendipity: a case with personal digital photos. In: Proceedings of the 25th BCS conference on human-computer interaction. British Computer Society, Swinton, pp 385–394

McCarthy J, Wright P (2004) Technology as experience. MIT Press, Cambridge, MA

Norrick NR (2000) Conversational narrative: storytelling in everyday talk. John Benjamins Publishing Company, Amsterdam/Philadelphia

Pearson M (1998) My balls/your chin. Perform Res 3(2):35–41

Peesapati ST, Schwanda V, Schultz J, Lepage M, Jeong S, Cosley D (2010) Pensieve: supporting everyday reminiscence. In: Proceedings of the SIGCHI conference on human factors in computing systems. ACM Press, New York, pp 2027–2036

Petrelli D, Whittaker S, Brockmeier J (2008) AutoTopography: what can physical mementos tell us about digital memories? In: Proceedings of the SIGCHI conference on human factors in computing systems. ACM Press, New York, pp 53–62

Reason M (2004) Theatre audiences and perceptions of 'liveness' in performance. Particip@tions 1(2):1–24

Reason M (2010) Asking the audience: audience research and the experience of theatre. About Perform 10:15–34

Sellen AJ, Whittaker S (2010) Beyond total capture: a constructive critique of lifelogging. Commun ACM 53(5):70–77

Spence J, Frohlich DM, Andrews S (2013) Performative experience design. In: CHI '13 extended abstracts on human factors in computing systems. ACM Press, New York, pp 2049–2058

Spence J, Andrews S, Frohlich D (forthcoming) *Collect Yourselves!*: risk, vulnerability, and intimacy in participatory performance. In: O'Grady A (ed) Risk, participation and performance practice, Palgrave

Taylor R, Schofield G, Shearer J, Wallace J, Wright P, Boulanger P, Olivier P (2011) Designing from within: humanaquarium. In: Proceedings of the 2011 annual conference on human factors in computing systems. ACM Press, New York, pp 1855–1864

ten Bhömer M, Helmes J, O'Hara K, van den Hoven E (2010) 4Photos: a collaborative photo sharing experience. In: Proceedings of the 6th Nordic conference on human-computer interaction: extending boundaries. ACM Press, New York, pp 52–61

Van House NA (2011) Personal photography, digital technologies and the uses of the visual. Vis Stud 26(2):125–134

Chapter 8
Looking Forwards

Abstract This chapter looks outwards and forwards, presenting PED as a framework or perspective for understanding the large and growing class of interactions with technology that involve personal media, identity, interpersonal relationships, social connections, ever-increasing (though far from universal) connectivity, and digital enhancements to the objects of everyday life. After claiming a lineage for PED in a range of existing work, it explains how PED frames concepts of performativity and performance in terms of experience as an emergent event whose parameters can be designed for, even if the event itself cannot be directly designed. It indicates how PED can bring performance studies and HCI into conversation with each other, as for example the four properties of autobiographical performance identified as part of the case study described in Chap. 5 illuminate concerns and possibilities from the perspectives of both fields. The chapter concludes by looking to potential future applications of PED, including the developing discussions around critical design, the political and ethical concerns of interaction, a surge of research into active spectatorship, a continued exploration of game and play, an exploration of the tensions between fiction and experience, and a reimagining of the concept of dramaturgy in the context of intermedial performance. PED is a new means of creating insights that I believe can drive a better informed and more consciously shaped relationship to our emerging, technologically expanded world.

Looking Forwards

In many ways, this is a speculative text. It originated in a desire to engage in a more sustained way with performance studies than many HCI researchers had done to date (with several exceptions noted earlier). This wish for engagement quickly gave way to the idea that performance should not be used simply to bolster the depth and rigour of performance references within an HCI context, although of course that is one of the aims of this work. Rather, performance can shape, and be shaped by, HCI and design research, resulting in the new sub-discipline of PED. Together, performance and HCI can form their own context, in which the insights of each field contribute to a holistic approach to the phenomenon of performing—whether professionally or conversationally, fictionalising or soul-baring—with digital technologies.

J. Spence, *Performative Experience Design*, Springer Series on Cultural Computing, DOI 10.1007/978-3-319-28395-1_8

At a fundamental level, PED is the setting of technological and social parameters to create opportunities for performative experiences with interactive technologies. I argue that the move towards PED has been under way for some time, in much of the work of mixed reality performance (Benford and Giannachi 2011), Digital Live Art (Sheridan and Bryan-Kinns 2008), the work of Robyn Taylor and colleagues (Taylor et al. 2008, 2011, 2014), the projects discussed in the 'Performance art and digital media' special issue of Digital Creativity (see Nitsche 2013), the work on performative interactions by Julie Williamson and colleagues (e.g. Williamson and Hansen 2012; Williamson and Brewster 2012; Williamson et al. 2014), and several others. The case study presented here complements these works by moving performance from the public realm to the private, personal, and enclosed. As a whole, though, PED aims to bring together what I identify as the driving forces behind all of these projects—experience design, performance, and performativity—into a cohesive framework that foregrounds performance as a lens for understanding and developing further work along these lines.

The diagram of the PED space (Fig. 1.3) may be easier to work with after following the explanations of performativity and performance in Chaps. 2 and 3. One can argue that performativity is inherent in every action a person takes, whether consciously or unconsciously. PED is founded on this understanding of performativity, which permeates both the intentionally 'performancey' and the unselfconsciously personal. However, when exploring options for design, it can be helpful to tease apart those experiences that mark themselves out as culturally and/or aesthetically worthy of the name 'performance' from those that draw less attention to themselves. In terms of the technologies to be employed, it is also critically important to think in terms of the complexity of the *experience* design—primarily in terms of user roles, though perhaps other important parameters will soon emerge. The complexity of the interactions with any given technology may or may not follow from the complexity of the interpersonal experience. PED encourages thinking in terms of increasing or decreasing both the degree of 'performance' and the complexity of the experience design, and always bearing in mind the performativity in even the smallest and most private of actions.

The chapters on performativity and performance lay out critical issues for PED and a set of starting points from which to investigate further. I have every expectation that the list of relevant theories and practices will continue to grow, especially given the bias in the case study towards narrative as a primary mode of interaction and the rich tradition of HCI research involving dance (see e.g. Schiphorst 2011). Similarly, Chap. 4 lays out the PED methodology as it has emerged from early work, but further research will undoubtedly lead to refinements, expansions, and/or alternative models. Chapters 5 and 6 spell out my own experiences with PED in a case study dedicated to co-located digital media sharing, which is of course only one of the many areas in which performative interactions with technology take place. Chapter 7 presents guidelines that I have derived from my own work, generalised in the hope that they will spark fresh ideas, but again ready to be modified and added to as PED research moves on.

The PED methodology contributes to both HCI and performance studies, in part through the development of the hybrid method of coded performance analysis, and in part through exposing methods of one field to the other. Performance methodologies can offer a new way for designers to think through their processes and ultimately better understand the theories and frameworks to be derived from them. Conversely, design practices can contribute a new way of approaching the devising or composing of performance, including in the context of current areas of interest such as scenography (see e.g. Kershaw and Nicholson 2011b) or dramaturgy (see e.g. Trencsényi and Cochrane 2014). Design-oriented research might also provide a more productive way of examining the use of digital technology in performance, which existing perspectives can fail to see, as argued by Salter (2010).

Additionally, methods from one field can be used to confirm—or question—findings from the other. For example, performance analyses can be used as an independent means of corroborating HCI conclusions such as Van House's finding that co-located photo sharing enables people to enact identity and relationships, and that '[c]o-present viewing is a dynamic, improvisational construction of a contingent, *situated* interaction between story-teller and audience' (2009, p. 1073, my emphasis). Similarly, HCI findings can corroborate performance theories. For example, the findings of Balabanović et al. (2000) that people invariably narrate when presenting digital photos or other mementoes to co-present audiences (2000, p. 570) can help to explain the tendency for autobiographical performances to include narration, usually in a relaxed and conversational style, even in performances otherwise marked by poetic or multimodal approaches.

The four properties of autobiographical performance offer an example of how concerns of performance can inform a design process that in turn creates performances to be understood from the perspectives of performance studies, HCI, and PED. Self-making proved to be difficult to pin down initially, as nearly any communication could be seen as an expression of the self. The vertical axis of the PED space (see Fig. 1.3) understood in terms of 'performance' and 'performativity' as laid out in Chaps. 2 and 3 guided the development of that concept through the design process, indicating where elements of self-making could be framed as more or less public and conscious. Ways of establishing individual identity within a group, as well as group identity, can be understood in terms of individual behaviours in combination with the way these behaviours are received and generate new behaviours in turn—including attention and energy. The parameters within which these behaviours are encouraged or discouraged can then be altered by design decisions.

Heightened attention is a rich area for design exploration and can be applied to many different types of experience design. By focusing individually on the objects—including digital objects—involved in performance, the people performing, and the overall structure of the performance event, it is possible to construct opportunities for these elements to grab the attention of the audience (and participant/performer). This in turn has the effect of opening the door for the performance to develop an emotional or aesthetic charge, including the potential for liminality and transformation.

Design for situatedness refers to paying attention to the physical, temporal, and social aspects of the performance experience. Particularly interesting for interaction design is the way in which interactions with technology constitute a significant part of the site, scene, or situation that shapes each experience. By carefully crafting the device or system to prompt particular types of performance, the designer can treat the performance 'frame' (Goffman 1974) as an element to be considered alongside physical, temporal, socio-cultural elements. In other words, the framework of performance can be a unifying factor when other elements, such as location, cannot be fixed.

Design for the aesthetics of the event is a new venture that pushes designers and researchers to consider the potential for their work to create experiences not only of 'beauty' but of challenge, risk, intimacy, and liminality—a temporary frame of mind in which a person's beliefs or attitudes might soften or even change. This concept in particular benefits from the concrete example of *Collect Yourselves!* used in Chaps. 5 and 6, which explains how design choices led to behaviours and emotions that created a fully aesthetic event.

Overall, the PED methodology is valuable for its ability to accommodate overlapping, key concerns of both HCI and performance studies. Its approach brings together political, ethical, and artistic concerns of performance practice with design-led understandings of novel interactions. The analysis of a performance created through the PED methodology opens up interaction to discussion on multiple levels. In this methodology, performance values of reflexivity and unpredictability are brought together with what Stolterman refers to as being '*prepared-for-action* but not *guided-in-action*' (2008, p. 61), allowing for research methods, and even research questions, to shift as the exploration unfolds.

One consequence of intertwining performance and HCI and design methodologies is an increasing tendency (though not an obligation) to consider the ethical and political implications of a given project. Underlying a large part of the performance work discussed in this text is an explicit or implicit political stance. For example, in a text that directly addresses the confluence of performance and technology with personal identity, Schiphorst identifies the potential political results of making the familiar strange again, a practice that can contribute 'to the design and development of our social digital identities and technologies of production' (2012, p. xvi). Such political aims form a common perspective for many performance researchers (e.g. Dolan 2005; Heddon 2008; Chatzichristodoulou 2011). As Kershaw and Nicholson explain:

> Research methods in theatre/performance studies … at best are not concerned with legitimating the cultural authority of the researcher or the research. Rather, they are about the engaged social-environmental production of systems and the cultural production of flexible research ecologies wherein tacit understandings, inferred practices and theoretical assumptions can be made explicit and can, in turn, be queried and contested. (2011a, p. 2)

This expectation that methodology might attempt to subvert authority or contest assumptions is familiar to many performance researchers, but perhaps less familiar to HCI researchers outside the area described as critical design (Bardzell and

Bardzell 2013)—whether those researchers identify with or strongly critique the approach of the Bardzells and their colleagues. Critical design is driven by a 'herme-neutics of suspicion' (Bardzell and Bardzell 2013, p. 3301, a phrase borrowed from Noël Carroll) that aligns closely with the emancipatory political and ethical aims of much performance studies research (e.g. Phelan 2004; Dolan 2005; Fischer-Lichte 2008). Performance methodologies can therefore contribute important methodolog-ical perspectives of reflexivity, unpredictability, and an implicitly political engage-ment with the wider world to discussions of critical design. Making the familiar strange again and working closely with non-professional performers are two spe-cific methods that further those aims and can be clearly understood in the context of design-oriented research and experience design. The case study in this book actively seeks to challenge emerging norms of digital media sharing, not necessarily because I, as the researcher, have decided that they are bad, but because I see value in ques-tioning assumptions behind this rapidly evolving 'social practice by which images, audience, and subject come together for both individual and group self-understanding and relationships' (Van House 2009, p. 1084). Taking an overtly political, critical stance is not a requirement of PED, but the performance orientation of the discipline certainly strengthens the perspective of researchers wishing to contribute to an ethi-cal, critical, exploratory, and humane understanding of the ways that people can engage meaningfully with digital technology.

After giving so many hints as to the potential for PED to expand and develop, I would like to offer a few specific areas that seem ripe for exploration: active specta-torship and audience response, game and play, fiction, and dramaturgy. The idea of active spectatorship is burgeoning in performance studies and may extend work within HCI on the relationship between performance and spectatorship (Dalsgaard and Hansen 2008) or on participatory experience design (McCarthy and Wright 2015). People using an interactive system or involved in performance are under-stood through the roles they play. The 'user' of a design might take on the role of a performer or audience member, 'orchestrator' (Benford and Giannachi 2011) or 'bystander' (Benford et al. 2006), or shift between roles. It is easy to see how per-formers or participants move out of their comfort zones and into the risky space of 'making special' (Dissanayake 2003) by holding themselves up for evaluation by others (Bauman 1975), creating 'protoselves' (Barclay 1994, pp. 71–72) suitable for the unique context of each performance. However, performance studies is increas-ingly interested in theories of active spectatorship, where audiences or bystanders in non-participatory performance can be said to take an active part in the performance and therefore, potentially, in this same risky and emotional territory (e.g. Oddey and White 2009; Fearon 2010; Ginters 2010; Reason 2010; Rancière 2011; Boenisch 2012; Fensham 2012; Lavender 2012). Similarly, in intermedial performance research, performance is arguably located in the 'body' (Nibbelink and Merx 2010, p. 220) or 'perception' (Boenisch 2006, p. 114) of the spectator, opening up new ways of understanding these less overtly active or performative roles. Any of these theoretical perspectives might reveal new ways of designing or understanding per-formative experiences as performers and audience members co-create the 'autopoi-etic feedback loop' (Fischer-Lichte 2008, p. 165), the self-generating and emergent performance event. Additionally, some of the research being done is empirically based and accessible to those with an HCI background (e.g. Reason 2010). It would be worthwhile to develop methods that could more accurately pinpoint spectator reactions in reaction to various types of performance and/or digital media (e.g. Katevas et al. 2015), or as they shift in and out of the role of performer or participant. Also, the PED framework of 'attending' and 'marking' may help to identify the work being done by those taking on various roles in performance.

Game and play were central to structuring and framing the case study in this book; these are also key framings in most of the other work I identify as sharing the aims of PED, such as mixed reality performance (Benford and Giannachi 2011). In *Collect Yourselves!*, the verb 'play' was often ambiguous, implying both playing a game and playing on a stage. The more the directions emphasised game mechanics and the language of games, the more likely the participants would be to focus on winning (Myers et al. 2014). However, the more the directions emphasised the 'performance' implication of the word 'play', the more likely I suspected the participants would be to making their contributions overtly theatrical. Further PED research could pursue different levels of orientation to gameplay, performance, and play for its own sake, as in the cases of Humanaquarium and Nightingallery (Taylor et al. 2011, p. 1859; 2014).

While it was critically important to use presentational performance rather than mimetic theatre to develop the concept of PED, the response of *Collect Yourselves!* participants to prompt four (lie) indicates that there are interesting tensions at work in the creation of a 'lie' or fiction based on one's own personal digital media. Future PED research could explore different methods of creating fictional stories for intermedial performance. With a clear distinction between the presentation of 'the self' or 'protoselves' (Barclay 1994, pp. 71–72) in performance and the representation of a fictional world—paradoxically predicated on the fact that there is no clear distinction to be made between fact and fiction, memory and imagination—it should be possible to pursue research into performative interactions that lean towards the fictional. One possible instigation for such research could be the performance of digital media that has been altered, mashed up, or created without physical referent, perhaps from a perspective that combines the media studies concept of bricolage (Deuze 2006) with postmodern performance techniques of fragmentation and collage (see e.g. Auslander 2004).

Finally, a recent upsurge in research into dramaturgy indicates that using it in place of devising might open a number of new vistas for PED. 'New dramaturgy' is defined as 'the inner flow of a dynamic system' emerging in part from new media and from 'changing relationships with both space and audiences' (Trencsényi and Cochrane 2014, p. xi). According to this definition, new dramaturgy is 'postmimetic', 'intercultural', and 'process-conscious' (2014, p. xii), including everything from devising practices to scenography (Lotker and Gough 2013) to spectatorship, with a particular emphasis on the felt experience of both performers and audience members (Trencsényi and Cochrane 2014). Not only are these ideas very much in line with PED, but new perspectives on dramaturgy were highlighted as a key concern of the Intermediality Working Group at IFTR/FIRT 2013.[1] Dramaturgy as a framework might offer a greater depth and breadth of perspectives on a participant's preparatory work on performance than even the vast array of devising processes can provide.

Thinking from the perspective of PED requires a subtle but fundamental shift from the perspectives of either HCI or performance studies on their own. Performance is much more than a simple tool for improving the user experience or increasing engagement, as many of the researchers and practitioners mentioned in this text have shown. And by the same token, HCI and its related technological pursuits are much more than a source of the latest digital tools for artistic experimentation. PED aims to understand and to challenge the ways in which digital technologies are woven into people's sense of self and how that self is experienced, created, performed, perceived, and shaped through interaction. Each PED project will fall somewhere on Wilson's 'performance continuum' (2006, p. 9) between the conversational and the cultural, informal and formal, with varying degrees of intensity, intentionality, risk, and reward. This ensures that all performative interactions can be understood using the same frameworks, whether they take the form of a small-group private encounter (such as *Collect Yourselves!*) or a culturally validated and artist-led performance (as with the works of Blast Theory), and whether the people involved are construed as performers, participants, audience members, bystanders, or roles yet to be discerned. Performance and performativity are the next means of riding the waves of HCI research, from single users accomplishing a single task, to multiple situated users working together, to recreational and social explorations of increasingly fluid and pervasive technologies. Performance and performativity push the boundaries of both the deeply felt personal experience of self and the construction of public faces and human relationships, both online and in person. The combination of performance studies and HCI allows for an extraordinarily rich perspective on how humans can, might, and do relate to each other using digital technology, particularly those technologies that have become embedded in our sense of self. PED is founded on a critical perspective and a corresponding interventionist attitude that is expressed through designed interventions into everyday life—whether through direct interaction with a technology, a culturally framed performance, or something between the two. PED contributes a new way of conceptualising both the devising and the creation of intermedial performance, which focuses less on the technology used 'on stage' and more on emerging ways of 'seeing, feeling, and being in the contemporary world' (Nelson 2010, p. 18) as it is increasingly saturated with digital media. Where the HCI side of PED is willing to let in some of the perspectives of performance studies, and the performance side of PED is willing to stretch itself to include some of the aims and means of HCI research, the result is a wealth of new insights that I believe can drive a better informed and more consciously shaped relationship to our emerging, technologically expanded world.

---

[1] IFTR/FIRT, held 22–26 July 2013 in Barcelona.

References

Auslander P (2004) Postmodernism and performance. In: Connor S (ed) The Cambridge companion to postmodernism. Cambridge University Press, Cambridge/New York, pp 97–115

Balabanović M, Chu L, Wolff G (2000) Storytelling with digital photographs. In: Proceedings of the SIGCHI conference on human factors in computing systems. ACM Press, New York, pp 564–571

Barclay CR (1994) Composing protoselves through improvisation. In: Neisser U, Fivush R (eds) The remembering self: construction and agency in self narrative. Cambridge University Press, Cambridge, pp 55–77

Bardzell J, Bardzell S (2013) What is critical about critical design? In: Proceedings of the SIGCHI conference on human factors in computing systems. ACM Press, New York, pp 3297–3306

Bauman R (1975) Verbal art as performance. Am Anthropol 77(2):290–311

Benford S, Giannachi G (2011) Performing mixed reality. MIT Press, Cambridge, MA/London

Benford S, Crabtree A, Reeves S, Sheridan J, Dix A, Flintham M, Drozd A (2006) The frame of the game: blurring the boundary between fiction and reality in mobile experiences. In: Proceedings of the SIGCHI conference on human factors in computing systems. ACM Press, New York, pp 427–436

Boenisch PM (2006) Aesthetic art to aisthetic act: theatre, media, intermedial performance. In: Chapple F, Kattenbelt C (eds) Intermediality in theatre and performance. Editions Rodopi B.V, Amsterdam/New York, pp 103–116

Boenisch PM (2012) Acts of spectating: the dramaturgy of the audience's experience in contemporary theatre. Crit Stages (7):np

Chatzichristodoulou M (2011) Mapping intermediality in performance. Contemp Theatr Rev 21(2):230–231

Dalsgaard P, Hansen LK (2008) Performing perception: staging aesthetics of interaction. ACM Trans Comput Hum Interact (TOCHI) 15(3):1–33

Deuze M (2006) Participation, remediation, bricolage: considering principal components of a digital culture. Inf Soc 22(2):63–75

Dissanayake E (2003) The core of art: making special. J Can Assoc Curric Stud 1(2):13–38

Dolan J (2005) Utopia in performance: finding hope at the theater. University of Michigan Press, Ann Arbor

Fearon F (2010) Decoding the audience: a theoretical paradigm for the analysis of the 'real' audience and their creation of meaning. About Perform 10:119–135

Fensham R (2012) Postdramatic spectatorship: participate or else. Crit Stages 7:1–8

Fischer-Lichte E (2008) The transformative power of performance: a new aesthetics. Routledge, London

Ginters L (2010) On audiencing: the work of the spectator in live performance. About Perform 10:7–14

Goffman E (1974) Frame analysis: an essay on the organization of experience. Harvard University Press, Cambridge, MA

Heddon D (2008) Autobiography and performance. Palgrave Macmillan, Basingstoke

Katevas K, Healey PG, Harris MT (2015) Robot comedy lab: experimenting with the social dynamics of live performance. Front Psychol 6:1253

Kershaw B, Nicholson (2011a) Introduction: doing methods creatively. In: Kershaw B, Nicholson H (eds) Research methods in theatre and performance. Edinburgh University Press, Edinburgh, pp 1–15

Kershaw B, Nicholson H (2011b) Research methods in theatre and performance. Edinburgh University Press, Edinburgh

Lavender A (2012) Viewing and acting (and points in between): the trouble with spectating after Rancière. Contemp Theatr Rev 22(3):307–326

Lotker S, Gough R (2013) On scenography: editorial. Perform Res 18(3):3–6

McCarthy J, Wright P (2015) Taking [a]part: the politics and aesthetics of participation in experience-centered design. MIT Press, Cambridge, MA/London

Myers M, Griffiths D, Sabnani N, Joshi A, Mahapatra S (2014) Sustaining lived practices through serious play. DRHA 2014, University of Greenwich, London, 31 Aug–3 Sept 2014

Nelson R (2010) Introduction: prospective mapping. In: Bay-Cheng S et al (eds) Mapping intermediality in performance. Amsterdam University Press, Amsterdam, pp 13–23

Nibbelink LG, Merx S (2010) Presence and perception: analysing intermediality in performance. In: Bay-Cheng S et al (eds) Mapping intermediality in performance. Amsterdam University Press, Amsterdam, pp 218–229

Nitsche M (2013) Performance art and digital media. Digit Creat 24(2):93–95

Oddey A, White C (2009) Modes of spectating. Intellect, Bristol

Phelan P (2004) Marina Abramović: witnessing shadows. Theatr J 56(4):569–577

Rancière J (2011) The emancipated spectator. Verso, London

Reason M (2010) Asking the audience: audience research and the experience of theatre. About Perform 10:15–34

Salter C (2010) Entangled: technology and the transformation of performance. MIT Press, Cambridge, MA

Schiphorst T (2011) Self-evidence: applying somatic connoisseurship to experience design. In: CHI'11 extended abstracts on human factors in computing systems. ACM Press, New York, pp 145–160

Schiphorst T (2012) Foreword. In: Broadhurst S, Machon J (eds) Identity, performance and technology: practices of empowerment, embodiment and technicity. Palgrave Macmillan, Basingstoke/New York, pp xi–xvi

Sheridan JG, Bryan-Kinns N (2008) Designing for performative tangible interaction. Int J Arts Technol 1(3):288–308

Stolterman E (2008) The nature of design practice and implications for interaction design research. Int J Des 2(1):55–65

Taylor R, Boulanger P, Olivier P (2008) dream.Medusa: a participatory performance. In: Proceedings of the 9th international symposium on smart graphics. Springer-Verlag, Berlin/Heidelberg, pp 200–206

Taylor R, Schofield G, Shearer J, Wallace J, Wright P, Boulanger P, Olivier P (2011) Designing from within: humanaquarium. In: Proceedings of the 2011 annual conference on human factors in computing systems. ACM Press, New York, pp 1855–1864

Taylor R, Schofield G, Shearer J, Wright P, Boulanger P, Olivier P (2014) Nightingallery: theatrical framing and orchestration in participatory performance. Pers Ubiquit Comput 18(7):1583–1600

Trencsényi K, Cochrane B (2014) Foreword. In: Trencsényi K, Cochrane B (eds) New dramaturgy: international perspectives on theory and practice. Bloomsbury Publishing, London/Delhi/New York/Sydney, pp xi–xx

Van House NA (2009) Collocated photo sharing, story-telling, and the performance of self. Int J Hum Comput Stud 67(12):1073–1086

Williamson JR, Brewster S (2012) A performative perspective on UX. Commun Mob Comput 1(1):1–5

Williamson JR, Hansen LK (2012) Designing performative interactions in public spaces. In: Proceedings of the designing interactive systems conference. ACM Press, New York, pp 791–792

Williamson JR, Hansen LK, Jacucci G, Light A, Reeves S (2014) Understanding performative interactions in public settings. Pers Ubiquit Comput 18(7):1545–1549

Wilson M (2006) Storytelling and theatre: contemporary storytellers and their art. Palgrave Macmillan, Basingstoke

Index

A
Abramović, M., 56, 57, 66, 112, 113, 130, 154
Activities, 13, 67
Aesthetics, 4, 5, 8, 12, 13, 15, 18, 19, 30, 33, 37, 39, 40, 47, 50, 51, 55–59, 63, 64, 66, 71, 73, 82–84, 86, 87, 89, 90, 93, 96, 99, 126–129, 135, 145, 146, 165, 173–176, 179–181, 183, 187, 188, 194, 195, 196, 204, 208–210
Affect, 3, 5, 8, 16, 38–40, 56, 57, 60, 72, 132, 158
Applied theatre, 63, 68, 69
Attending, 53, 126, 133, 135, 180, 187–189, 212. *See also* Marking
Audiences, 2, 5–9, 11, 13, 17, 18, 27–31, 33, 35, 36, 40, 46–58, 60, 61, 63–69, 71, 72, 74, 82, 83, 86–90, 94–96, 98, 99, 105, 107, 110, 112–114, 117–119, 121–130, 133, 134, 136, 137, 140, 143, 146, 147, 153–155, 157, 161, 162, 164–166, 168–178, 180–189, 194, 196–199, 201, 202, 204, 209, 211, 212. *See also* Spectators
Auslander, P., 27, 34, 114, 171, 212
Austin, J.L., 1, 26, 27
Autobiographical performance, 13, 19, 20, 27, 50, 53, 59–62, 65, 66, 68, 71, 72, 111–116, 122–130, 134, 135, 144–147, 159, 179–182, 184–185, 187, 193
Autopoietic feedback loop, 5, 62, 99, 189, 197, 211

B
Baker, B., 13, 45, 50, 51, 54, 56, 62–64, 66, 94, 126
Balabanović, M., 16, 62, 106, 108, 180, 181, 197, 209
Bardzell, J., 10, 12–14, 30, 73, 90, 110, 129, 211
Bardzell, S., 12–14, 211
Bauman, R., 19, 26, 30, 58, 59, 63, 72, 109, 124, 127–129, 146, 147, 157, 163, 188, 189, 211
Benford, S., 5–7, 9, 10, 14, 17, 18, 29, 38, 41, 48, 49, 63, 67, 82, 86, 154, 175, 189, 195, 202, 208, 211, 212
Blast Theory, 7, 38, 48, 86, 110, 112, 114, 154, 213
Bødker, S., 36, 37, 108, 110
Bubbling Tom, 45, 49–54, 60–62, 64, 66, 72, 112, 130
Butler, J., 1, 26–28, 62, 109, 123, 129

C
Cape Wrath, 66, 114–116, 118–122, 125, 126, 128, 134, 143, 144, 154
Challenges, 5, 12, 14, 15, 18, 31, 32, 39, 53, 66–69, 82, 99, 108, 131, 145, 165, 166, 173, 177–179, 187, 188, 194, 195, 202, 210, 211, 213
Chatzichristodoulou, M., 9, 48, 70, 123, 210
Class of '76, 66, 114, 115, 119, 130
Coded performance analysis, 19, 20, 70, 84, 95, 98–99, 165–176, 194, 197, 204

© Springer International Publishing Switzerland 2016
J. Spence, *Performative Experience Design*, Springer Series on Cultural
Computing, DOI 10.1007/978-3-319-28395-1

Printed in the United States
By Bookmasters